Good Policy, Good Practice
Series Editors: Kirsti Nilsen and Martin Dowding

1. *Library Collection Development Policies: Academic, Public, and Special Libraries,* by Frank Hoffmann and Richard Wood. 2005.
2. *Library Collection Development Policies: School Libraries,* by Frank Hoffmann and Richard Wood. 2005.

D0121707

Library Collection Development Policies

Academic, Public, and Special Libraries

Good Policy, Good Practice Series

Frank W. Hoffmann and Richard J. Wood

THE SCARECROW PRESS, INC.
Lanham, Maryland • Toronto • Oxford
2005

SCARECROW PRESS, INC.

Published in the United States of America
by Scarecrow Press, Inc.
A wholly owned subsidiary of
The Rowman & Littlefield Publishing Group, Inc.
4501 Forbes Boulevard, Suite 200, Lanham, Maryland 20706
www.scarecrowpress.com

PO Box 317
Oxford
OX2 9RU, UK

British Library Cataloguing in Publication Information Available

Library of Congress Cataloging-in-Publication Data

Hoffmann, Frank W., 1949–
  Library collection development policies : academic, public, and special
libraries / Frank W. Hoffmann and Richard J. Wood.
      p. cm. — (Good policy, good practice ; no. 1)
  Includes bibliographical references and index.
  ISBN 0-8108-5180-6 (pbk. : alk. paper)
  1. Collection development (Libraries)—United States. 2. Collection
development (Libraries)—United States—Policy statements. I. Wood,
Richard J. (Richard John). II. Title. III. Series.

  Z687.2.U6H64 2005
  025.2'1—dc22
                                                    2005006525

∞™ The paper used in this publication meets the minimum requirements of American
National Standard for Information Sciences—Permanence of Paper for Printed Library
Materials, ANSI/NISO Z39.48-1992.
Manufactured in the United States of America.

Contents

v

Acknowledgments

We would like to thank those libraries and related facilities that permitted the reproduction of portions of their collection development policies within this book. A complete institutional list can be found in Appendix A: Inventory of Excerpted Library Policies.

We also appreciate the willingness of the American Library Association to permit reproduction of many of its intellectual freedom policy statements in Appendix B. Many additional related statements can be found at ALA's official website, www.ala.org.

In addition, we would like to acknowledge the ongoing care and support provided by both of our wives, Lee Ann Hoffmann and Lynne Wood. They have been very understanding about the huge investments of time required to carry out this project.

Preface

This work—and a projected companion volume devoted to school library collection development policies—represent an outgrowth of our *Library Collection Development Policies: A Reference and Writers' Handbook*, published by Scarecrow Press in 1996, which attempted to (1) ascertain why a well-organized policy makes good sense, (2) outline the strategies behind their creation and getting them implemented, (3) examine the key elements comprising such documents, and (4) provide useful models culled from a wide range of library settings. These updated sourcebooks will focus on the latter two concerns in even greater detail, dissecting policies part-by-part, and then incorporating exemplary components from existing library manuals.

While collection development policies remain as vital to the integrity of library collection building as ever, the process also warrants reexamination in light of the many changes occurring in the information industry, libraries, library consortia, and scholarly communication since the mid-1990s. The professional literature, our own experiences within the library world, and feedback from others in the field underscored that those changes and their impact on library collection development policy had been significant.

Not too many decades ago, collection development librarians only had to consider monographs and print journal subscriptions for the vast majority of their acquisitions. Matters remained relatively simple even as the imperatives for selecting and acquiring new audio, video, and micromedia formats increased. Nearly all selection and acquisition processes were handled using paper forms until the 1990s in most libraries. Some of the audio, video, and micromedia formats have come and gone over the decades, but books, documents, and serials are now available in both print and electronic formats.

For music, we considered that the compact disc (typically known as CDs) became the preferred format in libraries for music since the early 1990s, but had not become the preferred format for reference books. By that time, the vast majority of librarians, in fact, seemed to be leary of the CD-ROM format for reference tools because hardware, software, archival, and other issues had not been resolved. Compact discs themselves were inexpensive, but they required the use of computer hardware and software that required ongoing maintenance and upgrading, as well as annual licenses in many cases. The picture has been further complicated by the rise of various forms of enhanced CDs, the closely-related DVD medium, and various electronic forms of storage available via online or wireless transmission.

Monographs, audio, visual, and some non-subscribed electronic resources can be purchased not only traditionally (directly from publishers and indirectly through jobbers), but also electronically through the Internet. Books may be acquired by libraries from jobbers who accept traditional paper orders or electronic ordering systems that may allow selectors to build and transmit electronic book carts. Collection development policies should certainly address these developments.

These types of ordering processes do not apply to subscribed electronic resources because signed license agreements must be negotiated and signed by authorized agents of the respective companies and libraries or library consortia. Electronic formats and how they are acquired or licensed has become very complex and often requires the combined attention of selectors, collection developers, users, library administration, lawyers, and library consortia staff. Let us examine a few cases in point.

Books are not just available in print format, but also in non-print or digitized formats such as CD-ROM. Digitized books may also be downloaded through the Internet by library users based on the terms of license agreements. Internet accessible electronic text services have revolutionized how information is accessed by anyone with a networked personal computer. The vast majority of information seekers today look to the Internet, not libraries, as their initial information source whether it is a company's webpage, a university's catalog, a virtual tour of a museum, a telephone directory, or a commercial database. Nearly every library and household these days use the Internet to access information about nearly any topic anywhere in the world. When we wrote the *Writers' Handbook* in 1995, very few library policies were available electronically and few library directors and collection development librarians used electronic mail and Listservs. Now librarians, like the authors, can now use the Internet to access collection development policies of thousands of libraries, find their e-mail addresses, and write them with questions or comments about their policies. These approaches have the potential for bypassing the library altogether, as well as significantly impacting library collection development policy.

As the most revolutionary change since the invention of the printing press centuries before, the Internet is ushering-out the use of CD-ROM reference tools and books in libraries. Questia by 2002, for example, digitized over 60,000 electronic books that the company makes available to students or other users for a modest monthly fee paid by the individual or for a per-student fee paid by an institution. Some larger and better funded libraries or library systems have found it advantageous to license Questia, though most libraries feel that it is the responsibility of their clientele to pay Questia's monthly rates. Another innovative company, ebrary, sells digitized content by the page.

The Internet is now the preferred way to access journal articles from remote databases produced by library industry giants like EBSCO, InfoTrac, Elsevier, Wiley, and LexisNexis. Their full-text journal article databases were licensed to individual libraries, library systems, and groups of libraries (consortia) at a premium (percentage) above the cost of their print subscriptions. The premiums for electronic access set by these companies vary widely, as do their annual increases and pricing models. With respect to collection development policy, it is nearly impossible to develop anything other than a very general approach to dealing with the unpredictability.

Multi-year consortial agreements are, nonetheless, often preferred by vendors and libraries alike to contain their respective costs and, for member libraries, to increase the number of accessible titles. A member library of a consortium, that is, could often gain access to all of the titles held in common by the members and increase the total number of accessible titles by cancelling duplicates and adding unique titles for an overall increase in the number of accessible titles. The cost of such licenses, however, has tended to increase nearly as much as the underlying journals. So, libraries have tended to pay for the licenses by cancelling print subscriptions where feasible. The feasibility of cancelling print subscriptions when licensing full-text equivalent titles, however, means different things to different librarians. Ideally, most librarians could agree that it is easier to cancel a print subscription that is common to several vendors such as EBSCO, ProQuest, and Gale, but harder for titles that are unique to a single vendor such as Elsevier, which has a history of higher than average journal price increases. The problem for those libraries that cancelled print subscriptions in order to pay for such licenses will come if there is insufficient funds to continue the licenses and the libraries end up with fewer print subscriptions and lose the electronic access to hundreds of others.

An additional problem may be the archival policy (or lack thereof) of the companies that license such full-text article databases and the impact on collection development policy. Many libraries that have acquired JSTOR databases, for instance, have confidently withdrawn print backruns when they have serious space problems because they trust the archival practices of JSTOR and because research libraries also are preserving print copies to assure permanent availability. Many of the other vendors we have mentioned above do not inspire the confidence of librarians and users because they are motivated by and depend upon profit to stay in business.

While these companies chiefly made journal literature available to end-users through libraries by means of license agreements, these companies may also make journal articles and electronic books available directly to the end-users in their homes or offices. Additionally, any scholar, writer, or individual with an Internet accessible computer may make their own publications available for free to the end-user. Scholars, academicians, doctors, government agencies, businesses, and others have been posting reports and drafts of their publications on their websites since the 1990s at an increasing rate. The Internet, therefore, has room for individuals, companies, governmental agencies, and jobbers to make the entire array of scholarly and non-scholarly literature available to anyone who has access to a networked personal computer. An increasing percentage of the world's literature usage is, therefore, accessible from non-subscribed journals or databases and outside of libraries. This trend is bound to influence scholarly communication, as well as library collection development policy.

All of these issues have come to the forefront since we wrote the *Writers' Handbook* in 1995. We could not recall examining many library collection development policies in 1994 that included selection criteria and policies addressing either CD-ROM databases or electronic access to remote information databases. Few library collection development policies in the *Writers' Handbook,* in fact, addressed selecting, archiving, accessing, or the licensing of electronic resources. Internet search engines, company websites, and library home pages as we know them today were not in use then. Like other large university and research libraries, California State University's policy—included in the *Writers' Handbook* (pp. 79–142)—recognized the development of end-user electronic services and resources. The CSU policy statement included a section on network-based materials (pp. 99–100) and envisaged the widespread, nearly ubiquitous, use of the full-text article databases now common in libraries of all sizes and types. CSU's policy also referenced the use of HyperCards, multimedia, CD-ROM towers, or multiple disc drives that were not yet prevalently used in smaller and mid-sized academic and public libraries. Tarlton Law Library's policy statement in the *Writers' Handbook* (p. 405) acknowledged not only CD-ROM formats from West and other publishers as a growing component of its collection, but also the disadvantages. Tarlton's policy statement also acknowledged "difficult searching software, the need to change disks, the inability to down-load searches, etc., are reasons to decide against electronic formats even where the access and price criteria have been met." Mediated database searches by librarians were still the norm in the early 1990s even in the largest academic libraries, so few library policy statements addressed selection criteria for electronic databases or license agreements.

Since 1995, of course, EBSCO, LexisNexis, Elsevier, Wiley, Gale, ProQuest, and other large companies have been developing their full-text digitized article databases and search engines for Internet access. An added impetus for these companies has continued to be the distance education programs that have been growing like Topsy. Such advances are noteworthy because they have affected how users want to retrieve information and how libraries provide it. The licensing of full-text article databases from these and similar companies has altered how libraries provide access to the journal literature and how users look for information. The now common practice of public, academic, special, and school libraries of licensing electronic resources by the year has altered reference, interlibrary loan, collection development, collection assessment, and other library programs. Providing electronic databases has also altered how users retrieve, disseminate, and think about information.

In further reflecting about how full-text article and journal index databases licensed by most libraries today have impacted library collection development practices and policies, we quickly concluded that we should be able to find many good examples to include in our new edition. We saw our task now as trying to show how library collection development policies have been impacted significantly by advances in the technology and telecommunications. A major portion of our book is, in fact, devoted to criteria for selection of electronic resources and licensing databases. The last part of this book is about virtual collection development and represents a fundamental difference between this and previous editions.

The development of the "virtual library" has, in a word, caused many libraries to develop their first policy statements, or to update their existing collection development policies to account for the advances in information technology we have been discussing here. Whether the impetus for writing or revising is concern about illegal electronic access, filtering, privacy, copyright, plagiarism, archiving, preservation, or other issues, it is a good idea to have a comprehensive collection development policy. Censors have, in fact, been a leading reason why librarians look to their collection development policies for defense against using filtering software.

A basic and perplexing issue, of course, is whether these practices will be perpetual. At this time, there is so much variability and instability in the information industry that few librarians are likely to count on the permanency of any license, not to mention technical and archival issues that complicate the entire environment. Users want free and easy access, libraries want good value at a good price, and vendors want to recover their initial costs and at least realize a reasonable profit at some point. Users, libraries, and vendors alike probably would like a stable and sustainable, if not growing, business that is mutually beneficial.

Another motivation in reorganizing the format employed in the *Writers' Handbook* was the fact that many library collection development policies are accessible through the Internet via simple web search strategies. Readers who wish to see a given document in its entirety can find the library's policy through the Internet, using either the accompanying web address supplied at the end of each excerpt, or simply searching with keywords such as "collection development policies" and the institution name. However, we believe that the close-up lens approach of providing background information devoted to the various policy components, complemented by representative excerpts from existing library documents, will spur greater facility in upgrading collection development policies in addition to composing them in complete form.

Introduction

This work represents an ongoing effort to fill the void in the library litera-ture relating to collection development policies. Our experience spans four decades as library educators and practitioners, and we created the book, as well as a projected companion volume devoted to school libraries, to assist both library school students and professionals in the field in the compilation, revising, and implementation of policies. Given the premise that a well-rounded policy reflects all activities concerning the collection management process — including the evaluation, selection, acquisition, and weeding of in-formation resources — we hope that the work will also prove useful to non-librarians possessing some kind of stake in high-quality library holdings. Such users might include library board members, politicians and adminis-trators directly responsible for library operations, and institutional patrons.

The text focuses on academic (undergraduate through post-graduate lev-els), public, and special-purpose libraries, the latter of which serve busi-nesses and corporations, governmental agencies, museums and other types of archives, health-care facilities, law firms, religious institutions, and mass media entities. While widely diversified as to appearance and purpose, these libraries — when contrasted with school media centers — share several impor-tant features: (1) a largely adult clientele; (2) a tendency towards greater staff specialization; and (3) less outside interference, in general, regarding collec-tion building issues. These rough similarities are recognizable in the archi-tecture of collection development policies themselves, from the broad head-ings employed to the more detailed textual passages.

The work is divided into two major sections: Part 1: Components of Collec-tion Development Policies, focuses on elements which enable these documents to serve as a blueprint for building library holdings, while Part 2: Virtual Collection Development, featuring Jane Pearlmutter's chapter, "Policy Components for Online Electronic Resources," and Chapter 31, Resource Sharing in the Digital Age, examines more recent trends in collection management. Appendix A: Inventory of Excerpted Library Policies identifies the institutions providing material that serves either as exemplary examples or to aptly illustrate the function of various policy statements. Addresses and phone numbers have been provided so you can contact these libraries for further information—most notably complete or updated copies of their respective policies. In cases where the policy has been published on the Internet, web addresses are included following the excerpted portion in Part 1. Appendix B: Intellectual Freedom Statements and Forms includes the text of American Library Association documents frequently included in collection development policies. ALA has long advocated that libraries promulgate policies and apply them to the ongoing process of collection building. To this end, ALA encourages libraries to incorporate these statements—and other information resources available from its website—into their respective policies.

Part 1

COMPONENTS OF COLLECTION DEVELOPMENT POLICIES

Chapter One

Introduction to Collection Development Policy Components

Considering the diversity of libraries by size, type, and service philosophy, it follows that the architecture of collection development policies should vary considerably from one institution to another. The general character of a given policy is determined by a number of factors, most notably the sections comprising the document; the arrangement of these sections; the style of writing; the degree of reliance upon outside guidelines, forms, procedures, etc.; and mode of presentation (i.e., a traditional print layout as opposed to mounting on an institution's website, complete with hyperlinks to individual sections). As is demonstrated by the policy examples provided under the respective component breakdowns in Part 1, even when libraries share a similar outlook regarding collection building they are likely to differ as to how they organize information as well as in the actual language of the headings they employ.

The headings in Part 1 constitute standardized sections most likely to be found in library collection development statements. After surveying literally thousands of policies either available for in-house library use, within monographs, or posted on the Internet, the authors feel safe in proposing that there is nothing approaching consensus regarding the structure of these documents. In Chapter 1 of *Library Collection Development Policies: A Reference and Writers' Handbook* (Scarecrow, 1996), we discussed at length the advantages to libraries of formulating collection development statements. Despite the efforts of library schools, scholars, professional associations, and other organizations to spread the gospel regarding written policies, many libraries continue to carry out the vital function of collection management without any form of documented plan. The bewildering array of policies available to the beginning collection developer may be in part responsible for their absence in some libraries.

We have covered all components considered necessary for good policies, including the following:

- Purpose statement
- Background statement
- Responsibility for collection development
- Mission, goals, and objectives statements
- Target audiences
- Budgeting and funding
- Evaluative criteria
- Format statement
- Government publications
- Treatment of specific resource groups
- Special collections
- Resource sharing
- Services statement
- Selection aids
- Copyright statement
- Intellectual freedom statement
- Acquisitions
- Gifts and exchange statement
- Collection maintenance statement
- Weeding statement
- Collection evaluation section
- Policy revision statement
- Definition of terms and glossary
- Bibliography
- Appendixes

These headings—along with the introductory discussion and excerpted policies—represent an attempt to impart some sense of clarity and uniformity to this rather chaotic state of affairs.

Chapter Two

Purpose Statements in Policies

Regarding collection development policies, Gorman and Howes state that "few—if any—of the great librarians of the past ever bothered with anything so mundane; they simply relied on their genuine passion for literature and inbred instinct for what was 'right' when collecting." (1) However, these same authors go on to admit that the volume, complexity, flux, and blurring of boundaries characterizing information in the present day has spurred most of the world's great libraries—whose unparalleled collections were built largely through the application of vision and sound instincts—to formulate their own written, publicly available policy statements. (2)

Nevertheless, many libraries today still do not possess written policies. Accordingly, it would seem imperative that existing documents construct a lucidly worded justification for such an expenditure of time and energy. The literature provides ample arguments for compiling—and utilizing—policies. Richard K. Gardner has provided perhaps the most comprehensive rationale, noting that policies facilitate accomplishment of the following tasks:

- forcing staff to think through library goals and commit themselves to these goals, helping them to identify long- and short-range needs of users and to establish priorities for allocating funds;
- helping assure that the library will commit itself to all parts of the community, both present and future;
- helping set standards for the selection and weeding of materials;
- informing users, administrators, and other libraries of collection scope, facilitating coordination of collection development among institutions;
- helping minimize personal bias by selectors and to highlight imbalances in selection criteria;

- serving as an in-service training tool for new staff;
- helping assure continuity, especially in collections of any size, providing pattern and framework to ease transition from one librarian to the next;
- providing a means of staff self-evaluation, or for evaluation by outsiders;
- helping demonstrate that the library is running a business-like operation;
- providing information to assist in budget allocations;
- contributing to operational efficiency in terms of routine decisions, which helps junior staff;
- serving as a tool of complaint-handling with regard to inclusions or exclusions. (3)

As implied by many of Gardner's points, a library collection development policy serves primarily as a planning document. This perspective is underscored by Gorman and Howes:

> Devising a policy is a means of engaging in self-examination and reflection, which today is essential for rational, coherent growth of a collection. All work in a library becomes routine, and routine often becomes a substitute for vision, especially in smaller libraries where one may lack the support of professional colleagues. Users change, needs change and resource availability changes; a policy can help one to be aware of these changes by acting as a collection of baseline data for current operations and, ideally, a starting point for future development. (4)

The library's purpose statement often focuses on the communication function: internally, with users, staff, and administrators, and externally, with other libraries and institutions. Communication embraces a wide range of vital operations, including training, budgeting, cooperative acquisitions, and shared services.

Critics often argue that policies tend to be inflexible in application. Unless these documents are reviewed and updated on a regular basis, changing factors—e.g., the emergence of new disciplines, alteration of the community profile, budget cuts—combined with staff inertia, can have a negative impact on the overall collection management program. Therefore, it is advisable that this section cite the role of a policy in defining how stability and flexibility enhance collection building.

The following excerpts represent model approaches for purpose statements developed by academic, public, and special libraries, respectively. Unless compromising the book layout or possessing an online appearance that is impossible to replicate, the samples here—and elsewhere—retain the character and format of the original documents. Additional examples of equal merit can be found on the Internet; for example, the Santa Fe Community College

(http://cisit.cc.fl.us/~library/col_policy.htm) purpose statement is comparable
to that included in the Lake Sumter Community College policy (following).

PURPOSE STATEMENT FOR ACADEMIC LIBRARIES

James Madison University Libraries: Collection Development Policy

JMU Libraries, which include Carrier Library and branch libraries in the Music Building and CISAT, support the mission of James Madison University to provide a comprehensive and quality undergraduate educational, cultural, and social experience for students. The University's mission further encompasses research and graduate education. JMU Libraries supports this mission, in part, by building local collections and providing access to appropriate and diverse collections of information.

The purpose of this document is to guide departmental faculty and librarians in developing and maintaining a balanced collection responsive to the changing needs of a dynamic institution.

The Libraries, in carrying out their collection development activities, adhere to the principles expressed in the following statements from the American Library Association's Library Bill of Rights: "Books and other library resources should be provided for the interest, information and enlightenment of all people of the community the library serves. Materials should not be excluded because of the origin, background, or views of those contributing to their creation. . . . Libraries should provide materials and information presenting all points of view on current and historical issues. Materials should not be proscribed or removed because of partisan or doctrinal disapproval." [p. 1; http://library.jmu.edu/forfaculty/cdpolicy.htm]

PURPOSE STATEMENT FOR COMMUNITY COLLEGES

Lake-Sumter (Leesburg, Florida) Community College Libraries: Collection Development Policy

Purpose of Collection Development

This policy is designed to guide the systematic development and management of Lake-Sumter Community College library collections of print, audiovisual, and electronic materials. Since the nature of information dissemination, networking, and library resource sharing are undergoing revolutionary change, this policy will consider collection development and management issues within the dynamic framework of global access to information resources, and will require regular assessment and adjustment. This policy applies to collection development and management at all Lake-Sumter Community College libraries.

Purpose of Collection Development Policy

This policy is intended to define a collection development and information access program to meet the following objectives:

* To assist librarians in providing current, diverse, balanced collections of materials to support the instructional, institutional and individual needs of students, faculty and staff.
* To provide access to electronic resources, including web-based resources, for faculty, staff and students, based on the college's fiscal resources.
* To insure faculty participation in collection development and management.
* To consolidate and centralize access to resources whenever appropriate to serve all college campuses.
* To serve traditional and distance education students and faculty by providing integrated access to collections of materials in all appropriate formats in the most cost-effective manner.
* To assist with short-range and long-range fiscal planning.

[revised April 16, 2001, pp. 1–3; http://lscc.cc.fl.us/library/coldev/htm]

PURPOSE STATEMENT FOR PUBLIC LIBRARIES

Granby (Connecticut) Public Library: Collection Development Policy

The purpose of a written Collection Development Policy is to guide the library staff in the selection of library materials and to inform the Library Board and the general public of the principles upon which selections are made. [adopted December 21, 1992, last revised June 26, 2001, pp. 1–2; http://www.cslib.org/cdpgra.htm]

Kitsap (Washington) Regional Library: Collection Development Policy (Third Edition)

This policy serves as a broad guide for all those involved with Collection Management for Kitsap Regional Library. Its purposes are to:
1. inform the Library's internal customers (the staff) and external customers (the people of Kitsap County) of the scope and nature of the collection, the

philosophies underlying collection decisions, and the plans for the continuing development of resources;

2. provide guidelines, which when combined with the application of professional judgment by trained staff, may be used to evaluate the collection on an ongoing basis;
3. define the relationships of various parts of the collection to the whole;
4. enable selectors and others involved with collection management to work toward defined goals, thus strengthening the collection and making the best use of available funds; and
5. assist Library staff in the responsible expenditure of funds for resources.

[adopted May 19, 1998, p. 2; www.krl.org/administration/policies/colldev.html]

SAMPLE PURPOSE STATEMENT FOR SPECIAL LIBRARIES AND RELATED INSTITUTIONS

Colorado Department of Education, Colorado Talking Book Library: Collection Development Policy

PURPOSE: The purpose of this statement is to define policies for selection of materials for the collection of the Colorado Talking Book Library (CTBL) which are not produced by National Library Service for the Blind and Physically Handicapped (NLS). Such materials may be obtained through commercial sources or produced on tape. The CTBL follows the criteria for selection guidelines stated in the NLS "Selection Policy for Reading Materials," as well as the "Library Bill of Rights," and "Freedom to Read" statements adopted by the American Library Association. [last modified October 11, 2000, page 1; www.cde.state.co.us/ctbl/tbcolldevpolicy.htm]

NOTES

1. G. E. Gorman and B. R. Howes, *Collection Development for Libraries* (London: Bowker-Saur, 1990, c1989), 4.

2. Gorman and Howes, *Collection Development for Libraries*, 4–5.

3. Richard K. Gardner, *Library Collections: Their Origin, Selection, and Development* (New York: McGraw-Hill, 1981), 222–224.

4. Gorman and Howes, *Collection Development for Libraries*, 5.

Chapter Three

Background Statements in Policies

The background statement once typically referred to the institution engaged in collection building and/or the community it served. By the 1980s it often included cooperative arrangements with other libraries that involved some type of resource sharing. More recently, however, separate sections devoted to such agreements have appeared in the revised editions of many written policies.

Public libraries seem most inclined to include community descriptions. This is perhaps because they function as an open institution serving essentially all citizens of a defined political jurisdiction (and beyond, if one considers consortia agreements and regional systems). In contrast, academic institutions generally possess a more homogenous audience; that is, affiliated students, faculty, and staff possessing circumscribed informational, instructional, and research needs.

Typically, community statements include one or more of the following features:

- geographical data;
- a demographic breakdown of the constituency as a whole;
- a listing of the notable business, political, educational, and cultural entities located in the immediate (or surrounding) area;
- the social services required by citizens;
- the location of library facilities and general statement of purpose; and
- a description of networking agreements.

The background statement serves to inform the entire collection building process, from the promulgation of a mission and goals for the library to the selection process itself. For this reason, it is usually located near the beginning of the policy, immediately following the Table of Contents or Introduction and Purpose Statement.

Elizabeth Futas, in *Collection Development Policies and Procedures* (Third Edition, 1995), noted that a new type of community description was gaining favor.

> Until [1990], coordinated collection development was a dream of many, but a dream without any substance. Slowly, the libraries of the 1990s have had to come to grips with some hard financial realities, and those realities are bringing coordinated collection development into the arena of the possible. (1)

The onset of the digital revolution in recent years has further facilitated what Futas considers, in all likelihood, to be "the next great movement within our field—the library without walls, the institution reaching beyond the near community into the global community." (2)

While all institutions within this section have done a competent job of communicating background information relating to their clientele (or potential clientele), the Kitsap Regional Library is notable for providing an especially detailed statement. It could be argued that much of the material covered by KRL is relevant as well to most professionally-run libraries; however, Kitsap seems to view the policy as a vehicle for educating its users regarding the collection building process as a whole. Furthermore, document size is not a valid consideration in an era where many library documents are posted on the Internet and feature internal hyperlinks to facilitate access.

BACKGROUND STATEMENT FOR ACADEMIC LIBRARIES

Drexel University, W. W. Hagerty Library: Collection Development Policy

University Background and Community Profile

Drexel University is Philadelphia's technology-based, co-operative education university. Founded in 1891 by financier Anthony J. Drexel, the University is nationally recognized for its excellence in preparing students for graduate studies and careers. A leader in curriculum innovation, in 1983, Drexel became the first university to require that all students have personal access to a microcomputer. The pioneering Engineering Curriculum has been designated a national model by the National Science Foundation.

The University is organized into six colleges and three schools. The colleges are: Arts and Sciences; Business and Administration; Engineering; Information Science and Technology; Nesbitt College of Design Arts; and

Evening and Professional Studies. The schools are Education; Biomedical Engineering, Science and Health Systems; and Environmental Science, Engineering and Policy. Drexel offers 53 bachelor's, 41 master's, and 17 doctoral programs. The University enrolls 11,000 students from 100 nations and has more than 65,000 alumni worldwide. [last updated October 27, 2000; p. 3]

BACKGROUND STATEMENT FOR COMMUNITY COLLEGES

Albuquerque Technical Vocational Institute: Collection Development Policy

Albuquerque TVI provides occupational, general, and basic education for a population which includes a broad spectrum of ages, cultural backgrounds, and intellectual abilities. Courses in these programs are delivered from four campuses in the Albuquerque metropolitan area. Distance learning programs reach students across the state of New Mexico via television broadcast, audio and video links, correspondence, and the Internet.

Main Campus and Joseph M. Montoya Campus have libraries on site. There are currently no facilities at either the South Valley or Rio Rancho campuses dedicated to library services.

It is the mission of the TVI Libraries to build collections in support of the occupational, general, and basic education programs of the Institute. The collection secondarily supports other academic and community programs, and provides academic library service to residents of the TVI district, which includes all of Bernalillo county and part of Sandoval county. [last updated June 28, 2001, p. 1; http://planet.tvi.cc.nm/library/P&P.cd.htm]

BACKGROUND STATEMENTS FOR PUBLIC LIBRARIES

Kitsap (Washington) Regional Library: Collection Development Policy (Third Edition)

Kitsap Regional Library serves a steadily growing population that is rapidly changing from predominantly rural to some of the fastest growing communities in the state. The County has experienced an 18 percent growth rate from 1990 to 1996, and the current population stands at approximately 240,000 people. While the County is one of the smallest in the state, covering only 393 square miles, this population figure places it as one of the top seven most populous counties in the state.

Kitsap County remains predominantly Caucasian in make-up, with only 14.8 percent of the population non-white. There are frequent fluctuations in the population with the arrival and departure of various naval vessels, and while there is a national trend towards military downsizing, 1996 figures for Washington were very close to 1990, and military personnel comprise approximately 7 percent of the total Kitsap population. This population is expected to continue to fluctuate as the Everett Port facility grows, although military personnel currently working at Everett are living in Bremerton. An additional carrier is expected to reside in Bremerton in 1998, thereby potentially boosting the population in the next few years.

From an age standpoint, 10.53 percent of the 1996 Kitsap population is over 65, which reflects national trends towards older populations and mirrors the total percentage of people who are 65 and over statewide, which is 11.49 percent. In a 1992 usage survey, slightly over half of the households reported having one or more children at home, with the largest percentage having elementary school-aged children. Additionally, there is a long-established community college in Bremerton and three active university extension programs being used in the area. Median age for the County was calculated at 44 years in 1992.

Kitsap County's median household income in 1996 was $38,931, making it the sixth highest in the state. Thirty-nine percent of the population is employed by government, according to 1995 statistics, with the next largest employment sectors being services and wholesale and retail trade. Per capita income in 1994 was estimated at $19,190, which represented a 1.6 percent increase from the previous year. However, from region to region within the Library's district there are significant pockets of high income, with Bainbridge Island being one of the most affluent communities in the Puget Sound area.

This statistical snapshot portrays a county in transition from its heavy dependence upon the military to a more urban, service, and trade-based community. The presence of two significant military bases supposes a transient element; however, a significant number of military dependents, mostly women with children, remain in the area. As noted, the military presence is not expected to decline over the next years, despite the national trend towards a declining military population. The Puget Sound Naval Shipyard is one of four operational naval shipyards in the country, and Bangor is one of four operating submarine bases nation-wide. The Naval Undersea Warfare Engineering Station at Keyport also provides a unique military industry for the area.

The City of Bremerton has long been in a period of declining growth, but recent interest in developing the waterfront, in conjunction with the promised faster ferries in 1998 and general growth of the County, may herald a new period of development for the city. On the other end of the County, by contrast, Bainbridge Island has grown significantly over the past decade, quadrupling its population.

Kitsap Regional Library, in order to respond to an increasing, more urbanized population, and in order to accommodate the most rural pockets of the County, provides remote access to information. The Library boasts 49 percent of the population holding library cards, an usually high percentage for a public library. Of this number, approximately 20 percent are registered with LinkNet, the library's on-line computer service, which includes e-mail, electronic reference resources, and Internet access.

Collection building for this population is also influenced by the disparate elements of an educated, urbanized population (personal investment, home decorating, gardening, popular literature); an alternative, back-to-nature population (magnetic healing, organic gardening, house construction, new age writing, and spiritualism); and a long-established, conservative older population (famous biographies, classic videos, history, travel, retirement). The natural beauty and ruggedness of the County, with 229 miles of saltwater shoreline and proximity to the Olympic Mountains, also attracts a sports-oriented population that wants to learn about boating, fishing, hiking, and sailing. Finally, the cultural activities of the area combined with its proximity to the larger urban center of Seattle, create a diverse and sophisticated population that enjoys opera, contemporary theater, and the visual arts. While it would be erroneous to draw these distinctions too narrowly, Kitsap Regional Library has distinguished itself within the state as being a net lender, rather than borrower, or materials from other libraries. The Library's acknowledgment of the breadth of its users' interests is reflected in this unique collection.

The above is a synopsis of statistical information. The Kitsap County Statistical Profile in the appendices contains more detailed information. [adopted May 19, 1998, pp. 7–9; www.krl.org/administration/policies/colldev.html]

Washoe County (Nevada) Library: Collection Development Policy

Washoe County is an area of diversity with congested urban areas and large tracts of rural land. Its people vary greatly in age, ethnic background, and in educational and economic levels.

The Washoe County Library System is the largest public library in Northern Nevada. The Library system consists of three major branches—Sparks, Reno, and Sierra View; two community branches—Peavine and Incline Village; seven partnership branches—Senior Center; Gelena High School Community Library, Verdi Elementary School, Gerlach High School, Mendive Middle School, Billinghurst Middle School, and Traner Middle School. The University of Nevada, Sierra Nevada College, and Truckee Meadows Community College are within Washoe County, as are smaller business colleges. There is great diversity between areas served. Gerlach is located 100 miles north of Reno and is a small community of ranchers and industrial workers. Incline Village is located in the Sierra Nevada Mountains by Lake Tahoe and has a larger professional population.

Because of these diversities in culture, economics, and location, the branches of the Washoe County Library must provide many different levels and quantities of materials. Other area libraries are available to provide additional library services to the community. The County Library does not need to collect "in-depth" in certain areas because of the complementary collections of the area libraries.

The branch collections will strive to meet the needs of the patrons in their service areas. It is also the responsibility of the Branch Managers, coordinating with the Collection Development Librarian, to meet the needs of all patrons of Washoe County to provide a full range of information. Each branch has system responsibilities requiring that information important to the needs of the patrons will be purchased and made available through intralibrary loan. [policy excerpted from Collection Development Plan approved August 16, 1995, updated January 5, 2001, pp. 1–2; www.washoe.lib.nv.us/ycolldev.htm]

NOTES

1. Elizabeth Futas, ed., *Collection Development Policies and Procedures*, 3rd Edition (Phoenix, Ariz.: Oryx, 1995), 194–95. Coordinated collection development has taken on sufficient importance within the overall umbrella of services for some institutions that it is accorded its own section in the book.

2. Futas, *Collection Development Policies and Procedures*, 194.

Chapter Four

Responsibility Statements in Policies

A fixture in most written policies, the Responsibility Statement should clearly state the title of the individual ultimately responsible for collection building decisions. This responsibility is usually vested in the Library Director or, in larger organizations, another administrator with line authority over collection development (e.g., Assistant Director for Technical Services). Higher level officials — Vice President for Academic Affairs, corporate CEO, Board of Trustees, etc. — may also be mentioned, especially in institutions where the library functions as a departmental unit. If any documents (e.g., applicable standards), beyond the policy itself, help govern collection building decisions, they are often cited in this section.

In many instances, the designated authority delegates responsibility to the staff involved with the day-to-day selection decisions. Whether department heads, branch managers, reference librarians, or subject bibliographers, the professional qualifications required of personnel in these positions should be noted by means of terminology easily understood by laypersons.

Some policies include a chart or figure outlining collection areas along with the staff member responsible for collection building within each category. As elsewhere, position titles should be employed rather than names of personnel since staff turnover generally occurs more frequently than the need to undertake a policy revision.

Additional details relating to the selection process are sometimes included; e.g., the use of professional reviewing tools and consideration of purchase recommendations from library clientele (particularly faculty in academic institutions). Such information can prove useful in diffusing outside criticism, particularly in cases of attempted censorship. If lengthy explanations are considered necessary, however, they probably should be included in their own sections.

[The above introduction to "Responsibility for Collection Development" was written by Debbie Cox, Reference Librarian/Collection Developer, Montgomery College, The Woodlands, Texas]

The variety of approaches in responsibility statements generally reflects the differing governance of the respective libraries. However, as the excerpts below make clear, libraries without exception advocate the administration of library affairs by trained professionals.

RESPONSIBILITY STATEMENTS FOR ACADEMIC LIBRARIES

Fitchburg State College: Collection Development Policies

The library director is responsible for managing the library and ultimately the material that is added to the collection. The librarians will meet as a committee once a month to decide on the selection of certain materials which will be added to the collection. This includes selections that will cost over $100; all standing orders; and all periodical suggestions.

Each librarian will be responsible for developing and maintaining a liaison relationship with an academic department of their choosing. Each department will in turn designate one of their faculty as their liaison. In selecting material, each librarian will need to maintain a department profile which will explain the needs and requirements of the department, the classes within the department, and the needs of the faculty; a subject file or profile which will briefly summarize the literature of the subject covered by the departments; and finally a holdings profile which would summarize the holdings of the FSC Library for the subjects covered by the departments.

The Collection Development Policy also recognizes and adopts the Guidelines of the Resources and Technical Services Division of the American Library Association. The librarians have met and decided the levels of collection for each of the academic departments.

All requests for material should be channeled to the appropriate librarian, no matter who initiated the request. The librarians have responsibility for selection.

In selecting material it will be the responsibility of each librarian to use the standard or appropriate titles.

The Library staff also adhered to the American Library Association Library Bill of Rights and the statement on Intellectual Freedom. [revised April 5, 2001, pp. 2–3; http://raven.fsc.edu/library/development.htm]

Kenyon College Library and Information Services: Collection Development Policy

Library Faculty Liaison Program

The College Librarians and Faculty share responsibility for developing the library collection. By way of the liaison program, they coordinate their efforts to ensure that the Library collects to meet the needs of the College. Most librarians, including the Director of Information Resources and the Acquisitions Librarian, serve as liaisons to several academic departments. The main responsibility of the liaisons is to maintain communication between the library and the faculty. As the library subject specialists, the liaisons serve as materials selectors, monitor the approval plan, and assess collection strengths and weaknesses. Liaisons also review gifts, provide advocacy for their disciplines in the Library, study collection use, and endeavor to understand community needs.

Library Collections Subcommittee

The Library Collections Subcommittee of the CPC is composed of four faculty members, two students, the Acquisitions Librarian, the Director of Information Resources, and the Vice President for Library and Information Services. The Subcommittee collaborates with the Library on policy matters relating to collection development. [updated May 25, 2000, p. 2; wysiwyg:// 85/http://lbis.kenyon.edu/colldev/]

RESPONSIBILITY STATEMENTS FOR COMMUNITY COLLEGES

Finger Lakes Community College, Charles J. Meder Library: Collection Development Policy

Ultimate responsibility for the development and maintenance of library collections rests with the Director of the Library. The Director will assign selection responsibilities to librarians who serve as liaisons to academic departments. In addition, suggestions are strongly encouraged from faculty to support their current and planned courses. Student, staff, and community requests for the acquisition of materials are also welcomed and encouraged. [adopted August 1998, p. 2; http://library.fingerlakes.edu/colldev.htm]

Oakton Community College: Library Policies

Selection of library materials is primarily the responsibility of the librarians under the direction of the Acquisitions Librarian. Problems will be resolved first in consultation with the Department Chair for Library Services, and then by the Director of Library Services. In addition, books requested by classroom faculty and by administrators will be ordered unless the request does not conform with the materials selection policy of the Library, or unless continued purchases in a particular subject area would create an undesirably large quantity of material in that subject area. [*Library Selection Policy*, adopted September 1995, pp. 3–4; http://servercc.oakton.edu/~wittman/find/policies.htm]

RESPONSIBILITY STATEMENTS FOR PUBLIC LIBRARIES

Eugene (Oregon) Public Library: Collection Development Policy

Ultimate responsibility for the EPL materials collection resides with the Library Services Director. The Head of Adult Services and Head of Children's/Extension Services are responsible for overseeing collection management. Reference and children's librarians, the Assistant Head of Adult Services and the Head of Adult Services all have collection development responsibilities for specific subject areas and formats. All librarians have a professional responsibility to be inclusive, not exclusive, in developing materials collections. [adopted by the Library Board September 2, 1992, updated November 2000, p. 4; www.ci.eugene.or.us/Library/hour . . . tions_cards/collection_development.htm)

Morton Grove (Illinois) Public Library: Collection Development and Materials Selection Policy

Ultimate responsibility for materials selection rests with the Library Director who operates within the framework of policies determined by the Board of Trustees. The Library Director delegates to the Head of Public Services/Assistant to the Director, who is responsible for collection development, the responsibility to work with the various sections within the Library to accomplish mutual goals and responsibilities regarding the acquisition, cataloging, and processing of materials, and to promote consistency in the selection and maintenance of the materials collection. All professional staff members may participate in the selection of library materials.

The authority and responsibilities of the Head of Public Services/Assistant to the Director consists of the following:

- Authority to approve or disapprove selection recommendation from the selection librarians, other staff, and the public.

- Authority to make final decisions on the withdrawal of circulating materials, the rebinding of books, repackaging of audiovisual materials, replacement orders, and the addition of gifts to the cataloged circulating collection.
- Authority to review various collections in the Library, evaluate the contents, and submit written reports to the Library Director.
- Authority to initiate any weeding projects as a result of collection evaluations.

[*The Webrary*, first published on the web January 26, 1998, last updated August 2, 2000, pp. 1–2; www.webrary.org/inside/colldevtoc.html]

Chapter Five

Mission, Goal, and Objective Statements in Policies

Although widely employed within written policies, this section poses a number of problems for anyone referring to these documents. In many instances, libraries don't utilize mission, goal, and objective statements in tandem; this despite the fact that these three concepts are interrelated and vital to the overall collection building plan. This shortcoming may be a result of confusion in the way some libraries interpret these concepts. Elizabeth Futas has alluded to the lack of consistency from one library to another in the application of these terms, noting that policies "often called them mission statements when they were goals, goals when they were objectives, and objectives when they were goals." (1)

Some libraries opt for including mission, goal, and objective statements which address the full spectrum of library services. In such cases, those statements specifically geared to collection development may be hard to discern or absent altogether. Furthermore, it is doubtful that many of the statements appearing in policies have been formulated based on sound data. Therefore, the likelihood of a library achieving published goals and objectives is subject to question.

Given the widespread misuse of these terms, it would seem instructive to delineate their meaning and application. According to Futas, a mission statement "should be short, general, and long-lived," while complementing the mission of the parent institution, if there is one. (2) In order to fulfill the mission, goals should articulate library priorities in the form of broad, albeit focused, purpose statements. Typically beginning with words like "develop," "provide," "encourage," or "support," goals should be achievable within a ten-year period. Best seen as incremental steps which enable an institution to achieve its goals and mission, objective statements should be measurable, specific, determinate, and action oriented. (3)

The contrast between general statements, incorporating issues which encompass more than collection development, and those focusing on collection building proper is reflected in the documents cited here. Furthermore, examples can be seen to vary considerably regarding the depth of coverage devoted to delineating this operation. SUNY's Charles B. Sears Law Library limits this section to a paraphrase of its mission statement; collection building is noted only in a peripheral manner. The City of Louisville Public Library places an even greater emphasis on brevity, outlining its community service role in one concise sentence, with no mention of information resources at all. On the other hand, Lake-Sumter Community College Libraries has opted for a more detailed approach, quoting the parent institution's multi-faceted mission, and then citing its particular role, including the provision of services as well as collection development. Both the Newark Public Library and Kitsap Regional Library have addressed their respective mandates in more complex fashion. Newark attempts to delineate its purpose and mission statements within the context of various service roles, whereas the Kitsap cites a series of planning documents in relating its mission to collection management and service imperatives.

MISSION, GOAL, AND OBJECTIVE STATEMENT FOR ACADEMIC LIBRARIES

State University of New York at Buffalo, Charles B. Sears Law Library: Collection Development Library

The Law Library's primary mission is to support the research and educational needs of the U.B. Law School community. Additionally, it serves the legal information needs of the University community, the practicing bar, and the public at large. As the only research level law library in Western New York, it is an important anchor and archive.

The Law Library is committed to providing easy access to information in an atmosphere conducive to study and research, a collection development policy that includes print, electronic, and other non-print material, and expert information access services that promote the effective use of the library's resources. [last updated May 2001, p. 2; http://ublib.buffalo.edu/libraries/units/law/cdpol.htm]

MISSION, GOAL, AND OBJECTIVE STATEMENTS FOR COMMUNITY COLLEGES

Lake-Sumter Community College Libraries: Collection Development Policy

College Mission

The mission of Lake-Sumter Community College is to provide:

1. High quality post-secondary academic education, leading to an Associate in Arts degree, which parallels the first and second years of a baccalaureate degree program.
2. High quality post-secondary career education, leading to an Associate in Science degree and/or certificate, which offers students comprehensive education in specific vocations.
3. High quality non-credit continuing education programs that develop skills necessary for entry into a vocational/technical field, for advancement in a current occupation, or for a career change, and customized programs designed for business, industry, and other organizations.
4. High quality college preparatory courses designed to help prepare students for college-level courses.
5. High quality credit and non-credit courses for persons desiring fulfillment of personal educational objectives.
6. High quality credit and non-credit courses using alternative instructional methods to provide flexible access for students.
7. Student development and support services that encourage and enhance the success and well-being of a diverse and ever-changing student population.
8. An intellectual atmosphere which is conducive to the pursuit of knowledge and the examination of ideas.
9. Cultural, social, community service, and intercollegiate activities intended to enrich not only the lives of the students but also the lives of residents throughout the district.
10. Active participation in and support of local and state-wide economic development.
11. Other programs and/or activities as may be authorized by the State Board of Education, State Board of Community Colleges and District Board of Trustees.

Mission of the College Libraries

In accordance with the college's mission, the college libraries recognize their responsibility to serve as an integral part of the college's instructional program. The primary purpose of the college libraries, and the mission of the collection development and management program, is to serve the academic community by providing access to resources that support the college curriculum, by stimulating the intellectual development of students and faculty, by motivating students to acquire life-long learning and reading skills, and by assisting faculty in maintaining awareness of current information resources and information literacy skills.

The college libraries also strive to provide continuing education opportunities that will enrich the entire community by making resources and facilities available to community residents. Materials will not be specifically acquired for community residents or groups, except for links to Internet resources and government documents which meet LSCC government documents selection criteria.

Collection development for the joint-use libraries at the Sumter campus and South Lake campus are a shared responsibility of Lake-Sumter Community College and the Sumter County Public Library System at the Sumter campus, and Lake-Sumter Community College and the University of Central Florida at the South Lake campus. The college is responsible for selecting only materials intended for college use in the joint-use libraries. [revised 16, 2001, pp. 1–3; http://lscc.cc.fl.us/library/colldev.htm]

MISSION, GOAL, AND OBJECTIVE STATEMENTS FOR PUBLIC LIBRARIES

Glenview (Illinois) Public Library: Collection Development Policy

The Glenview Public Library, supported by Glenview taxpayers, provides service to all individuals and groups in the community regardless of age, race, sex, religion, or political belief. The Library's mission, briefly stated (see the Long Range Plan), is to serve and promote the informational, cultural, educational, and recreational needs of all the residents of Glenview, providing access to the universe of information. To carry out this mission, the Board has directed the staff to select and provide books and other materials which will assist the residents of Glenview in the pursuit of knowledge, information, education, research, and recreation. The Glenview Public Library is a repository for the free expression of individuals where residents of the community may come to examine, study, read, and evaluate all sides of issues. Freedom to read is essential to maintain democracy in our village, state, and country. The Glenview Public Library does not necessarily advocate the ideas found in its collection, nor does the presence of an item indicate any endorsement of its contents. It is in the community's interest that the Glenview Public Library make available the widest diversity of views and opinions, including those which may seem unorthodox to some or be unpopular. [last updated May 1, 2000, p. 2; www.glenview.lib.il.us/coldev.html]

City of Louisville Public Library: Collection Policy

The mission of the Louisville Public library is to provide effective delivery of library and information services that meet the informational, educational, and recreational needs of the community. [last modified February 28, 2001, p. 1; www.ci.louisville.co.us/library/collect.asp]

Newark Public Library: Collection Development Policy

The Library's purpose, mission statement, and service roles, as articulated in its long range plan, are the key principles that shape the development of the collections.

Purpose Statement

The purpose of The Newark Public Library is to empower Newark residents, students, and workers to enrich their own lives with knowledge, information, education, and culture.

Mission Statement

The mission of The Newark Public Library is to provide for the people of Newark an easily available local collection of and global access to the universal record of human thought, wisdom, ideals, information, experiences, and artistic expressions.

The Library provides information useful for daily living, supports formal education and independent learning efforts, and assists researchers and scholars.

Deriving its principal support from the City of Newark, the Library emphasizes services for Newark's residents and students. Affirming its belief in the power of education and in the potential of libraries to change lives, the Library strongly supports the children of Newark in their efforts to learn and grow and achieve.

As a major resource for New Jersey, the Library strives also to serve those who work in the City, and libraries and people throughout the state.

In support of this mission, the Library selects, collects, organizes, and makes available for use a broad, deep, and diverse collection of materials in a variety of formats; provides excellent personal information services and guidance in the use of library resources; and offers programs for personal enrichment.

In pursuing this mission, the Library strives to fulfill its unique responsibility to ensure free, open, and equal access to information for all the people that the Library serves.

The Library actively seeks to serve and reflect the diverse Newark community in its collections, services, programs, and staff. It affirms a commitment to preserve, promote, and celebrate the multicultural heritage of the people of Newark.

The Newark Public Library contributes to the economic life of the City, the vitality of its neighborhoods, and the quality of life of its citizens.

Service Roles

In accord with its stated purpose and mission, the Library is focusing its principal efforts during this planning cycle on fulfilling these primary service roles.

Information Center

Newark residents, students, and workers have access to current, accurate, practical information useful for daily living.

The public will benefit from easy access to quick and accurate answers to the questions and decisions they face daily. Information and assistance that is not publicly available elsewhere will be available on any subject for anyone. Individuals, businesses, and government agencies will find the information they need.

Formal Education Support Center

Students in Newark schools and colleges are able to meet educational objectives established during their formal course of study.

After school and on weekends the Library serves as a major homework assistance center. The Library's collections and staff expertise are strong in this area, in response to traditional and continuing heavy use by students. This area is also appropriate for development of collaborative efforts with the schools and recognition and support for the services provided. This role is strongly tied to the Library's commitment to children.

Research Center

People doing research have access to the Library's research collections and staff expertise.

Over the term of its long history, the Library has developed many and diverse subject specialties. Researchers need the unique resources, the primary sources, the special collections, the breadth of the Library's collections, and the assistance of staff subject specialists to create new knowledge.

Independent Learning Center

Newark people of all ages can pursue learning and self improvement in reading, languages, and their individual interests.

The Library is uniquely suited to support lifelong learning—efforts that precede, follow, or supplement formal schooling. This concept of the library as "the people's university" echoes a function first articulated by Thomas Jefferson but specifically applied to the particular needs of the Newark community. The Library identifies literacy, career information, English as a Second Language, and adult basic education as priority activities for this role.

The Library has targeted two areas for growth and development as important secondary roles during the current planning cycle.

Preschoolers Door to Learning

Young children develop an interest in reading and learning through services for children and for parents or caregivers and children together.

Fifty percent of a child's intellectual skill is developed before the age of four. This is a critical time to instill a love of learning and reading and to foster a child's identification of the Library as an appealing and useful part of life. For preschool children, who are served by no other community agency, the Library is their first experience of a structured educational environment. For parents and caregivers, the Library is a place to find support, guidance, and a "community" of other parents and children. By encouraging reading aloud as a shared activity, the Library strengthens family bonds and nurtures the child's association of parental interest, comfort, and support with the pleasure and excitement of reading and learning.

Community Information Center

The public has current information on community organizations, issues, services, and activities.

In a city the size and complexity of Newark, a myriad of organizations and agencies provide an array of activities, programs, and services. Citizens often must battle through a maze of bureaucracies to gain information and services essential to their lives. Their task can be complicated by barriers of language, lack of mobility or transportation, infirmity, or special needs. The Library transcends these barriers to become the one place to call or visit to get vital information or to be quickly and accurately referred to the appropriate agency.

Finally, the Library also maintains support for two other service roles.

Popular Materials Library

Library users have popular materials readily available in a variety of formats consistent with their interests and demands.

The people of Newark enjoy the benefit of free use of popular materials to read, to listen to, and to view. Rather than having to buy materials for leisure and cultural enrichment, library users can turn to the Library to borrow what they want.

Community Activities Center

The Library serves as a center for community activities, meetings, and services, and as a cultural leader in the City.

Community life is enriched by library-sponsored opportunities to meet and discuss important issues, participate in recreational activities, hear distinguished speakers, attend cultural programs, and view art and historical exhibits. The library facilities are used by community groups to provide social services and promote civic activities. The library collaborates with community groups and provides leadership for cultural activities. [adopted September 24, 1997, pp. 3–6; Roles are excerpted from *Gateway to Information/Door to Learning, The Newark Public Library's Service Plan for 1994-1998*]

Kitsap (Washington) Regional Library: Collection Development Policy (Third Edition)

Kitsap Regional Library's Mission Statement

As an advocate for its customers, Kitsap Regional Library provides and promotes access to information for the people of Kitsap County.

The "Mission Statement" is part of Kitsap Regional Library's Strategic Plan.

"Customers" are those people who live in Kitsap County and use the Library and its services. The Library is primarily supported by property taxes and is committed to providing excellent service for its customers.

"Information" consists of knowledge, facts, and ideas relevant to the people of Kitsap County. It is provided in a variety of formats: it complements, rather than duplicates, information available through other agencies. Information may be practical, educational, cultural, and entertaining and includes the history of civilization, the detail of the current world, and the speculations of the future. Information can be found in both the non-fiction and fiction collections of the Library. The Library focuses on providing information when it is asked for ("just in time") rather than storing it for potential future need ("just in case").

The Library actively promotes access to information for its customers beyond its own collection by initiating and supporting liaisons with other agencies and institutions that also provide information. Cooperative agreements allow agencies to make the most effective use of traditional and electronic information delivery so that they can best meet their customers' needs.

Vision Statement

"Kitsap Regional Library is the dynamic and evolving center of information access for the people of Kitsap County. The Library is an inviting place where individuals, families, and organizations may explore the world of knowledge and the record of culture. In the foreseeable future, books and other traditionally acquired materials remain a vital part of the Library's base of information. The Library also responds to the changing needs of its customers and continues to move beyond the walls, providing an increasing range of information resources that are electronically linked and available to people in their homes and businesses. The Library informs the public of its range of services. People view the Library as a well-managed organization and an integral part of their lives."

Service Vision 2000

[Resolution 1990/6, adopted by the Kitsap Regional Library Board of Trustees on August 21, 1990]

Whereas, the Kitsap Regional Library is committed to serving as an informational gateway which facilitates independent pursuit of knowledge; and

Whereas, our principles of service are:

- to encourage an interest in reading and learning in members of the community, and
- to provide equal access to the spectrum of recorded knowledge relevant to the interests and priorities of the community,

Therefore, be it resolved that it is the intent of the Kitsap Regional Library Board of Trustees to increase the organizational emphasis on information technology and user discovery service, and be it further resolved that the Kitsap Regional Library Director is directed to propose steps to be taken to refine these goals and to implement them.

Values

Customer Service: Kitsap Regional Library values its customers. We listen to our customers and focus our resources and energy on their service needs and expectations. Each customer is regarded as an individual with innate worth and dignity.

Excellent Service: Kitsap Regional Library values its ability to provide excellent service to its customers. The Library is the primary information provider in the County and its services are recognized for their quality and responsiveness.

Cost-Effective Service: Kitsap Regional Library values its ability to find cost-effective ways to provide materials and services to its customers. The Library is seen as a conscientious and responsible steward of taxpayers' resources.

Continued Improvement: Kitsap Regional Library values its commitment to ongoing service improvements. The Library is an evolving entity that constantly evaluates its service and strives, within the boundaries of its resources, to meet the changing needs of its customers.

Best Tools for the Job: Kitsap Regional Library values a commitment to cost-effective methods for promoting and providing access to information, including tools in the forefront of technology.

Mission Statement

Reference and Information Services enables the people of Kitsap County to find answers to their questions.

The Reference and Information Services Division is made up of two departments: the Reference Department and the Collection Development Department.

Vision for Information Services in the Year 2000

This is a key document to collection development and information delivery at Kitsap Regional Library. Developed by a staff team, which included the Director, it is an integral part of Kitsap Regional Library's Strategic Plan. The document includes a vision statement describing the provision of information services to the people of Kitsap County in 2000, a mission statement for the Reference and Information Division, and ten goals to put the vision into effect (see Appendices).

To support its mission [includes only those goals relating to collection development]:

Goal 1: The Reference and Information Services Division provides county-wide service. Concentrated resources, leadership, expertise, and staff training are provided through one or more strategically located support sites.

Goals 2: The emphasis of the Reference and Information Services Division is on providing access to information that is of interest to the people of the County as a whole. This service units consists of basic, expanded, and support service levels. Basic information and reference services are available at all sites with expanded and support level service available at designated sites.

Goal 6: Reference and Information Services continues to move beyond the walls of the traditional Library by employing electronic and other technologies that improve people's access to information.

Goal 7: Reciprocal contractual agreements are established with other agencies for the sharing of networked resources.

Goal 8: Resources and access provided by Reference and Information Services complement, rather than duplicate or replace, those of educational institutions.

Goal 10: People may be offered additional access and specialized or expedited services for a fee, as long as the provision of such services or access does not detract from meeting the needs of the general public.

Provision of On-Line Information, 1997–2000: Vision Statement and Recommendations from the Networked Information Team

"The expectation is that (1) the amount of information provided on-line will have doubled during the next four years and that (2) the number of people using on-line information will also double during that time. . . . Information that is now provided through print and other formats will be increasingly provided on-line. Books, videos, and sound recordings are not likely to disappear, but much of what they contain will be available from new technologies. . . . The print collection will steadily begin to decrease in size over the next four years in response to more widely available and cost-effective electronic alternatives. For example, the print collection supporting reference services may be reduced by as much as ten percent by the year 2000 as on-line alternatives become available . . .

The Library manages its on-line information as it has traditionally managed its other collection resources, with a focus on both cost-effectiveness and diversity.

"Provision of On-Line Information, 1997–2000" was approved by Library Council in August 1997 (see Appendices).

Using the "Mission Statement," "Vision Statement," "Service Vision 2000," goals of "I-2000," "Provision of On-Line Information, 1997–2000," and the "values" of the Library as its framework, the "Collection Development Policy" guides the selection of materials for Kitsap Regional Library. This includes their format, their age appropriateness, their location in the system, the means by which they are delivered, and the number of titles duplicated to meet their interest. The collection is an active one, meeting the current needs of the Library's customers. Items are expected to be used frequently, or they are withdrawn from the collection. A substantial percentage of the collection has been purchased within the past five years. Combined with an active annual assessment process, this assures that the collection satisfies the interests of those who use it.

Information found in electronic sources, both within the system and from outside resources, increasingly impacts the size of the print collection. As online alternatives become user-friendly and can be selected, catalogued, and presented so that our customers can find them useful, or superior to the print collection, they are included in the Library's collection. On-line information will be increasingly included in the collection when it offers a wider cost-effective distribution of access throughout the County than can be achieved with print resources.

Because information involves the accumulation of knowledge, the Library's collection reflects diverse points-of-view and a wide range of ideas spanning recorded history. The selection of materials for the Library is based on the broad backgrounds, interests, and needs of Kitsap County residents and library customers. [adopted May 19, 1998, pp. 3–7; www.krl.org/administration/policies/colldev.html]

MISSION, GOAL, AND OBJECTIVE STATEMENT FOR SPECIAL LIBRARIES AND RELATED INSTITUTIONS

The Newark Museum Library and Archives: Collection Development Policy

The main purpose of the Library and the Archives of The Newark Museum is to meet the research needs of the professional staff of The Newark Museum. This staff includes the art curators, the scientists, the educators, the exhibition staff, and the administrative staff. The Library and the Archives also serves the docents, volunteers, and members of The Newark Museum. Secondarily, the Library and the Archives is open to the general public, by appointment only, particularly to serious researchers, university professors, graduate students, and undergraduates. (p. 1; www.arlisna.org/Newark.htm)

NOTES

1. Elizabeth Futas, ed., *Collection Development Policies and Procedures*. 3rd ed. (Phoenix, Ariz.: Oryx, 1995, 184–5.
2. Futas, *Collection Development Policies and Procedures*, 184.
3. Futas, *Collection Development Policies and Procedures*, 184.

Chapter Six

Target Audience
Identification in Policies

Audience statements range from broad-based descriptions of clientele to highly focused user groups. General discussions of patrons—as opposed to the demographic breakdowns characterizing Community Statements—tend to address exactly who is eligible to use the library collection.

Collection development statements are more likely to mention specific types of clients. According to Elizabeth Futas, patron categories seem to be included because "library materials specific to their needs form a special or large segment of their collection, and they wish to bring this particular group to the attention of the readers of the policy." (1) Academic institutions tend to emphasize student constituencies, whereas public libraries generally concentrate on children and young adults. Some public libraries go into considerable detail outlining responsibilities to area students. For example, the Colusa County (California) Library includes the following guidelines:

> Both the adult and young adult collections will serve as supplementary sources for student use, but materials selected for students must also be useful to the general reader. Textbooks will not ordinarily be purchased, as the public library is not designed to provide school library service. Although school curriculum demands are considered, the public library should be a supplement, not a substitute, for the development and use of school library resources. (2)

Given the federal government's legislative mandates addressing the needs of disabled citizens, it is not surprising that many institutions have singled out the homebound, individuals with learning disabilities, and the visually, physically, and mentally challenged in recently published documents.

The following excerpts reflect the contrasting approaches taken by libraries regarding service to patrons. Whereas some policies focus on specific client groups, others—most notably, the Clatsop Community College and Victoria and Albert Museum policies—take a more generalized approach.

TARGET AUDIENCE STATEMENT FOR ACADEMIC LIBRARIES

Springfield College, Babson Library: Collection Development Policy

Collection Development for Persons with Disabilities

Under the provisions of the Americans with Disabilities Act (ADA) and Section 504 of the Rehabilitation Act of 1973, persons with disabilities have equal access to information and sources to the extent possible within the mission guidelines of the Babson Library. Materials that are designed for use by individuals with disabilities will be purchased by subject liaisons; e.g., a large print version of a psychology text would be purchased by the Psychology liaison librarian. Materials about disabilities will be purchased within the appropriate existing subject funds. [copyright 1997, last modified October 26, 2000, p. 25; www.spfldcol.edu/homepage.nsf/]

TARGET AUDIENCE STATEMENT FOR COMMUNITY COLLEGES

Clatsop Community College Library (Oregon): Collection Development Policy

All adults may use the materials in the library. Students must be currently registered. County patrons must be 18 years of age. If under 18, they may not check materials out and must be accompanied by an adult. Patrons under 18 will be redirected as feasible to their high school libraries. Patrons requesting a library card must show proof of continuing residency in Clatsop County or one of the other counties in Clatsop Community College's service area.

Clatsop Community College is a rural college in an economically depressed region. There are few public libraries available locally. It is important that collection development at CCC Library take into consideration the specific local needs of the student population that arise from these factors. [drafted June 24, 1999, revised October 31, 2000, p. 1; http://library.clatsop.cc .or.us/cd00-01.htm]

TARGET AUDIENCE STATEMENTS FOR PUBLIC LIBRARIES

Dane County Library: Selection Policy

Adult and Young Adult

Items in the adult collection are selected primarily for persons 14 years of age and older. Selection is as broad in scope as the interests of the residents of Dane County. Besides aiming at variety and depth in content, it must recognize a wide range of reading abilities.

Through carefully chosen materials, young adults are introduced to the Library's complete resources and are encouraged to continue using them — materials which help young adults understand themselves and others, broaden their viewpoints and knowledge of the world, stimulate their curiosity, and expand both their reading ability and reading enjoyment. Emphasis will be on popular browsing materials, primarily paperbacks, rather than on school-related materials.

Responsibility for the reading of children rests with their parents or legal guardians. Selection of material will not be inhibited by the possibility that books may come into the possession of children. The selection criteria for young adult material will be the same as stated for books and other print material.

Children

In selecting materials for children, the objective is to make available a collection that satisfies the informational, recreational, and cultural reading needs and potentials for children from pre-school age to age 14. Books and other materials are included which meet the general demands of the majority of children along with special needs or talents. Children have full access to adult and young adult materials both on the bookmobile and through interlibrary loan. The selection criteria for children's material are the same as for adult materials with the addition of vocabulary suitable to the age of the intended audience and, for children's fiction, the quality of the illustrations.

Students

It must be recognized that the primary obligation for providing library services in support of formal education rests with each educational institution. For this reason, the Library Service does not develop its collections in response to curriculum-based requests. Textbooks are purchased only when they provide the best coverage of a subject and are useful to the general public; they are not purchased or duplicated to satisfy the demands of a specific course of study.

Visually Handicapped

For individuals whose reading is limited by poor eyesight, the Library Service maintains a collection of large print books on topics of general interest. The Library Service assists qualified individuals to obtain talking books and other services from the Library Service for the Blind and Physically Handicapped. [adopted September 1988, amended December 7, 2000; www.scls .lib.wi.us/del/policies.html]

Middleton Public Library: Collection Development Policy

Materials for Children

1. In selecting materials for children, the library's goal is to make available a collection which satisfies their informational and recreational needs.
2. Materials are selected which meet the general needs of the majority of children. Materials whose qualities make them valuable to children with special needs, talents, problems, or interests are also considered.
3. Criteria for materials selection are the same as for adult and young adult materials with the addition of vocabulary suitable to the age of the intended audience and quality of the illustrations in children's fiction.
   A. Materials for adult new readers will continue to be purchased and displayed in a separate section. These materials are designed to allow adult readers to pursue their studies independently or with the assistance of a tutor.
   B. Materials and equipment for the visually impaired, such as large-print books and magnifiers, are acquired according to patron demand. The library also encourages patrons with special needs to use the resources of the Milwaukee Regional Library for the Blind and Physically Handicapped.
   C. The library will continue to work with other area libraries and organizations in the planning or expansion of services for those with special needs not currently being met or adequately met. [updated October 16, 1997, p. 8; www.scls.lib.wi.us/middleton/policies/midpolcol.htm]

TARGET AUDIENCE STATEMENT FOR SPECIAL LIBRARIES AND RELATED INSTITUTIONS

National Art Library, Victoria and Albert Museum: Collection Development Policy

Analysis of a survey of Library users in 1985/86 showed that students, both undergraduate and postgraduate, comprised 50% of the readership, the other

50% being made up of artists, designers, academic and private researchers, art history lecturers, teachers, picture researchers, writers, curators of other museums and galleries, art and museum library professionals, staff of professional associations, auction house staff and antique dealers, and the general public.

In 1985/6, 56% of all users came from London and South East England, the rest from elsewhere in the UK and abroad, with the single largest group being from the United States and Canada. Most users had a reading knowledge of French, German, or Italian in addition to English.

It is probably safe to assume that the pattern has changed [since that time] in that a greater number of undergraduate students use the library, the budgets of their own libraries having been drastically reduced over the last three years. However, the NAL is not funded to assume the role implied by the uncontrolled admission of undergraduates. The staffing levels of the NAL oblige it to ensure that only such students are admitted as can show that the materials they require are unobtainable elsewhere. In practice, this restricts admission of undergraduates to those involved in extended essays or theses. Nevertheless, the NAL welcomes group visits of students to view materials with their tutors or NAL staff. [copyright 1993, Chapter 1, pp. 4–5; www.nal.vam.ac.uk/pubs/nalcdp1.htm]

NOTES

1. Elizabeth Futas, ed., *Collection Development Policies and Procedures*, 3rd ed. (Phoenix, Ariz.: Oryx, 1995), 244.

2. Ibid.

Chapter Seven

Budget Allocation and Funding Statements in Policies

Although a core feature of collection management, the allocation of funds has only recently become a fixture in policy statements. Elizabeth Futas, in *Collection Development Policies and Procedures*, attributes this change to the following factors:

- processes once carried out behind closed doors are now appearing in public documents; and
- procedures once a part of manuals attached to policy documents are today more likely to be inserted into the policy proper. (1)

The rationale for discussing collection funding allocations within policies is twofold:

1. increased calls for accountability on the part of public institutions; and
2. the desire of library administrators for ammunition in budgetary hearings. (2)

In order to be effective, the funding section should focus on the sources for the materials budget, whether or not supplementary monies are available, and the basic breakdowns for acquiring library holdings. This involves addressing the following questions (sometimes located elsewhere in the policy):

- Exactly what kinds of resources are being purchased through mainstream budgetary allotments?
- How does the library determine its collection priorities?
- Assuming essential services are in no way compromised, can funds be saved by substituting one format for another?
- Will a cooperative acquisitions program facilitate fiscal savings?

• Has the library made a reasonable effort to obtain support through grants, philanthropy, and other outside sources?

A problematical undercurrent to the funding statement is the inclusion of extraneous procedural details and complicated allocation formulas which detract from the essential information required for public consumption. Extensive line item breakdowns and thoroughgoing discussions of performance-based budgets are better placed in an all-encompassing procedures manual.

The growing importance of the budget within collection development policies is reflected in the excerpts below. In the case of academic institutions, conspectus analysis—a definitive survey is provided in *Collection Assessment: A Look at the RLG Conspectus*, edited by Richard J. Wood and Katina Strauch (Binghamton, NY: Haworth, 1992)—is often integrated into the funding process.

BUDGET ALLOCATION AND FUNDING STATEMENT FOR ACADEMIC LIBRARIES

University of Evansville Libraries: Collection Development Manual

Budget Allocation

With the recommendation of the University Librarian, the University Administration allocates the overall library materials budget. The materials budget is divided between nonrecurring ("Books") and recurring ("Periodicals") expenditures with the exact division determined by agreement between the University Librarian and the Administration. The terms *books* and *periodicals* are historic legacies, and electronic and other nonprint expenditures are included in these categories based on their budget characteristics.

The Periodicals budget is administered by the librarians in consultation with the faculty and includes continuing online resources. The book budget is divided among Standing Orders, Collection Development, Reference, and the departmental units. Initially, Standing Orders are allocated their projected cost and the remaining funds are then divided between the library and the departments with the percentage of the division decided by the University Librarian. The library portion is controlled by the librarians and used for Reference or other works, particularly interdisciplinary materials. Each departmental unit is allocated funds from the remainder based upon a formula devised by a Faculty Senate committee which uses weighted criteria such as enrollment, number of professors, level of courses/students taught, and cost of materials in each discipline.

Supplemental Funds

The library has a limited amount of supplemental money regularly available to it. Generally referred to as "gift money," most of it consists of the proceeds of bequests from which the library receives the income. The funds are limited and most have restrictions. The major funds are:

Wheeler. Walton M. Wheeler was a prominent attorney and a member of the Board of Trustees. Since 1960, the proceeds from a trust in his memory have been awarded annually to one or more faculty members for special library purchases. Proposals are solicited in the Fall Semester.

Harding. The Harrison H. and Jesse L. Harding funds are to be used for titles in American history and civilization.

Eades. The Alvin Q. Eades funds may be used for general library acquisitions.

Orr. The Drs. Samuel and Jane Orr Unitrust may be used for books and other educational materials.

Cox. Donated in memory of Eva V. and Ting Cox by their son and husband, respectively, Warren M. Cox, Jr., proceeds from this endowment are for the purchase of library books.

Clifford. The James L. Clifford Endowment is to be used for materials relating to Samuel Johnson and 18th-century life.

[web edition November 1995, above section revised May 23, 2000, 2 pp.; http://www2.evansville.edu/libweb/libservices/cd/pm94-6.htm]

BUDGET ALLOCATION AND FUNDING STATEMENT FOR COMMUNITY COLLEGES

Clatsop Community College Library: Collection Development Policy

Funds are allotted at this time by format: AV materials, Books, and Periodicals. Funds are not allotted by topic, or department. After automation has been completed, the result of a conspectus analysis should determine the areas that need special focus. Going into the second year of using the automation system, all items added to the collection will be given a statistical category based on the department that requested the item and/or the topic of the item. This information will help in the conspectus analysis that will be conducted every budget year.

Classic materials in literature, of high quality and lasting value, and in high demand for the instructional needs, will be purchased if available in several formats: AV and print and/or electronic (which includes CDs). Only a certain percent of the budget can be used to that effect, as stated below. The first and primary purchase of an item will be in its primary format.

Books and AV materials: Approximately 40% of the book budget is allotted to standing orders at this time, mainly for reference books.

Fifty-five percent of the combined AV/Book budget will be allotted to maintaining level 3a of the conspectus for the main departments of instruction of the college: nursing, business, microcomputer applications and programming, fine arts, arts and letters, maritime science, applied technology, physics, chemistry and biology, criminal justice.

Five percent of the AV budget is allotted to providing alternative formats in high demand for instructional needs as mentioned above.

At this time, the AV budget is focused primarily on requests from instructors, to support their class demonstrations and their teaching. Large purchases are rotated among disciplines. The analysis of the collection with the conspectus after the automation is complete, will be done with AV and print formats combined. As stated in section XII of this Collection Development Policy, this analysis will guide the staff on what areas to target as a team. [adopted October 31, 2000, p. 2; http://library.clatsop.cc.or.us/cd00-01.htm]

BUDGET ALLOCATION AND FUNDING STATEMENT FOR PUBLIC LIBRARIES

Marshall (Idaho) Public Library: Collection Development Policy

1. The overwhelming majority of funds expended for materials are budgeted annually through the Library Fund received from the City of Pocatello from property taxes.
2. The library solicits and welcomes donations of funds and grants from the Friends of the Marshall Public Library and a variety of other sources.
3. The Pocatello Public Library Endowment Fund, an Agency Fund of the Idaho Community Foundation, has been established to provide a perennial source of funds for the purchased of library materials.

[revised January 18, 2000, p. 5; www.lili.org/marshall/gen_collect.html]

NOTES

1. Futas, Elizabeth, ed., *Collection Development Policies and Procedures*, 3rd ed. (Phoenix, Ariz.: Oryx, 1995), 199.
2. Futas, *Collection Development Policies and Procedures*, 199.

Chapter Eight

Evaluative Criteria
Identified in Policies

This section, sometimes referred to as Selection Criteria, represents the core of the collection development policy. It provides a blueprint as to why certain information resources are chosen over others for library holdings. Therefore, listing criteria employed by collection developers informs an institution's constituency regarding the decision-making process and expenditure of funds.

Policies vary to a considerable degree in the presentation of this information. Most notably, libraries do not always clearly differentiate between general and specific criteria, choosing instead to provide an inventory of points for consideration during the evaluation process. Libraries offering a more segmented layout may have contrasting perceptions of exactly what constitutes "general" criteria. Some institutions equate them with collection building *objectives*; that is, a mechanism for viewing holdings as a single entity, whereas specific criteria are applied on a title-by-title basis. In other words, such general criteria serve as a corrective mechanism to ensure that collections remain focused on overriding institutional goals and objectives. Typical examples of these general criteria would include:

- The collection will attempt to provide a balance of viewpoints on all controversial issues.
- The collection will attempt to include a cross-section of media formats, topics, and viewpoints representative of patron needs and interests.
- The library will attempt to meet all relevant collection standards, whether issued by governmental agencies, professional associations, or regional accrediting bodies.

The majority of libraries, however, view general criteria as possessing the broadest possible application, whereas specific criteria are employed with particular media, categories, etc. For instance, the East Gwillimbury (Canada) Public Library supplements its "general considerations" listing with "special considerations" sections for the evaluation of non-fiction, fiction, and non-book materials. (1) Specific criteria may also be organized by age levels, subject areas, and special collections. (2)

Some policies include additional irregularities worthy of note. Evaluative criteria are occasionally found in other portions of the document; e.g., the format statement, gifts, and weeding guidelines. In other instances, the library will apply the same set of criteria for both the selection and weeding functions. Elizabeth Futas provides the following justification for such a strategy:

> What differs, after all, is the community for which it was selected versus the community for which it will be rejected, and the time it was selected versus the time it will be discarded. The process and the criteria remain the same. (3)

The Fermilab Library's "Evaluation" excerpt (later in this chapter) illustrates this approach.

The varied approaches noted above—use of general vs. specific criteria, fragmented integrated presentation of criteria, etc.—are reflected in the following policy examples.

COLLECTION DEVELOPMENT OBJECTIVES
FOR ACADEMIC LIBRARIES

University of Southern Mississippi: Collection Development Policy

The library attempts to acquire all types of library materials to meet its major objectives. In order to meet the objectives, cooperation between faculty, staff, and students is necessary. The objectives are as follows:

1. To obtain and make available those library materials needed for the instructional programs offered by The University.
2. To acquire and make available those library materials required by the students, faculty, and staff for their general research.
3. To make provision for access to information needed to support the instructional and research needs of The University community, but not available on-site.
4. To develop collections in areas in which new and expanded responsibilities of The University are anticipated.

5. To collect and preserve all printed materials relating to the history, development, and character of The University of Southern Mississippi. To acquire and preserve all publications of departments, schools, and agencies of The University.

In an effort to meet its obligations, USM Libraries follows these general guidelines:

1. Allocated funds are spent for materials to be housed in Cook Library, in Special Collections, in the Music Resource Center, in Gunn Education Materials Center, and on the Gulf Coast campus in Cox Library, and in the Curriculum Lab. Library funds are not spent for materials to be housed outside the official library locations and/or the electronic access systems.
2. When lack of funds limits purchases, first priority is given to current publications rather than retrospective items.
3. Publications in the English language are given first priority.
4. Materials are acquired in an alternative format if originals are not available or if they are too expensive.
5. A duplicate of any item is purchased only by justification of heavy and continued use. Multiple copies for classroom use are not purchased.
6. Holdings of other libraries in the region are considered before purchasing expensive items or collections.
7. The library does not purchase extensive in-depth materials for specific thesis topics of graduate students or for short-term research of faculty members.
8. Works of contemporary authors who have achieved critical recognition will be purchased; otherwise current popular fiction and non-fiction will not be purchased.

[last modified January 24, 2001, pp. 1–2; www.lib.usm.edu/policy/cdpolicy .htm]

COLLECTION DEVELOPMENT OBJECTIVES FOR PUBLIC LIBRARIES

Fort Vancouver Regional Library: Policy for Selecting and Discarding Materials

The Library collection will be selected and maintained to enable each person to find the library materials and information that she or he wants according to her or his own free choice. No material will be excluded because of the race, nationality, religion, gender, sexual orientation, political or social view of either the author or of the material.

The collection, taken as a whole, will be an unbiased and diverse source of information representing as many viewpoints as possible. Subjects and viewpoints will be covered in sufficient depth and breadth to meet anticipated and expressed individual and community needs.

The Board recognized that library resources are not unlimited. Selected materials must adhere to budget allocations. Resource sharing with other libraries, and electronic and other methods of information access, are valid and necessary ways of meeting patrons' needs.

Selection of materials by the Library does not mean endorsement of the contents or the views expressed in those materials [adopted November 29, 1972, revised August 14, 2000, pp. 1–2; www.fvrl.org/selectingdiscarding.html]

Oneida Public Library: Material Selection Policy

The primary objectives of book selection shall be to collect materials of contemporary significance and of permanent value. The Library will always be guided by a sense of responsibility to both present and future patrons in adding material which will enrich the collections and maintain an overall balance. The Library also recognizes an immediate duty to make available materials for enlightenment and recreation, even though such material may not have enduring interest or value. The Library will provide a representative sampling of experimental material, but will not always attempt to be exhaustive. The Library does not consider it necessary or desirable to acquire all books on a subject if these books tend to duplicate each other. [p. 2; www.midyork.org/oneida/libwebmaterialsselect.htm]

SPECIFIC EVALUATIVE CRITERIAS
FOR ACADEMIC LIBRARIES

Albion College, Stockwell-Mudd Libraries: Library Collection Development Policy

Selection Criteria

The Library acquires materials of both permanent and current interest in all subjects, based upon the merits of a work in relation to the needs, interests, and demands of the community. Each of these criteria may not and need not be used to evaluate each item, but they are applied as general guidelines for consideration of all materials. While a single standard cannot be applied to each work, the following general criteria are used in selecting materials for purchase.

Selection Guidelines

The following guidelines should be considered in selecting and adding materials to the collection:

- Subject matter and scope:
  - suits the purposes of the curriculum for which it is intended
  - is significant
  - is of local interest (subject, author, or publisher)
  - has present and potential relevance to community needs and preferences
  - is related to the existing collection and to other titles and authors dealing with the same subject
  - has historical value
  - is of permanent and timeless interest
  - serves specific research needs of faculty
- Literature:
  - is written by an author in any language considered to be important to our curriculum
  - represents the best of its author or genre
  - includes all works by major authors
  - includes reading copies and critical editions
- Treatment of subject or material:
  - suits the needs of students and faculty studying the discipline
  - can be introductory, speculative, scholarly, technical, or popular
  - may provide partial or complete coverage
  - may be current or retrospective
  - may be of timely and/or popular interest
  - should be of an appropriate level of difficulty
  - should be suitable and useful in subject and style for the library's intended audience
  - may be important as a document of the times
  - may have unique and/or special features
- Validity/accuracy:
  - information presented is accurate, current, and authoritative
  - author, artist, or publisher has good reputation or qualifications
  - literature titles have literary merit as expressed in critical reviews
  - other criteria to consider include availability of indexing, date of publication, primary versus secondary source, fact or opinion, observation or research
- Point of view:
  - is fair and balanced in its point of view, but we may select titles of a partisan or sectarian nature, even some that may have unredeemable bias
  - contributes to community values and citizenship

- has alternative viewpoints
- has social significance
- Elements of quality:
  - is the best of its type for addition to the collection
  - is suitable format for its message
  - shows originality and creativity in its presentation and content
  - is well written
  - is cited frequently in standard bibliographies
- Formats:
  - consider all formats for selection, providing the content falls within the guidelines set forth in this document
  - consider the condition and durability of the materials
  - consider the font style and size, indexing, paper quality, binding, and the suitability of the format for library use
  - when selecting electronic resources, consider Web-based versus Telnet/ CD, Windows or Mac version, IP address checking, archiving, free trials, full-text availability, indexing, etc.
- Textbooks (textbooks are defined here as works whose published form clearly indicates its intended use as a principal teaching aid):
  - consider textbooks when they are important for reference purposes, selected alternative textbooks to those adopted by Albion College courses, or where the textbook is considered a definitive or classic work in the subject
- Price:
  - select paperback editions when deemed appropriate
  - select high priced items when deemed essential to the collection
- Demand:
  - acquire only one copy of a title unless high demand requires additional copies
- Regional availability:
  - avoid unnecessary duplication of titles
  - pursue cooperative collection agreements with other libraries in Michigan

[approved by the Library Advisory Committee March 14, 2000, pp. 3–4; www.albion.edu/library/collect2.htm]

Fitchburg State College: Periodicals Collection Development Policy

A. Current Subscriptions
1. Title(s) must meet the appropriate academic code level as detailed in the Collection Development Policy. The collection developer aims to purchase the core journals in all academic programs.

2. Access to the journal articles has to be assured through library-owned indexes, abstracts, or CD-ROMs.
3. Reviews and recommendations from the professional library literature sources such as *Magazines For Libraries*, *Choice*, and literature reviews from the subject area will be consulted.
4. The existing holdings in the periodicals collection shall be consulted to provide a profile of holdings for the subject area and to see if the title is relevant.
5. Interlibrary loan request statistics will be consulted to ascertain use and demand.
6. The various library-owned union lists will be consulted to ascertain the availability of the title in the geographic area.
7. The price of the subscription will also be considered.

B. Retrospective Holdings
1. When finances permit we will annually purchase back issues of journals in microform to expand the library's holdings.
2. The retrospective issues need to be indexed in the library-owned indexes, abstracts, and CD-ROMs.
3. Generally, FSC will purchase two years of back issues as a minimum order.

[revised April 5, 2001, p. 6; http://raven.fsc.edu/library/development.htm]

SPECIFIC EVALUATIVE CRITERIA FOR COMMUNITY COLLEGES

North Harris Montgomery Community College District: Collection Development Policy

The following criteria are considered in the selection of resources:

- Support of the curricular needs of the specific colleges' instructional programs.
- Enrichment and support of the existing collection.
- Appropriateness for undergraduate use in general education and/or occupational programs.
- Timeliness.
- Lasting value.
- Quality of content and presentation.
- Literary merit or artistic quality.
- Presentation of alternative viewpoints.
- Physical quality and durability.

- Appropriateness of format, based on intended use.
- Relative cost in relation to the budget and other available materials.
- Availability.
- Acceptibility based on professional selection tools.
- Reputation of author/producer.
- Frequency of requests for item.
- Program accreditation requirements.
- Only or best available resource on subject.
- General information for college community.
- Coverage in library-owned indexes.
- Clearly-identified sources of information.

Additional criteria for selection of nonprint and/or electronic resources:

- Technical quality.
- Compatibility with college equipment and software.
- Availability with college equipment and software.
- Additional costs such as archiving, updating, training, furniture, space, technical support, and maintenance.
- Cost effective replacement for existing resources.
- Unique or more efficient information.
- Licensing and/or contractual restrictions.
- Vendor technical and training support.
- Ability to produce archival/backup copies.
- Updated on a regular basis by producer/author.
- Complete records in citation, abstract, or full-text formats that can be downloaded, emailed, and printed.
- Logical and readily navigable user interface.
- Online and hard-copy documentation easily located, useful, and logical.
- Continuous access with minimal downtime.
- Collection and dissemination of usage statistics by vendor in useful format.
- Stability of product software and content.

[last updated March 27, 2000, p. 4]

SPECIFIC EVALUATIVE CRITERIAS FOR PUBLIC LIBRARIES

Fresno County Library: Materials Selection Policy

Each acquisition, whether purchased or donated, is considered in terms of the following standards. Clearly, however, an item need not meet all of the criteria in order to be acceptable. In general, materials which are produced primarily in advocacy of a specific group are not added.

A. General criteria:

- Insight into human and social conditions.
- Suitability of subject and style for intended audiences.
- Present and potential relevance to community needs and interests.
- Contemporary significance or permanent value.
- Relation to existing collection.
- Attention of critics, reviewers, and public.
- Scarcity of information in subject area.
- Availability of material elsewhere in the community. (Holdings of specialized libraries within this community are considered in developing the library's collection.)
- Price and format.

B. Specific criteria for the evaluation of works of information and opinion:

- Authority.
- Comprehensiveness and depth of treatment.
- Clarity, accuracy, and logic of presentation.

C. Specific criteria for the evaluation of works of imagination:

- Representation of significant literary or social trends.
- Vitality and originality.
- Artistic presentation and experimentation.
- Authenticity of historical, regional, or social setting.

Because the library must serve as a resource for the individual to examine issues freely and make his/her own decision, the collection must contain the various positions expressed on important, complicated, or controversial questions, including unpopular and unorthodox positions. [www.sjvls.lib.ca.us/fresno/select/html]

Hart/Battelle Memorial Library of West Jefferson (Ohio): Collection Development Policy

General Selection Criteria

1. Suitability of physical format for library purposes.
2. Suitability of subject and method of presentation for intended audience.

3. Relationship to existing collection in the same subject field.
4. Relevance to present and projected community needs and demands.
5. Competence and reputation of author and/or publisher.

Selection of Fiction (Adult and Juvenile)

1. Works of fiction are evaluated on the following elements:
   a. realistic representation of some aspect of life chosen by the author for description.
   b. effectiveness in sustaining the interest of the reader.
   c. structural soundness.
   d. clarity of style.
   e. vitality and consistency of characterization.
   Although the quality of materials will be judged on the work as a whole, not by excerpts, incidents and language in the work should be in keeping with the social, moral, and emotional background of the characters.

Selection of Nonfiction (Adult and Juvenile)

1. Works of nonfiction are chosen on the basis of the following elements:
   a. significance of the topic for the intended audience.
   b. sufficient scope for intended audience.
   c. accuracy and effectiveness in the presentation of the information.
   d. current interest or relevance.
   e. acceptable format for the intended audience.

Selection of Non-Print Materials (Adult and Juvenile)

1. Selection of non-print materials is based on artistic and technical quality of the work as well as the value of the content for fulfilling the informational, recreational, and informational needs of our patrons.
2. No videos with a rating of NC-17 or X will be purchased for the Library.

Manitowoc (Wisconsin) Public Library: Policies & Procedures, Collection Development

One or more of the following criteria may be used to determine whether or not an item should be added to the library's collection: availability; suitability of subject, format, and level for intended audience; published and/or broadcast reviews; authority and significance of the author, composer, filmmaker, etc.; reputation of the publisher or producer; timeliness and/or permanence; quality of writing, design, illustrations, or productions; relevance to community needs; potential and/or known demand; comparison with our existing materials on the same subject; accessibility of the same material in the geographic area; and cost. [adopted March 28, 1988, p. 2; www.manitowoc .lib.wi.us/Collectiondevelopment.htm]

SPECIFIC EVALUATIVE CRITERIA FOR SPECIAL LIBRARIES AND RELATED INSTITUTIONS

Fermilab IRD: Library Collection Development Policy

Resources and services will be evaluated before purchase, and as part of periodic weeding, based on:

- Relevance
- Usage
- Cost-effectiveness
- Currency of material
- Authority (i.e., is it a trusted source?)
- Coherence of series

Library Advisory Committee (LAC) members and other Laboratory staff will be consulted on questions of authority, currency, and any other evaluation criteria as warranted. The literature of the library profession, especially science librarianship, will be consulted as warranted. [approved October 2, 1998, last modified January 24, 2000, p. 1; http://fnalpubs.fnal.gov/library/cdpolicy.html]

NOTES

1. Elizabeth Futas, ed., *Collection Development Policies and Procedures.* 3rd ed. (Phoenix, Ariz.: Oryx, 1995), 225–6.

2. "Selection Criteria," *Collection Development Policies*, 3–4; www.dlapr.lib.az.us/ cdt/colldev.htm.

3. Futas, *Collection Development Policies and Procedures*, 222.

Chapter Nine

Format Statements in Policies

A library's format statement generally refers to the types of information resources included—or *not* included—within its holdings. Although by no means a fixture in collection development policies, it is included as a response to one or more of the following issues:

- Delineation of the characteristics of those formats included in an institution's holdings.
- Affirmation of the absence of media bias in the collection building process.
- Citing limits to the acquisition of certain formats (as well as the rationale behind such restrictions).
- Documentation of specific features regarding the evaluation, acquisition, maintenance, servicing, etc., of a particular medium.

For some time, educators, librarians, and media experts in other fields have elaborated on the limitations of print resources—compared with other information formats—on the basis of criteria such as inherent appeal, effectiveness in communicating particular ideas and feelings, ease of use, timeliness, cost, availability, and durability. (1) Recognizing the limitations of a collection built exclusively around traditional print materials such as books and serials, some libraries (especially those serving educational institutions) operate under mandates to develop integrated multimedia holdings.

Perhaps the most concise—and open-ended—means of communicating receptivity to varied formats consists of a statement indicating that the library in question will acquire whatever information package is most appropriate to achieving institutional objectives. However, since many non-print formats require specialized hardware for playback purposes (and additional equipment for reproduction, projection to groups, and other everyday applications), collection developers may feel it necessary to include more detail regarding the use of various software within the overall service scheme.

In addition to documenting a commitment to a broad range of media, libraries may find a format statement instrumental in clarifying the thrust of future acquisition priorities. G. Edward Evans, in his work *Developing Library and Information Center Collections*, addresses the pitfalls that a collection developer faces in attempting to select the most effective form of information package:

> With each passing year, as multimedia computer systems combine text, graphics, audio, and video clips, the distinction between books and audiovisuals becomes more and more blurred. Information that once was available only in printed formats is now available in several forms, including books, microfiche, CD-ROM, and online. Book publishers, especially publishers of scholarly journals, are thinking about and (in more and more cases) actually publishing their material electronically. Many publishers expect to use, and are using, CD-ROM packages to distribute reference material. (2)

Format limitations typically cited by libraries include (1) the limited availability of certain types of software, (2) obsolescence, and (3) equipment problems (e.g., high cost, complexity of operation, lack of dependability). These limitations are a product of the highly volatile marketplace and sheer diversity of non-print media. The following listing illustrates the diverse array of sound recordings commercially available during the lifespan of many presently employed librarians (1950 and 2000). It represents a comparatively small slice of the overall entertainment and educational media empire; the output of other sectors (film, video, micrographics, realia, etc.) presents an equally confusing picture:

- 78 r.p.m. shellac discs (issued in a variety of sizes)
- Wire recordings (blank medium; spool sizes vary)
- Reel-to-reel magnetic tape (blank and prerecorded media; reel sizes vary)
- 45 r.p.m. vinyl discs (varied sizes; primarily 7 inches in diameter)
- 33 r.p.m. vinyl discs (varied sizes; primarily 12 inches in diameter)
- Soundpages/Soundsheets/Flexi-Discs/Talking Books (varied sizes and playback speeds)
- Audiocassettes (blank and prerecorded media; former available in 3 tape formulations as well as microcassette size)
- 8-track cassettes (blank and prerecorded media)
- Compact discs (3-inch and 5 ½-inch sizes; various spin-off formats, including CD-Video, CD-Graphics, CD-Interactive, enhanced CDs, CD-Read Only Memory, CD-Recordable and CD-ReWritable)
- Digital audio tape (DAT)
- Digital compact cassettes (DCC)

- Mini-Discs (blank and prerecorded media)
- Digital Video Disc-Audio (blank and prerecorded media)—Unlike DVDs, DVD-Audio releases are marketed directly to the audience for sound recordings; many other video formats—e.g., laserdiscs, half-inch videotape formulations—include titles (concerts, documentaries, video clips, etc.) which emphasize audio information.

A number of factors—most notably, the rapid turnover of AV technologies driven by an innovative climate, and unpredictability of media manufacturers and retailers regarding support of new products—have caused even the most open-minded, media literate librarians to move cautiously before shifting their allegiance to up-and-coming formats. At the very least, the presence of outmoded formats in a collection places an added imperative on efficient weeding practices and creates the general impression that collection developers have failed to spend funds in the most effective manner.

Much information continues to be reissued in new formulations; for example, the work of popular music entertainer Al Jolson has probably been issued on virtually every graphic medium devised over the past 125 years. However, in cases where valuable material is only available on outmoded formats, some libraries may feel obligated to add new configurations to the existing collection rather than simply allowing one medium to supercede another. In short, the format statement should cover all issues emanating from the decision of the library to include (or not include) particular types of media. An in-depth treatment of format-related concerns might include responses to the following questions:

- How will playback equipment for essentially obsolete formats be maintained, repaired, and replaced?
- Are there any special concerns relating to storage (climate considerations, protective containers, display cases, etc.), handling, and maintenance? Will staff training (and clearly-worded patron directives) be necessary to ensure that these concerns are properly implemented?
- Should particularly useful information available only on outmoded formats be copied to newer configurations? If so, are there any potential copyright violations?
- Should those libraries not actively engaged in archival practices consider shifting obsolete materials to another institution?
- Do evaluative criteria and acquisition sources of certain media vary to the extent that they should be separated from the general discussion of such matters in other portions of the policy?

A substantial number of policies place all or most format-related information within a section connoting something other than *types of material*, typically evaluative criteria, special collections, or a heading focusing exclusively on one configuration (e.g., serials, microforms).

The policy excerpts below illustrate the wide range of approaches employed by libraries in communicating exactly how the format issues noted above have been resolved. For example, the Babson Library, Albuquerque Technical Vocational Institute Libraries, and University of Miami Richter Library all focus on the limits in acquiring various formats, although the latter also outlines the criteria relating to the evaluation of specific types of media. On the other hand, the Central Piedmont Community College policy simply itemizes those formats considered—as well as those not considered—in collection building, while the North Vancouver District Public Library begins the section entitled "Audio Recordings Collections" with an affirmation of its commitment to the medium.

FORMAT STATEMENTS FOR ACADEMIC LIBRARIES

Springfield College, Babson Library: Collection Development Policy

Purpose of the Collection Development Policy

Collection development is a means by which Babson Library provides organized collections of information items that will meet institutional, curricular research, and instructional requirement, as well as the cultural needs of the college community. Library collections facilitate and enrich classroom instruction as well as providing information which represents the diverse and varied background of the college community.

The purpose of this collection development policy is to explain the basis for collection development decisions. The goal is to provide a clear set of guidelines for the building of a balanced and useable collection.

Types of Materials

Monographs. Monographs are selected if they support the needs listed in the purpose statement above.

Serials. Journals, newspapers, and other serials are selected if they support the needs listed in the purpose statement above.

Textbooks. The library does not ordinarily purchase textbooks used for courses at Springfield College, but focuses on supplementary materials to support the curriculum. However, textbooks may be selected if they enhance the collection as a whole.

Theses, Dissertations, and Physical Therapy Projects. Babson Library acquires, both for preservation and research purposes, copies of theses, dissertations, and other research projects completed at Springfield College. Theses and dissertations from other colleges are selected if they support the needs listed in the purpose statement above.

Format of Materials

The Library acquires many formats of material or media—microforms, video recordings, electronic databases, pamphlets, audiotapes, etc. All formats are considered potential resource materials for the library collection.

Microforms. As part of the Library's commitment to collect and provide access to significant collections of materials supporting campus and curricular needs, Babson Library acquires microform resources. These include subscriptions to individual collections deemed critical to research but either unavailable in paper or electronic form, or difficult to acquire and maintain in print or electronic form. Other microform acquisitions include maintenance of historical collections, such as journal back issues.

Electronic Resources. A resource is collected in electronic format if it fulfills a need for the resource in the collection, and the electronic form is the best format for the particular item, due to availability, accessibility, permanence, or interactivity of the electronic resource.

Video Recordings. Video recordings that support the curriculum (i.e., are used for courses) are acquired by Library Liaisons and the faculty. Only the originally purchased copy or copies made with the permission of the copyright holder will be added to the Library's collection.

Audiotapes. The Library will purchase audiotapes if that is deemed to be the best format for a publication. Recreational audiotapes (e.g., popular novels or self-help titles) are not purchased.

Miscellaneous. The library will occasionally acquire pamphlets but does not maintain a vertical file. The library does not acquire works of art but may accept them as gifts for the small circulating art collection at the discretion of the Director.

[copyright 1997, last modified October 26, 2000, pp. 2–4; www.spfldcol .edu/homepage.nsf/]

University of Miami Richter Library: Collection Development Policies

Dante B. Fascell Division of Government Information and Special Formats: Policy Statement

Government information is currently available in several formats: paper (books, posters, maps, brochures, etc.), microfiche, electronic (floppy disks, CD-ROMs, DVDs, World Wide Web and other Internet access), and to a lesser extent formats such as video and realia. Sometimes it is possible to choose between formats for a particular item. Most of the time, however, only one format of the title is available for selection.

Some criteria for selection include: frequency of use, space/storage capacity and frequency of publication, cost of providing access, resource sharing capabilities, and the Library's prior holdings. When selecting microfiche and electronic resources it is important to keep in mind the appropriateness of the material to the medium in which it is conveyed. Technical support for electronic resources is also a crucial consideration.

In keeping with the Library's shift toward electronic resources, the Internet is utilized to its fullest extent. CD-ROMs are selected; however, there are limits to the number and kind of CDs that can be supported within the Division. There is a general library trend away from supporting stand-alone CD-ROMs to maximizing access to information through networked CD-ROMs and the Internet. Due to space constraints, microfiche is selected for many materials, including Congressional publications. Paper is the preferred format for certain high use items such as desk reference materials. Floppy disks and posters are avoided when possible. [last updated May 19, 2000, p. 10; www.library .miami.edu/acqui/colldev.html]

FORMAT STATEMENTS FOR COMMUNITY COLLEGES

Albuquerque Technical Vocational Institute Libraries: Collection Development Policy

Hardbound versus paperbound books. For their greater durability, hardbound editions are generally the preferred format. Paperbacks, however, are purchased for topics which change rapidly, when duplicate copies of a specific book are needed, if a hardcover is unavailable, if the title requires frequent replacement, or if the paperbound appears to be a better value. Paperbacks are also purchased for the Libraries' leisure reading collection.

Textbooks. Textbooks are purchased only when they provide a good, general introduction to a topic. The library does not purchase the specific edition of textbooks used in Institute courses. It is neither financially feasible to purchase these textbooks each term nor within the scope of the Libraries' mission. Instructors may place textbooks on reserve at their discretion.

Periodicals. The Libraries give priority to relevant titles that are indexed in services to which the Libraries subscribe. The financial resources of the library, availability of titles elsewhere in the geographic area, and the availability of titles in electronic format in the Libraries are additional considerations.

Microforms. Microfilm and microfiche are purchased as a way of preserving information presented in newspapers and periodicals. For ease of use, microfiche is the preferred format.

Pamphlets, maps, and other ephemera. These items are added to the vertical file to provide concise and timely information, particularly on topics that change rapidly or are of current, short-term interest. Items on topics of local interest are also included in the vertical file.

Government information. The Libraries are not depositories for federal or New Mexico state government publications. International, federal, state, and local government publications are selected according to the same criteria as other library materials and are placed in appropriate locations in the collections.

Media. The Libraries maintain a media collection for faculty use in the classroom. Media are collected with extensive input from the Institute faculty with final approval from the Libraries.

Foreign language materials. Items written in languages other than English are purchased only when they support the language curricula of the Institute.

Library fiction. Items in this category are purchased according to the same criteria as other library materials.

Popular works. Popular fiction is purchased as funds permit for the Libraries' leisure reading collection.

Electronic information products. Online products are evaluated and purchased using the same criteria for printed materials. These products are also subject to evaluation based upon the Institute's technology infrastructure and vendors' licensing agreements.

Web links. Links from the Libraries' web pages are identified, evaluated, and selected using the same criteria for printed materials.

Multi-format items. Community Colleges Examples of these items include a book with computer disks, a book supplemented with audio-tapes, a video-tape and book set, or a book set with Internet links. These materials are selected using the same criteria for printed materials. Location of multi-format items is at the discretion of the Libraries.

Other materials. Art works, globes, and other similar items may be purchased to enhance the Libraries' collections and environment.

[last updated June 28, 2001, pp. 2–4; http://planet.tvi.cc.nm.us/library/P&P.cd.htm]

Central Piedmont Community College (North Carolina): Collection Development Policy

The Library collects:

1. Print materials
   - Books
   - Pamphlets
   - Serials, periodicals, newspapers
   - Selected government documents
   - Ephemeral materials

2. Non-print materials
   * Microforms
   * Audiovisuals
   * Electronic resources
   * Selected maps
3. Selected CPCC college history materials

The Library supplements its holdings by providing access to a variety of external resources. The Library does not systematically collect:

1. Textbooks currently adopted at CPCC
2. Realia, specimens
3. Games
4. Theses, dissertations
5. Pictures, photographs
6. Manuscripts and archival materials, incunabula
7. Laboratory manuals
8. Instructor's manuals
9. Course outlines
10. Galley proofs
11. Foreign language materials with the exception of dictionaries, grammars, and audiovisual materials
12. Desk copies (material used routinely in a secretary's or faculty member's office; e.g., word processing software, utility software, dictionaries)

The Library no longer purchases:

1. Reel-to-reel video
2. Reel-to-reel audio
3. Phonodiscs
4. Film loop

[adopted 1994, last modified May 5, 1999, pp. 9–10; www.cpcc.cc.nc.us/Library/general/policy/cd.htm]

FORMAT STATEMENTS FOR PUBLIC LIBRARIES

North Vancouver District Public Library: Audio-Visual Collection Development Policy

Audio Recordings Collections

North Vancouver District Public Library recognizes that there is a whole body of information that can best be appreciated or acquired in the audio form. The information most characteristically preserved by audio recording is music, but there are also many other types of information which can be expressed through this medium. The Library makes every effort to keep abreast of the new audio technology as it is adopted by its patrons, in order to provide the medium most appropriate at any given time.

Adult Music Collection

As an integral part of our overall mission as an agency of information, culture, informal education, and entertainment, the North Vancouver District Public Library has established a core collection of music recordings for its patrons. The collection is intended to cover generally the broad spectrum of music, historically over time, including significant works, composers, performers, and performances. Our goal is to provide a balanced view of all genres and styles within this collection. Classical music, jazz, world music, and current popular music of all categories are included.

Collection Criteria

All recordings will be selected with professional judgment, using criteria based upon reviews, discographies, recommendations by community subject specialists, and patron requests. Availability, demonstrated community interest, and budgetary constraints will also be considered. While demand is an important criterion in most selection decisions, other factors relating to the existing collection, broad relevance to the community, and the artistic and technical quality or historical significance of the recording/music are also taken into account. While current popular "hit parade" recordings are certainly not precluded, in general our goal is to provide musically enduring recordings.

Media Choice

Compact Discs: Selections for the Adult Music Collection are currently being purchased in the compact disc format only.

Audiocassette Tapes: These are not currently purchased by the Library for the adult music collection.

Policies

General policies concerning intellectual freedom, donations and withdrawals, loan limits, holds, and damage and loss are not included here, but rather in the Adult Materials Collection Development Policy and Staff Policy and Procedures handbooks. The adult music collection is for circulation only and is available to registered borrowers of all ages. There is no associated equipment available for circulation or library use. Duplication of any sound recording borrowed from this library is a violation of Canadian copyright law. Music sound recordings are fully catalogued with multiple subject headings and performers' names. In most cases a full contents note is included.

Adult Non-Music Collection

There is a great variety of non-music information that can be expressed through this medium, and our goal is to select those recordings which best suit it. Our collection may include examples of the following:

- Fiction
  - classics [unabridged]
  - contemporary [abridged and unabridged]
  - short stories
- Non-fiction
  - sound effects
  - self-development programmes
  - business and careers
  - humour, nostalgia, old radio programmes
  - speeches, debates, lectures, interviews
  - foreign language learning and instruction
  - poetry readings, literature
  - theatre arts—monologues, accents
  - medical and similar self-help programmes
  - music instruction

Collection Criteria

All recordings will be selected with professional judgement, using criteria based on reviews, bibliographies, recommendations by subject specialists, and patron requests. While demand is an important criterion in most selection decisions, other factors relating to existing collections, broad relevance to the community, budgetary constraint, and artistic and technical quality are taken into account.

Media Choice

Compact Discs: Selections will be purchased in this format where it is deemed to be the most appropriate.

Audiocassette Tapes: Selections will be purchased in this format where it is deemed to be the most appropriate.

Policies

General policies concerning intellectual freedom, donations and withdrawals, loan limits, holds, and damage and loss are found in the Adult Materials Collection Development Policy and Staff Policy and Procedures handbooks. This collection is for circulation only and is available to registered borrowers of all ages. There is no associated equipment available for circulation or library use. Non-music recordings in the general adult collection are purchased in the English language versions only, except in the case of language instruction recordings. Duplication of any sound recording borrowed from this library is a violation of Canadian copyright law. Non-music sound recordings are fully catalogued with multiple subject headings and contents notes as required. [approved by Library Board August 17, 1996, revised March 11, 1999, last updated January 31, 2001; www.nvdpl.north-van.bc.ca/about/policies_2000/av_coll_pol.htm]

Pioneer Library System (Oklahoma): Collection Development Policy

Materials are chosen for the information, interest, and entertainment needs of the people of the community. The emphasis in all collections, print and non-print, will be on current and popular treatment of subjects, with a view to maintaining lively and active collections for the citizens of Cleveland, McClain, and Pottawatomie Counties.

System materials are purchased for use by all system agencies, either by format, distribution, or temporary/permanent location. Some examples of system materials include systemwide electronic products, circulating large print books, Staff Collection, Big Books for storytimes.

Selection of nonprint materials will follow the guidelines for collection development in general, with special consideration given the appropriateness of the various formats available. Choice of format may be based on such factors as whether the information is particularly well-conveyed through a certain format, if a format might enhance different learning styles, or if the information is to be preserved in an enduring format.

Works by local authors will be given special consideration for selection, evaluating the format and focus of the item to determine placement.

Books (Print Format)

Nonfiction. The nonfiction collection is directed to those who use the public library as their first or primary resource. The library will provide materials in subjects of established or realistically anticipated demand. General treatment will usually be preferred unless there is an identified need for specific treatment of a subject in a particular community.

In general, textbooks are added only if they provide information on subjects where there is little or no material available in any other form or when the textbook makes a significant contribution to the collection. Books of a scientific or technical nature will be provided insofar as they do not duplicate existing collections in university or special libraries which are available to the public.

Branches maintain a general collection of historical and current materials about Oklahoma. Each library also develops a comprehensive collection of local history that meets General Selection Criteria. Published genealogical materials pertaining to the county or city may be collected as a part of the local history of the area.

Fiction. The library recognizes the importance of fiction as a source of enrichment and entertainment.

Home Services. Home Services is available to customers (adult, young adult, or children) who are unable to reach the library because of health, economic, or physical challenges or lack of transportation. Homebound individuals in Cleveland, McClain, and Pottawatomie Counties are eligible. There are no charges for use of the service. Home Services provides paperback, hardback, books-on-tape, and Large Print materials. Home Services provides a catalog of paperback books, or customers can check out materials owned by the Library System by calling Home Services staff. Home Services paperbacks are not considered a part of the system's holdings.

Newspapers and Periodicals

Current periodicals are used for source material not found in books and are intended for reference use, for recreational reading, and to balance the collection. Titles are chosen for timeliness of subject matter, accessibility of content through periodical indexes, subject need, popular demand, and recreational value. Gift subscriptions are accepted subject to the approval of the Collection Development Coordinator.

The branch libraries retain back issues of periodicals as their space permits. Back issues may be available in a variety of formats. Local newspapers are made available at branch libraries along with selected state and national newspapers.

Video

Video recordings are purchased in VHS format. Each branch has a circulating collection of recreational, documentary, instructional, and cultural material which serves all ages. A non-circulating collection of videotapes is also maintained at the headquarters library for staff training and is not intended for the public.

Most of the videos purchased by the system are for home video use only. The material on the home video is protected by copyright. It is for private use only and any other use including performance in public, in whole or in part, is prohibited by law. A selected number of videotapes are purchased with public performance rights and may be shown, free-of-charge, to public groups. Both home videotapes and public performance videotapes are clearly labeled on the videotape case.

Audio Recordings

A variety of audio recordings are purchased to serve the recreational and informational needs of customers. Both spoken and music recordings are collected to provide a sampling of many interests.

Electronic Formats

Pioneer recognizes that the development of information available in electronic formats has become an important part of library collections. This format is especially convenient for sharing information systemwide.

Databases which provide access to magazines, journals, and other publications are provided to our customers, either through our automated library system, or as part of in-library network or individual work stations.

Information provided through on-line databases, CD-ROM applications, or other electronic formats are selected by the Collection Development staff using the General Selection Criteria for all library materials.

Multimedia Kits

Learning Kits are developed using a mixture of print and nonprint materials. Learning Kits and other types of multimedia kits are available for checkout to all library card holders.

Vertical File

The vertical file includes pamphlets, clippings, maps, brochures, pictures, and similar materials that are of a current or brief nature and that fill information gaps in the general collection. Placement in the vertical file is dependent on format and arrangement is by subject.

Computer Software

Branch libraries may develop circulating and non-circulating collections of software suitable for use by the general public.

The library will not accept copies of copyrighted software and related materials (except from owners of the copyright) as gifts. Branches will not duplicate copyrighted materials.

Films and Filmstrips

A non-circulating collection of children's films and filmstrips is available for use in all branches for programming purposes.

New Formats

Materials in new formats will be collected when feasible. [revised June 23, 1998, pp. 8–11; www.pioneer.lib.ok.us/colldev.html]

FORMAT STATEMENTS FOR SPECIAL LIBRARIES AND RELATED INSTITUTIONS

National Library of Canada: Collection Management Policy

Comprehensive Acquisition

The National Library collects the following types of published Canadiana comprehensively in all formats:

- agendas (with original text)
- annuals
- annual reports
- art portfolios (with title page)
- association/society literature
- atlases
- braille
- briefs
- broadsides published before 1900
- CD-ROMs and other databases in tangible form
- college and university calendars
- comic books
- computer software
- concert programmes
- conference proceedings
- directories
- electronic music
- encyclopedias
- exhibition catalogues

- foreign and international official publications (considered Canadiana)
- large print books
- livres d'artistes
- loose leaf services
- mass market paperbacks
- microforms (including all available newspapers)
- multimedia kits
- music
- music collections
- newsletters
- Native, ethnic, and student newspapers
- non-commercial talking books
- provincial and federal official publications
- pamphlets
- periodicals
- privately printed monographs
- public opinion polls
- published bibliographies
- publishers' catalogues
- recorded books
- recorded history
- research reports
- scores
- separately published translations
- sheet music
- sound recordings
- study guides
- technical reports
- textbooks
- theses
- video recordings

Selective Acquisition

- All areas of special emphasis
- catalogues of antiquarian dealers specializing in Canadiana
- non-government press releases
- unpublished bibliographies
- Canadian literature, publishing, and the book arts
- advertising material and trade catalogues
- one-of-a-kind livres objects, book works, or book objects
- twentieth-century broadsides

- photographs
- posters
- Canadian music and music in Canada
- advertising material and trade catalogues
- photographs of creative Canadians
- posters
- student papers
- Library and information science
- advertising material and trade catalogues
- posters
- student papers

The National Library maintains, in original format, a representative collection of Canadian daily newspapers of all regions of the country, in the two official languages.

Separately published television and radio guides or schedules are collected selectively where there is substantial original text.

School yearbooks and annuals are collected for post-secondary institutions at the institution-wide level. Departmental yearbooks are collected only for departments or faculties of music and library and information science.

Municipal documents would be acquired and preserved most effectively through a decentralized program. Until such a program is established with other institutions, the National Library will continue to collect municipal documents selectively.

Much of the above material is acquired only as unsolicited gifts or as part of a collection rather than through active acquisition.

Exclusions

The National Library does not collect the following types of published Canadiana:

- calendars of days and months
- dance programs
- ex libris (book plates)
- films
- film strips (unless part of kits)
- financial statements
- herdbooks
- mass market paperbacks, sound recordings and videos merely printed or produced or pressed in Canada with no Canadian creator, publisher, or subject
- maps (separately published single sheets)

- newspapers issued primarily for advertising purposes
- weekly newspapers in original format
- prospectuses
- publications of local organizations such as union locals, legion branches, individual schools, individual churches (e.g., annual reports, bylaws, constitutions, newsletters, yearbooks)
- reports promoting the sale of stock in one company
- reprints which do not differ bibliographically from originals
- service and operation manuals
- theatre programmes
- timetables
- translations of periodical articles

[February 1993, revised August 1999, pp. 10–13; www.nlc-bnc.ca/9/9/index-e.html]

Newark Museum Library and Archives: Collection Development Policy

The Library and the Archives will acquire materials in a variety of different formats. For the Library, it will acquire monographs, exhibition catalogs, handbooks of museum and private collections, conference proceedings, dictionaries, indexes and abstracts, auction catalogs, and periodicals. Rare books may also be acquired, usually through gifts or donations, but also upon the recommendation of the curators, if they fall within the primary subject areas of the Library. All reasonable attempts will be made to preserve them and to safeguard them for future use. This will include providing for their security. Ephemeral materials, such as pamphlets, newspaper clippings, press releases, publicity announcements, especially in regards to artists and exhibitions, will be added to the vertical file, whenever appropriate or useful. Whenever possible, the Library will attempt to acquire works in hardcover or another suitable format for long-term retention. It will give priority to current literature, but it will also acquire out-of-print materials, whenever requested, needed, and/or available.

For the Archives, it will acquire at least three copies of the publications of The Newark Museum, whether in the form of exhibition catalogs or publicity announcements. It will also acquire at least three copies of the publications relating to exhibitions organized by other institutions and hosted by The Newark Museum. It will eventually be the repository of the official records of The Newark Museum Association, as well as the official records of related organizations associated with The Newark Museum, such as the Volunteer

Organization, the Friends of the Decorative Arts, etc. These records are created in groups by working offices or organizations in the course of their normal operations. They are intended for the use of the originating office or organization, and are useful to others only incidentally. Consequently, they are not arranged in a library classification system, but are retained in the meaningful order in which they were deposited with only slight rearrangements in special cases as deemed necessary by the librarian.

Photographs, the bulk of which document the history of The Newark Museum's collections, exhibitions, or activities, are retained in the Library and the Archives as an important source of visual information. The special photographic collections, such as the Tibetan Photographic Archives and the Historical Photographics, as well as fine arts photography, are treated as collection materials under the care of the appropriate curator, registrar, or librarian. [p. 3; www.arlisna.org/Newark.htm]

NOTES

1. G. Edward Evans, *Developing Library and Information Center Collections*. 4th ed. (Englewood, Colo.: Libraries Unlimited, 2000), 273.

2. Evans, *Developing Library and Information Center Collections*, 273.

Chapter Ten

Government Publication Sections in Policies

Many collection development policies devote a substantial amount of space to discussing resources published by various governmental entities. G. Edward Evans provides one rationale for the importance of government documents to libraries of all types:

> Without question, governments are the world's number one producers of information and publications. Despite major efforts stemming from the U.S. Paperwork Reduction Act (1980) and the Government Printing Reform Act of 1996, the U.S. federal government still produces more publications than the combined total from U.S. commercial publishers. The relationship between the volume of government and commercial publications is probably the same in every country. In many countries, all levels of government generate information and publications, not just the national level. (1)

The importance of government information extends beyond the sheer quantity of material being produced by federal, state, local, and international agencies. Much of this material is unavailable through commercial, corporate, or private channels. In fact, many government publications are the result of research, task forces, committee hearings, etc., instituted precisely because specific information gaps (many of which pose potential risks to the health and security of the general populace) have been identified. Recognizing the importance of government information to U.S. citizens, Congress created a list of basic principles as part of the Government Printing Reform Act:

- The public has a right of access to government information;
- The government has an obligation to guarantee the authenticity and integrity of its information;

- The government has an obligation to disseminate and provide broad public access to its information;
- The government has an obligation to preserve its information; and
- Government information created or compiled by government employees or at government expense should remain in the public domain. (2)

As a complement to its large-scale publishing activities, the U.S. government instituted the Federal Depository Library Program. As of 1998, there were 1,365 full or selective depository libraries nationwide. (3) In addition, many libraries—either unable to qualify for depository status or unwilling to conform to federal guidelines regarding staffing, space, accessibility, etc., issues—are committed to purchasing government resources which fall within their collection building objectives. Furthermore, a considerable number of libraries have found the publications of local, state, and international government agencies worth acquiring.

The decision to include government-produced information raises a considerable number of questions, all of which should be addressed in the written statement. As a result, this section can include as many facets as the overall collection development policy itself. Important issues to consider include:

- Selection of formats. Federal documents, alone, are produced in print, CD-ROM, electronic, and various non-print configurations.
- Whether or not the library can qualify for federal or state depository status.
- Which sources to utilize in the acquisition of government titles. In addition to the depository systems, the options for federal materials includes GPO direct ordering, regional distribution centers, consumer catalogs, GPO Bookstores, specialized jobbers (e.g., NTIS), issuing agencies, legislators, and downloading information from agency websites.
- Organizing these resources as a separate collection versus integrating them into the general holdings. The former approach presumes the use of classification schemes tailored specifically for government publications (e.g., SuDocs for federal titles); however, segregated collections tend to be used less by both librarians and patrons. On the other hand, the integrated approach entails higher costs for full cataloging of government materials and compatibility problems regarding entry information (e.g., LC subject headings are not readily adaptable to federal titles).
- Subjects (or curriculum areas) to be accorded priority designation in the selection process; many academic libraries have chosen to incorporate government documents into the general conspectus review.
- For preservation purposes, the vast quantities of paper materials require binding or, at minimum, some form of economical storage such as file boxes.

The policy excerpts below reflect many of key issues relating to the evaluation and acquisition of government publications, including the role of depository programs, networking and interlibrary cooperation, format and subject breakdowns, and weeding policies. Academic institutions—represented here by the Perkins Library (Duke University) and Griffith Memorial Library (Sheridan College)—generally provide more in-depth coverage of this medium than public or special libraries. This is due in part to the depository status enjoyed by many universities and community colleges—an arrangement requiring a more thoroughgoing commitment on the part of participating agencies.

GOVERNMENT PUBLICATION SECTION FOR ACADEMIC LIBRARIES

Duke University, Perkins Library: Collection Policy for Federal Documents

Table of Contents

[In the original policy, each of the headings below is hyperlinked to the appropriate section of the document.]

Federal Depository Library Program
Depository History
Mission Statements
The Collection
    Scope
    Selection Responsibility
    Formats
    Non-Depository Collecting
    Management, Weeding, and Maintenance
Public Access
    Arrangement and Location
    Reference Service
    Lending and Borrowing Guidelines
Resource Sharing
Resources for Searching U.S. Government Publications
Depository History and Mission Statements

Federal Depository Library Program

In the late 19th century Congress established the Federal Depository Library Program, to be managed by the Superintendent of Documents at the U.S. Government Printing Office (GPO). The mission of the program is to provide free access to federal government information to the residents of the United States of America. Designated depository libraries select publications based on the needs of their primary clientele and the congressional district in which the library resides.

Depository History

Duke University Library received its Senate designated selected federal depository status in 1890. The primary clientele of the federal depository are the residents of the 4th Congressional district, and the students, faculty, and staff of Duke University. The depository was formerly located in the 2nd Congressional district. Therefore, it has historically provided depository service to residents of those districts. The Library currently selects just over 80% of the total number of items available through the Federal Depository Library Program.

Mission Statements Perkins Library System

In active support of Duke University's mission: we provide to the University and wider academic community a place for self-education and discovery; we promote scholarship and good citizenship through information literacy; we acquire, organize, preserve, and deliver information resources and assist users in their effective use; we create a great library for a great University.

Public Documents and Maps

The Public Documents and Maps Team advances the mission of the Perkins Library System through effective utilization of all available resources to meet user needs for government information and maps.

The Public Documents and Maps Department holds and provides access to approximately 2 million volumes in all formats from federal, state, and intergovernmental organizations. It is a depository for United States, North Carolina, and European Union documents, and collects broadly from intergovernmental organizations. Its map collection contains over 127,000 paper maps with local, state, national, and international coverage, as well as computer map programs and data.

The Collection Scope

Subject strengths include congressional and executive historical materials, economics, international relations, labor, military history, and social issues. Subject areas currently not collected include: technical reports in defense and energy; legal court reports and materials issued by the Judiciary (except U.S. Supreme Court Reports); and agricultural materials. Though established in the late 19th century, the federal collection includes materials from the founding of the Republic through the present time. Significant agency collections include:

- Department of Commerce (C)
- Department of Labor (L)
- Department of State (S)
- Independent Agencies (Y3)
- Publications of Congress and its agencies

Collections of historical interest include:

- Department of Navy (N)
- Department of War (W)
- U.S. Serial Set

The federal collection is a "research level" collection. That is, it includes supplementary material beyond depository items. The collection should be comprehensive particularly in areas supporting the curriculum and research of Duke University, and retain material for historical research.

Selection Responsibility

The Federal Documents Librarian develops the U.S. federal collection in consultation with other resource specialists, residents, students, faculty, and staff. The collection supports the academic programs and research interests of students and faculty at Duke University, and the federal information needs of the 4th Congressional District.

Patrons may request that the library acquire materials not currently held in the collection. All requests are evaluated to determine the appropriateness of the purchase and possible access issues. The library relies on neighboring depositories for comprehensive selection in areas such as law, agriculture, and technical reports.

Each year item number selections are reviewed. While a zero-base review each year is recommended by the Government Printing Office (GPO), this is very difficult in a large selective depository. Instead, the Federal Documents Librarian focuses on selected agencies or formats for yearly review. Individual items will be purchased, and item numbers added during GPO's Annual Selection Cycle at the discretion of the Federal Documents Librarian.

Formats

Duke selects federal information in all available formats including paper, microfiche, maps, and electronic materials. When determining formats to be selected, a decision is based on the content and purpose of the publication.

The library will select electronic material regardless of its ability to service the products. Electronic products not supported in the Public Documents department may be circulated.

Non-Depository Collecting

The library participates in the Documents Expediting of the Library of Congress through which it can obtain many government publications unavailable through the depository program. The department will also contact government agencies directly to receive materials not available from the GPO.

The department maintains deposit accounts with the GPO and the National Technical Information System (NTIS) for purchase of government materials which may not be otherwise available.

The Perkins Library also supplements the depository collection with commercial indexes, bibliographies, online services, directories, periodicals, and monographs of interest to the federal depository user and which aid in locating government material. Some services are, by contract, available only to the Duke University community; others are available to all users. A list of these resources may be found on the Resources for Searching U.S. Government Publications web page.

Management, Weeding, & Maintenance

The federal depository of the Perkins Library Systems is managed according to guidelines established by the Library Programs Service of the Superintendent of Documents at the U.S. Government Printing Office and the regional depository in the Government Documents Section of the Davis Library, University of North Carolina, Chapel Hill. Duke participates in the North Carolina State Documents Plan as established in 1985. The plan provides additional service, collection, and retention instruction which supplement those of the Federal Depository Library Program.

As a research library, Duke strives for a comprehensive federal collection. Weeding of the collection is performed judiciously and focuses on ephemeral items such as dated materials and pamphlets.

In order to preserve the collection, the federal documents staff selectively binds currently received printed materials. The department is committed to preserving federal materials in all formats and works with the appropriate library departments to ensure appropriate binding, storage, and handling of materials. The department makes every effort to replace badly damaged or deteriorating materials.

Public Access Policies

The primary circulating collection of U.S. federal documents is available to all members of the public during hours the library building is open. Federal materials located in the Documents Reference Room (reference materials, microfiche, CD-ROMs, current periodicals, maps, and the Census) as well as rare materials are available to the public during the hours the department is open.

Arrangement and Location

Primary Locations

Federal documents are located primarily in Perkins Library. The main collection resides in stacks on the basement level and is shelved in Superintendent of Documents (SuDoc) number order. Some older materials are located in compact shelving on the sub-basement level. Federal materials considered rare and valuable are located in locked areas.

Secondary Locations

Selected federal documents are distributed to other Duke libraries. Branches and professional libraries holding federal material include Biological-Environmental Sciences, Chemistry, Engineering, Math/Physics, and the Medical Center Library. Some items are reclassified into the Dewey Decimal Classification System while others remain in the SuDoc Classification System.

Offsite Stacks

Due to lack of space in the main library, a portion of the federal collection is located at Duke Off-Site Stacks (DOSS). Materials at DOSS are primarily long runs of older serials, Congressional hearings prior to 1980, and selected agency materials.

Reference Service

Reference service is provided to all during the hours the department is open. Phone and Internet questions are accepted, although complex reference requests will require that users come to the library.

Lending and Borrowing Guidelines

Most federal documents circulate to registered Duke borrowers. Some items are identified as non-circulating and must be used at the library. Those include many serials, rare or deteriorating materials, North Carolina maps, reference materials (including the Census), and the U.S. Serial Set. Triangle Research Library Network (TRLN) borrowers may check out federal material when the item is not available at their own depositories.

Federal documents are lent via inter-library loan at the discretion of the Federal Documents Librarian. The U.S. Serial Set and federal documents published prior to 1900 are not available for interlibrary lending.

Resource Sharing: Neighboring Depositories

The Research Triangle is blessed with a number of depository libraries. On the Duke campus, the Duke University Law School Library is an additional specialized depository with a collection which focuses on legal and judicial materials. The two depositories at Duke cooperate in collection development, consultations, and reference assistance.

Triangle Research Library Network (TRLN)

TRLN includes seven depository libraries:

- Duke University, Perkins Library
- Duke University, Law School Library
- North Carolina Central University, Shepard Library
- North Carolina Central University, School of Law Library
- University of North Carolina–Chapel Hill, Davis Library
- University of North Carolina–Chapel Hill, Everett Law Library
- North Carolina State University, D.H. Hill Library

The University of North Carolina–Chapel Hill, Davis Library is the state regional depository. North Carolina State University, D.H. Hill Library is the state Patent Depository Library.

Cooperation among these federal depositories include borrowing privileges for students, expedited lending of materials, purchases of large collections or electronic resources, and reference assistance. [last updated June 30, 2000; http://docs.lib.duke.edu/federal/fed_cdpo.html]

GOVERNMENT PUBLICATION SECTION
FOR COMMUNITY COLLEGES

Sheridan College, Griffith Memorial Library: Collection Development Policy

Appendix D: Collection Development Policy, Federal Government Publications

Because of constant change in the needs of the college and of the community, this policy should serve only as a guideline for decision-making. It should be reviewed annually by the library staff and then forwarded for review with advisory groups as appropriate and revised as necessary.

Space, cost, and staffing are ever-present factors to be taken into consideration. Other factors to consider include a definition of the geographic area and population; subject areas to be collected; the strengths and weaknesses of the collections of other nearby libraries; choices of format between microfiche, paper, or electronic; purchasing vs. depository; accessibility (including available indexing and in-house cataloging); and discarding of material.

This policy corresponds as closely as possible with the Collection Development Policy proper for Griffith Memorial Library.

Geographic Area and Population

Sheridan College is a two-year community college with an FTE of 1,351 (Sheridan Campus) and 780 (Gillette Campus). It is located in Sheridan, Wyoming (24,581 county population), in the northeastern segment of Wyoming near the Montana border. The Griffith Memorial Library houses a collection of 25,000 books, 2,100 audiovisual units, and 290 periodical/newspaper subscriptions and 4,500 periodical/newspaper subscriptions in computer databases. The library is one of 10 selective depositories in Wyoming that have formed a cooperative consortium of depository libraries. The nearest depository is located in Gillette at the Campbell County Public Library (101 miles). There is no longer a Regional Depository in the state. Instead, Wyoming is now served by the Regional at the University of Colorado in Boulder, Colorado. A map showing the depositories in Wyoming is attached [not included here]. Sheridan College has an extension campus located in Gillette. The Griffith Memorial Library provides consultation services for the Gillette Campus library. The people of Sheridan and Johnson (6,513 county population) counties, the small towns and reservations in southern Montana, as well as distance education students and faculty from various colleges including University of Wyoming and Regis College are periodic users of the library.

The Government Publications Collection

The majority of Government Publications in the library are shelved together and classified according to the Superintendent of Documents Classification System (SuDocs). However, standard reference sources such as the Statistical Abstracts, the Government Manual, the Zip Code Directory, etc., are given a Dewey classification number and shelved with the Reference Collection. Other books are integrated into the regular book collection when they cover a popular subject, especially if published in a hard-bound format. Popular periodicals and periodicals on topics frequently in demand are shelved in the Library's Periodical Collection. Pamphlets on popular subjects, received as gifts, are occasionally added to the Vertical File. All of the above are noted in the Government Publications shelf list, which shows the location of each title. Publications shelved in the Government Publications collections are also listed in the public access catalog in order to achieve greater accessibility.

Choice of Format

Government Publications are presently published in paper, microfiche, and electronic formats. We will select major reference publications in paper. If not available in paper through the depository system, a decision will be made whether or not to purchase commercially. Paper is also preferred for popular publications, pictorial publications, and maps.

For material less frequently used, microfiche is acceptable. Microfiche will also be selected for most Congressional material.

As electronic formats (CD-ROM, computer disks, and the Internet) are provided to depositories with supporting software and documentation, Sheridan College will continue to increase its electronic format holdings of government publications. Requests are currently submitted for upgrading computer hardware to enable the college to meet or exceed GPO standards for electronic publications.

Selection

The first priority for selection will be college curriculum and student research support, followed by college employee research requirements, with community being the third priority. College curriculum and employees include the entire Northern Wyoming Community College District (Sheridan College and the Gillette Campus). As the College is a two-year institution with many vocational programs, collection emphasis is on current material. The main subject areas collected retrospectively are geology and mining.

Survey/Item Selection Lists. Using the above priorities as a guide, the document assistant will select from each Survey, with final selection made by the college librarian. Additional publications may be selected throughout the year and ordered from the annual Item Selection List.

Selective Housing. A Selective Housing agreement with Sheridan Fulmer Public Library allows additional selections from the Item Selection List. These publications are shelved at the public library. A copy of each agreement is enclosed.

Direct Orders. Publications not selected through the depository system may be ordered through the library's USGPO Deposit Account. As a finite amount of money is available, these publications are carefully selected. A publication may be purchased rather than selected as a depository item because the title is one of several included under one item number and the library needs only the one title. If a popular or frequently requested publication is available only in microfiche through the depository system, a paper copy may be purchased. Another option is to purchase commercially, as when superior indexes are offered through a commercial source. A commercial source is sometimes the only way to fill in back issues.

Gifts. When a gift is received, the decision as to whether or not to keep it is again based on the above-mentioned priorities. If kept, it is classified with the proper SuDocs number and entered in the shelf list. A decision is also made as to whether it is more appropriate in the documents collection or in some other area, such as the Vertical File.

Exchange Lists. Exchange Lists are primarily used to fill in missing or lost publications. However, other items may be selected from the list if need is determined, according to the set priorities.

Subject Areas from Curriculum (If Covered in Government Publications)

A. College Curriculum
   1. Agriculture
   2. Business
   3. Computer Information Systems
   4. Health (including Dental Assisting, Dental Hygiene, and Nursing)
   5. Education
   6. Technical Areas, including Surveying, Engine Mechanics, Auto Maintenance, Drafting, Welding
   7. Natural Sciences (Biology, Geology, Astronomy, etc.)
   8. Physical Education/Recreation
   9. Police Science
   10. Social Science (Psychology, Geography, Sociology, etc.)
B. Examples of Institutional Requirements (other than college curriculum)
   1. Grants
   2. Statistics
   3. Labor and employment trends
C. Community Needs
   1. Agriculture
   2. Labor and Census (Economic Development)
   3. Geology and Mining
   4. Fish and Wildlife
   5. Laws and Regulations
D. Primary Areas of Selection (including rank and depth of collection): See table 10.1.

Table 10.1. Primary Areas of Selection, Including Priority Ranking (1=strongest and 4=lightest) and Depth of Collection

Rank	Subject Area	Depth of Collection
1	Agriculture Ag. business Animal science	AS and AAS degree level and certificate of completion, plus community Farm and ranch management Ag. chemicals Crops Aquaculture
1	Business and economics Office information management Business administration	AA, AS, and AAS degree level and certificate of completion, plus community Economics Finance management
1	Dental assisting Dental hygiene ADN and PN nursing	AS and AAS degree level and certificate of completion
1	Police science	AS and AAS degree level
1	Statistics (all areas)	Used by all populations, on any subjects
1	Current popular topics, including drugs, alcohol, child abuse, AIDS	Students and community
2	Education Elementary and secondary education	AA degree level
2	Geology and maps	Student/employee use Most use from the community (professional and recreational)
3	Geography	AA degree level
3	Fish and wildlife	Community
3	Mining	Community
2	Laws and regulations	College administration and community use Some student and community use
4	Physical education and recreation	AA degree level; some employee use
4	Sociology	AS degree level; some employee use
4	Sciences	AS degree level; some employee use

Interlibrary Loan

For requested Government Publications not available in our collection, Interlibrary Loan is an alternative. There are no restrictions for interlibrary loans from consortium libraries, but should a loan have to go out of the consortium there may be a charge from the lending library. If particular titles are frequently requested, then they are considered for future selection.

Discarding Procedures (Withdrawal of Items)

All depository publications must be retained for 5 years, except where superseded (Instructions to Depository Libraries, Appendix C, provides a list of superseded documents). Withdrawal of publications must be accomplished according to Sections 2 and 11 of Instructions to Depository Libraries.

Ideally, the collection should be weeded once a year. Items to be pulled include outdated information, especially on such topics as agricultural chemi-
cals and medicine and drugs. In such cases, outdated information can be dangerous. If any older material is historically important, it should be kept. Also,
all Wyoming census publications will be kept. Another criterion for weeding
is amount of use, or need. If a particular publication is not being used and/or
there seems to be no need for it, it is a candidate for discard.

The documents assistant makes the initial review for weeding. Library staff
and appropriate college employees are asked to review the potential discards.

Future

As mentioned in the introduction, this policy should be reviewed by library
staff annually and forwarded to advisory committees for approval when
changes are considered. Computers and other electronic formats are changing the way we organize and provide access to information. [adopted March
15, 1994, last revised February 2001, pp. 8–13; www.sc.whecn.edu/library/
services/scgml_colldev.html]

GOVERNMENT PUBLICATION SECTION
FOR PUBLIC LIBRARIES

Morton Grove (Illinois) Public Library: Collection Development and Materials Selection Policy

Government Documents. A dramatic shift, at both the federal and state
levels, to disseminating documents via electronic delivery or database and not
in print form, has greatly influenced how the Morton Grove Public Library
selects and purchases government documents in the fiscal year 1995–1996.

Influencing Factors. Government information sources provide the librarian and the patron with access to the function and product of various agencies, bureaus, and other governmental systems. The library's selection of print
materials is heavily influenced by several factors: the location of the IRAD
(Illinois Record Archives Depository) at Northeastern Illinois University, the
location of NARA (National Archives Records Administration) in Chicago,
complete or partial depositories of federal and state documents at several ac-

ademic and large public libraries, and the proliferation of Web sites on the Internet.

Selection Plan. Government information sources are selected according to the guidelines for selection established for the WWW sources and the Reference Collection. Some of the tools used to select resources at the federal level are the Superintendent of Documents Home Page on the U.S. Government Printing Office Web Site and the GPO Catalog available on FirstSearch. State resources are chosen based on the monthly publication, *Illinois Documents*, and the State of Illinois Web Site. Local (i.e., Morton Grove, Niles/Maine Township, or Cook County) resources are quite often given to the library at little or no cost. Therefore, each donation will be considered on an individual basis, using the selection criteria established for the pertinent area of the collection.

Retention & Weeding. Again, the significance of electronic information sources will be felt in this area of the collection. The majority of print resources may be considered permanent additions to the Reference or Local History Collections. Any weeding that is done will be based on continued timeliness, relevancy, and condition of the material. The Reference Coordinator will continually reevaluate the status of print information sources.

Development Plan. Information provided by various governmental entities is used primarily in the Reference and Local History Collections. The library will continue to choose government information sources, in print form, as long as they prove to be the most current, accurate source available. The library will also continue to select, using the established guidelines for selections, appropriate Internet Web sites to be added to the library's online presence, the Morton Grove Webrary.

(*The Webrary*, 1st web edition January 26, 1998, last updated March 20, 2001; www.webrary.org/inside/colldevadultgov.htm]

NOTES

1. G. Edward Evans, *Developing Library and Information Center Collections* (Englewood, Colo.: Libraries Unlimited, 2000), 238.

2. "Statement on H.R. 4280, The Government Printing Reform Act of 1996," *Documents to the People* 25 (March 1997): 11.

3. Evans, *Developing Library and Information Collections*, 257.

Chapter Eleven

Treatment of Specific Resources Identified in Policies

While format statements tend to discuss library media as a whole, many collection development policies include separate sections devoted to specific media formats. These sections may cover a wide range of concerns, such as selection criteria, acquisition issues, service imperatives, associated problems (e.g., preservation, hardware compatibility), and subcategories of interest to the library. Virtually any format found in library collections and archives might be emphasized in this manner; however, headings most frequently found in policies include serials, microforms, audiovisual resources (or more narrow media groupings; e.g., films, videotape, sound recordings), reference books, manuscripts, and government publications (covered in the previous chapter). Electronic information has become an increasingly popular topic since the mid-1990s. Many libraries' policies are likely to expand on the digital domain—perhaps focusing individually on various subtopics such as on-line commercial databases, laser optical software, computer software, floppy disks, and Internet websites—in future policy revisions.

The policy excerpts below are specifically concerned with serials, audiovisual materials, and realia. However, as previously noted, many other formats are covered as separate sections in existing library policies.

STATEMENT COVERING SERIALS FOR ACADEMIC LIBRARIES

College of St. Catherine: Collection Development Policy

Serials

Serials are defined as titles issued periodically and expected to continue indefinitely, often with numbered parts. The serials collection includes newspapers, journals, annuals, and monographic series. Because the ongoing nature of serial publications requires long-term commitments of money (unlike monographs which are one-time purchases), space, and maintenance, serial selection decisions are given close scrutiny. Titles are added very selectively, and serials are charged to special library-controlled budget lines. At present, because of budget constraints, when a title is added, one of equivalent value must be dropped.

Recommendation for serial purchase may be initiated by any member of the academic community. However, responsibility for serials collection development decisions rests with the Library Director, the Minneapolis Campus Librarian, and the Head of Technical Services, in consultation with Academic Departments.

Selection Guidelines for Serials

The Libraries' general framework for building, preserving, maintaining, and evaluating the collection is outlined in earlier sections of this document and forms the basis for these selection guidelines.

Specific Selection Guidelines for Serials

1. Relevance of the title to the curriculum. Normally, the Libraries do not purchase serials to support faculty research.
2. Strength of existing subject coverage in the collection and a title's ability to add significantly to the existing coverage.
3. Indexing availability. For most journals the Libraries acquire, there should be indexes available in sources the Libraries own.
4. Cost and projected availability of funds.
5. Audience for whom the title is intended.
6. Reputation of editors or publishers.
7. Language of the title: normally, titles will be acquired only in those languages in which academic programs are taught.
8. Currency of information.
9. Availability of the title in the other CLIC libraries, and the Twin Cities area.

[drafted October 30, 1994, last updated January 2000, pp. 4–5; www.stkate .edu/library/about/collpol.html]

STATEMENT COVERING SERIALS FOR COMMUNITY COLLEGES

Finger Lakes Community College, Charles J. Meder Library: Collection Development Policy

Serials differ from monographs in that a serial subscription is an ongoing financial commitment. In addition, serials prices have historically increased at a rate that far exceeds such standard economic indicators as the Consumer Price Index and great care must be taken to ensure that the Library's ongoing commitment to serials does not consume a disproportionate share of the total acquisitions budget. Therefore, requests for new serial subscriptions must be considered very carefully. Generally, a new serial subscription will not be entered unless another subscription of similar expense can be canceled.

Back runs of serials are purchased only when deemed necessary or as the budget permits.

Some or all of the following criteria are used in evaluating titles for acquisition or cancellation:

* Strength of the existing collection in the title's subject area
* Support of present academic curriculum
* Present use of other serials in this subject area
* Projected future use
* Cost
* Reputation of journal and the publisher
* Inclusion in a reliable indexing source
* Number of recent interlibrary loan requests for this serial

[August 1998, p. 3; http://library.fingerlakes.edu/colldev.htm]

STATEMENT COVERING SERIALS FOR PUBLIC LIBRARIES

Kitsap Regional Library: Collection Development Policy (Third Edition)

The Library provides two types of periodical collections:

1. A "browsing collection," consisting of a selection of popular, current print magazines and newspapers (that may or may not be indexed) of consistent and widespread interest within the community. While these periodicals may be used to find answers to specific questions, they are most generally scanned, leafed through, or read in their entirety. Many of them contain a high ratio of colored illustrations to text.

    Browsing collections of periodicals are available at all branches of the Library and are developed to meet community interest using the guidelines of the Library's tiered information delivery plan. Although all interests cannot be represented at any one site, an effort is made to provide diversity in subject and title coverage throughout the system. Periodicals of interest to both adults and children are included at each branch.

2. A non-circulating "reference collection" of print, on-line, and microfilmed magazines and newspapers that provide answers to specific questions. Because these periodicals are primarily used for information retrieval, it is of vital importance that they be well indexed, that the Library supplies indexing to them, and that both the index and subsequent retrieval of information be user-friendly and capable of producing relevant search results.

Reference collections of periodicals include:

• on-line collections that are available at all sites, including dial-in;
• selected print issues of specific titles that do not check out because of their reference value;
• older print or microfilmed issues that are not available on-line or are of reference value for other reasons; i.e., their illustrations. With the exception of the on-line collection, most reference periodicals are housed at the Central Branch.

On-line periodical databases are selected to meet a wide spectrum of user needs and interests. Emphasis is placed on ease of use, amount of full text, currency, consistency of accessibility, number of titles relevant to user interest, quality and relevancy of indexing, and cost-effectiveness.

Microform editions of individual periodicals are obtained to provide back files. In some instances, they are acquired to provide the only copy of titles used primarily for reference; i.e., when microform is the only available format or when it best suits space or use considerations.

A limited number of newspapers from nearby cities and out of the area are included in the collection because they are frequently and consistently requested. The emphasis is on those papers from West Coast regions. The Library attempts to acquire and maintain historical files of all Kitsap County newspapers and, as funding allows, to provide indexing for them.

The selection of periodicals is coordinated annually by the Collection Manager and is funded from the Information Budget. [approved May 19, 1998, pp. 32–33; www.krl.org/administration/policies/colldev.html]

STATEMENT COVERING SERIALS FOR SPECIAL LIBRARIES AND RELATED INSTITUTIONS

National Library of Wales: Statement of Collection Development Policy

Policy: To acquire and retain all non-academic serials published in Wales and the immediate Border areas possessing obvious Welsh and Celtic interest.

New non-academic periodicals published outside Wales will not normally be acquired except as part of any co-operative acquisitions agreement by the legal deposit libraries.

Means: The Library receives monthly a new Periodicals List and a New Annuals List from the Copyright Act. The effect of the policy is that few non-academic serials on the list will be selected. No purchases of such materials will normally be made. No donations or exchanges will normally be accepted.

It is important to note that there is sometimes considerable difficulty in identifying a new serial's subject relative to academic level from the information supplied on the New Periodicals and New Annuals Lists since these provide brief information about title and publisher. Once a serial title has been accepted it is not possible on preservation practice subsequently to cancel it.

Categories: The policy will not include serials in the following and any other non-academic categories unless they have a clear Welsh interest or unless they form part of a co-operative acquisition agreement by the legal deposit libraries.

- Local interest magazines
- Diary/What's on magazines
- Hobby and recreation magazines
- Popular magazines
- Light fiction magazines
- Domestic interest magazines (home-making, cookery, etc.)
- Sporting magazines
- Comics
- Erotic and pornographic magazines
- Occult magazines
- Magazines of specialized industries, trades, and businesses
- Student magazines
- School magazines
- Parish magazines and newsletters
- Newsletters of amateur societies
- Fanzines
- Magazines and newsletters produced in connection with the theatre, film, media, pop worlds
- Newsletters of Friends of societies and institutions
- Local genealogical newsletters

Notes: It is estimated that some 35% of new UK periodicals published annually fall within these categories. [copyrighted 1996-2001, last updated April 2001, pp. 3–4; www.llgc.org.uk/lp/lp0053.htm]

STATEMENTS COVERING AUDIOVISUAL MATERIALS FOR ACADEMIC LIBRARIES

Albion College, Stockwell-Mudd Libraries: Collection Development Policy

The Library considers all formats for selection, providing the content falls within the guidelines set forth in the Selection Guidelines section above. Other formats will be considered for adoption as appropriate. Currently the following types of non-print materials are being added to the collection:

1. Film and Video Recordings (VHS and U-matic cassettes, 16mm film, laser discs, DVDs)
2. Audio Recordings (cassette and reel-to-reel tapes, CDs, LPs). We no longer acquire LPs or eight track tapes for the regular collection. We may still acquire them for the Archives Collection.

[approved March 14, 2000, p. 11; www.albion.edu/library/collect2.htm]

Tufts University Health Sciences Library: Collection Development Policy

AV materials, including audio cassettes, videocassettes, slides, realia, etc., are purchased only on faculty recommendation to support the curriculum, with the exception of several current subscriptions to AV journals such as the Network for Continuing Medical Education (NCME) videos, Audio-Digest tapes, or other popular titles. [copyright 1997, updated November 13, 2000, p. 2; www.library.tufts.edu.hsl/colldevelopment.html]

STATEMENT COVERING AUDIOVISUAL MATERIALS FOR COMMUNITY COLLEGES

Griffith Memorial Library, Sheridan College: Collection Development Policy

The library orders audiovisual and computer software on a preview basis when possible. Preview requests are initiated via a Sheridan College purchase order. The library acquires materials in print, audiovisual and magnetic media and online digital formats: computer software for personal computers, maps, microforms, models, realia, CD-ROMs, audio CDs, laser discs, 35mm slides, and videocassettes or the licenses which support the acquisition of taped satellite programs. Formats acquired must be compatible with existing campus hardware and audiovisual equipment. [adopted May 4, 2001, last modified May 10, 2001, p. 3; www.sc.whecn.edu/library/services/scgml_colldev.html]

STATEMENT COVERING AUDIOVISUAL MATERIALS FOR PUBLIC LIBRARIES

Queens Borough Public Library: Collection Development Policy

The Library's film and video collections, housed in the branch agencies and Central Library, support ALA's Freedom to View Principle (see appendixes) and strive to provide a diversity of viewpoints without the constraint of labeling or prejudging film, video, and other audiovisual materials on the basis of the moral, religious, or political beliefs of the producer or filmmaker on the basis of controversial content.

Branch Collections

All age level interests are represented in these collections which consist of popular feature films, award winning films, documentaries, and films of instructional nature.

Central Library

The Central Library Film and Video Collection is divided into four major categories.

1. Fiction: Includes works of a theatrical nature, in English, of major international directors and performers, and adult animation.
2. Non-Fiction: Includes documentaries, instructional material, titles related to deaf culture, ESL, academic course work, crafts, sports and recreation, test preparation, and computer science.
3. International Films: Includes subtitled and non-subtitled material, although subtitled films are preferred over dubbings. Selection is guided by the demographic composition of the borough, the specific needs and interests of diverse cultural groups, and related outreach services provided by the Library. Theatrical and non-theatrical adult and children's films and award winning films of recognized quality in languages other than English are collected.
4. Children's Films: Includes video productions of folk tales, picture books, feature films (live action and animated), story-telling sessions, and music

for sing-along programs. Material acquired is appropriate for use in Library programs, classrooms, and workshops. The collection is relevant to study at the graduate level in elementary education, child psychology, and children's literature.

[copyright 2001, last updated March 22, 2001, pp. 6–7; www.queenslibrary .org/books/cdpol.asp]

STATEMENT COVERING REALIA FOR PUBLIC LIBRARIES

Bettendorf (Illinois) Public Library: Collection Development Policies

Children's Materials: Realia

The realia collection enables children to have hands-on experiences through the use of puppets and Learning-to-Go Kits. Puppets are selected as companions to children's literature rather than as toys. The Learning-to-Go Kits have topics that are mutually agreed upon by the staff of Youth Services and the Family Museum of Arts & Science. The kits have been designed to bring the resources and materials from each facility out into the community and into the hands of children. Some duplication of materials does exist within the general collection of library materials.

Special criteria (in addition to general criteria):

- Durability of materials
- Ability to clean and disinfect
- Pieces large enough to avoid injury
- Relationship to other material in a kit

[revised April 1999, p. 8; www.rbls.lib.il.us/bpl/policies/collect.htm]

Pasadena (California) Public Library: Collection Development Policy

The Toy Collection

A collection of educational toys, intended for use by preschoolers, is available at the Central Library and each of the branches. It provides this age group with a way of learning about their world through play and builds a foundation for reading through the development of motor and cognitive skills. The collection consists of items such as puppets, puzzles, and blocks. Each toy is accompanied by an educational card for the parents, detailing ways to use the toy to further enhance skill development. The foundation for reading is also strengthened by attendance at preschool story-times. To encourage this attendance, the toys are only available for check-out by parents one-half hour before and after storytime. [p. 14; www .ci.pasadena.ca.us/library/collection.asp]

Chapter Twelve

Special Collection
Statements in Policies

In the broadest sense, the term "special collections" refers to well-defined groupings of materials that stand in contrast with an institution's general holdings. The general holdings exist to meet the core needs of a library's clientele. Within an academic setting, for instance, this would entail basic information service and curriculum support for both students and faculty. At that same college, special collections would address the Research (Level 4) and Comprehensive (Level 5) categories of the Conspectus Outline developed by the Research Libraries Group. (1) These levels are defined as follows:

Research Level. A collection that includes the major published source materials required for dissertation and independent research, including materials containing research reporting, new findings, scientific experimental results, and other information useful to researchers. It is intended to include all important reference works and a wide selection of specialized monographs, as well as a very extensive collection of journals and major indexing and abstracting services in the field. Pertinent foreign language materials are included. Older material is usually retained for historical research and actively preserved. A collection at this level supports doctoral and other original research.

Comprehensive Level. A collection in which a library endeavors, so far as it is reasonably possible, to include all significant works of recorded knowledge (publications, manuscripts, other forms), in all applicable languages, for a necessarily defined and limited field. The level of collection intensity is one that maintains a "special collection"; the aim, if not the achievement, is exhaustiveness. Old material is retained for historical research with active preservation efforts.

Special collections are viewed from a completely different perspective in other types of libraries. Whereas special libraries based in corporations, law

firms, churches, and the like consider archives to be anathema, these resources often constitute the core holdings in museums, local historical societies, private foundations, professional associations, and governmental agencies. While these archival collections range in depth from piecemeal to world
class, most place an emphasis on the chief archival tenets of security, limited
access, and preservation.

Ever conscious of community attitudes, public libraries tend to focus their
energies on local history, genealogy, or resources by and about notable individuals (authors, celebrities, politicians, businessmen, etc.) affiliated with the
area. Like state universities, public libraries are careful to avoid using tax-
payer funding for special collections. Rather, they rely on private and corporate philanthropy, whether financial bequests or outright gifts of rare resources. However, unlike archival holdings in special purpose institutions or
universities, which generally emphasize the preservation function, special
collections in public libraries are geared to heavy use and are widely publi-
cized as a community asset.

Considerations as to type of institution notwithstanding, special collections
presume the existence of the following conditions:

* adequate space for housing the materials;
* staff expertise;
* accessibility—via physical location and document delivery—to potential
  users;
* sufficient prestige to attract philanthropy and grants;
* a funding base adequate to subsidize facilities, maintenance, and use of
  archival resources; and
* the flexibility to shift collection building priorities to capitalize on recent
  acquisitions.

Those factors dictate that only major federal archives (e.g., the Library of
Congress, Smithsonian Institution), state libraries, and large public and university libraries will be able to afford diversified special collections. Nevertheless, smaller institutions—or those possessing narrow subject interests—
are capable of developing outstanding specialized holdings.

S. Michael Malinconico and Jane C. Worth provided the following
growth rates for information sources from 1985 to 1994 during a 1995
IFLA presentation:

* between 2 and 7 percent growth for paper-based sources (books and print
  journals);
* more than 28 percent growth per year for online databases;

- nearly 40 percent growth per year for online databases which contain full text; and
- more than 100 percent growth per year for CD-ROM databases. (2)

The continued growth of electronic documents will undoubtedly influence the composition of special collections as well as the services provided by their parent institutions. Some prognosticators have argued that the Internet will put libraries out of the information dissemination business. Graham Cornish has expressed reservations, noting that this medium "has a limited range of materials available, often excluding the most valuable items for research. In any case, there is a serious question mark over whether free Internet access and services will continue to remain free." (3) In short, libraries—built in no small measure on the research materials provided in special collections—are likely to remain vital information providers for many years to come.

The policy examples below provide a mere sampling of the types of special collections developed and maintained by libraries. However, the selected areas—broad-based special collections, local history/genealogy, rare books, and subject archives—are representative of the depth and diversity of such resources as well as the relevant policy documentation provided by parent institutions. Other sections of Part 1—most notably, Government Publications and Treatment of Specific Resource Groups—contain material sometimes classified as special collections.

SPECIAL COLLECTION STATEMENT
FOR ACADEMIC LIBRARIES

Michigan State University: Collection Development Policy Statements

Purpose or Scope of Collection

Curricular/Research/Programmatic Needs

The Special Collections Division of the MSU Libraries supports the information, instruction, and research needs of MSU students, faculty, and staff as well as visiting researchers and the general public. The collections support programs in the humanities, the social sciences, and the sciences.

The Division has three principle charges or responsibilities: 1) Develop unique and/or special research collections of rare or other material in designated subject areas; 2) House and preserve library materials which require special custodial care and/or supervised use; 3) Provide access to materials within the guidelines regulating their use.

Development and implementation of collection policy for the Special Collections Division is the responsibility of the Head of Special Collections, in consultation with the Head of Collections Management. Within the guidelines of Special Collections policy, selectors from any department of the Libraries may be designated to participate in development of collections, under the direction of the Head of Special Collections.

With the approval of the Head of Special Collections, materials acquired by any subject selector in the pursuit of his/her collection development responsibility may be destined to Special Collections if rarity or other considerations dictate preservation in the original format. All pre-1801 imprints, U.S. imprints through 1830, trans-Mississippi imprints through 1850, first or signed editions by notable authors or others collected in Special Collections, and editions under 500 copies should be referred to the Special Collections librarian for evaluation. Fine examples of bindings, period bindings, unusual bindings and works with original art or photographs pasted in, and erotica or other illustrative material limited in number or likely to be mutilated should also be considered.

The Rare Book Collection

Some of the oldest and most distinguished rare book collections are in the fields characteristic to a land grant university. The Veterinary Medicine Historical Collections, for example, is among the finest in the world in terms of early veterinary works. There are also significant early holdings in agriculture, horticulture, landscape architecture, botany, gardening, ornithology, entomology, and herbals. The Mary Ross Reynolds Cookery and Domestic Arts Collection and the Beatrice V. Grant Cookery Collection combined with other cookery/domestic art holdings gives this popular field particular research strength. For over 50 years an important apiculture collection has grown thanks to an initial donation from Ray Stannard Baker.

After achieving university status in 1955, the Libraries acquired a number of outstanding rare book collections. These include the French Monarchy Collection, the German Criminology Collection, the Italian Risorgimento Collection, and a strong collection of eighteenth century British materials. There are significant collections of literary first editions of writers of the Irish Literary Renaissance, a number of American expatriate writers of the twentieth century, and selected American and English writers over the past two centuries. The written work of Argentine author Jorge Luis Borges is represented as well. American small press poetry; early travel literature, particularly accounts of European travelers in Africa and North America; and the Canadian Northwest are all considered important collections.

Most recently all the literary works of distinguished MSU writers have been collected. These writers include Richard Ford, Tom McGuane, Jim Harrison, Dan Gerber, Carolyn Forché, and Diane Wakoski among others.

The Special Collections

There are several special collections whose importance rests less on rarity than on comprehensiveness and breadth. The printing collection features works on The History of Printing, The Book Arts, and a fine collection of type specimen books. The Illuminated Manuscript Facsimile Collection has facsimile reproductions of European manuscripts from the sixth through the fifteenth centuries. The two largest special collections, the Russel B. Nye Popular Culture Collection, and the American Radicalism Collection give their own separate collection development policies.

Archives and Manuscripts

In addition to rare books and special collections, there are a number of manuscript and archival collections that give primary support to book collections. Thanks to a recent expansion in the Division there is now space to house all the manuscripts and archives together. Prominent holdings include: The Richard Ford Papers, The Thomas McGuane Papers, The Dan Gerber Papers, The Russel B. Nye Papers, The Ivan Ilyin Papers, The Smith Papers, The Eclipse Comics Papers, The Ahmed M. Kathrada Papers, The Ethiopian Collection, The Saul Wellman Papers, and the East Lansing Peace Education Papers.

Factors Influencing Collection Policy

Anticipated Future Trends

Recently much of the rare book market has become an arena for the very rich and select buyer. Wealthy individuals, consortiums, and well-endowed special libraries have pushed rare book prices upward often beyond the reach of public institutions like MSU. In this market great care must be taken to assess a book's worth versus its importance to the collections. It is important that areas of collecting interest are carefully defined. Only collections which already possess national strength or curriculum importance should be targeted for active collecting.

Relationships with Other Resources

1. Many of the holdings in Special Collections are supported by the general, circulating collection. Patrons are always urged to check the general collections for additional information.

2. There are a number of outstanding special libraries and collections in Michigan. Currently there are no formal co-operative agreements among these libraries.

Relationships to Resources Treated in Other Policy Statements

Analysis of the Subject Field: Levels of Collecting Intensity

Veterinary Medicine Historical Collection. An outstanding collection of some 1,200 manuscripts and printed works to 1900. Currently the subject of a comprehensive catalog to be published by the MSU Press. Level: 4.

University Authors. Over the past several decades a number of important literary writers have graduated from or been faculty members at MSU. While the list is always growing, the works of the following authors are collected: Richard Ford, Dan Gerber, Lev Raphael, Jim Harrison, Gary Gildner, William Penn, Thomas McGuane, Lee Upton, Hugh Fox, Diane Wakoski, William Barnhardt, F. Richard Thomas, Carolyn Forché, and Marcus Cafagña. Level: 5.

The Charles and Ruth Schmitter Fencing Collection. A distinguished collection of fencing, dueling, arms and armor, and related subjects donated by the Schmitters. Collecting will focus on early material (pre-1900) in all languages with an emphasis on very early fencing/dueling works (pre-1700). A recently created endowment fund will help in acquiring material. Fencing/Dueling books that include horsemanship will also be preferred as a complement to veterinary medicine. Level: 4.

Gastronomy/Cookery

Early English and American Cookbooks (pre-1900). While most of the important titles in this area are already held, several gaps exist. First editions preferred to fill these holes. Collecting may include herbals, dietary works, kitchen gardening, and beer making. Eighteenth-century English and America cookery manuscripts are collected intensively.

African-American Cookery. Collect available cookbook titles in any edition or time period which feature influence of African food on world cuisines. Areas include African-American, Caribbean, Brazilian, and African cookbooks.

Jewish/Kosher Cookery. Collect available cookbook titles in any edition or time period which exhibit influence of Jewish food culture on international cuisines.

Unusual Cookery. The odd or unusual cookbook in any edition or time period. The emphasis is twentieth-century American, but not exclusively.

Level 4 for all designated cookery levels. The Beatrice V. Grant Endowment Fund is available for cookbook acquisitions.

Early Agriculture

Collect primarily English and American agricultural works to 1850. First editions preferred, but not required. Special attention for works that include gardening and domestic arts to complement cookery and veterinary medicine. Emphasis also on apiculture, grasses, farm management, forestry, and husbandry. Level: 3.

Modern American Fiction. Collect the occasional "high spot" of current American fiction. First editions only of fiction printed since 1960. The collection serves to complement the University Authors Collection. Level: 2.

Eighteenth-Century British Studies. Collect courtesy (advice) books from the eighteenth century. Any edition is acceptable. Also, Johnsonian literary circle titles in any edition.

Fine Printing/Book Arts. Collect all available productions by Laura Davidson, a Cambridge book artist who attended MSU. Books produced by fine, small printing houses can be acquired through University Authors collection. Level: 5.

Manuscripts and Archives. (1) Where possible, collect the manuscript collections of designated University authors. Major acquisitions of material may be necessary. Comprehensive. (2) Collect manuscript and archival collections that complement and support existing print collections, especially Africana, Radicalism, Popular Culture, Veterinary Medicine, and Comic Art. Selective.

Collection Management Issues

Preservation. A good many books in the collections are plagued with problems of foxing, deteriorating bindings, or loose covers, while many others suffer from brittle paper. With the new compact shelving, light is less a problem, but drastic fluctuations in temperature and humidity still present deadly problems to the physical well-being of the collections.

Funding for rare book special treatment is only adequate. A new endowment for preservation, the Carter Harrison Endowment, will help.

Boxes and minor repairs are handled by a capable in-house preservation office. Digital conversion of at-risk material is of major importance. Steps need to begin at once to establish a digital text office with strong ties to Special Collections materials.

Security. A new security system was installed in 1997, with further study planned for a video/surveillance system.

Endowments. Endowment funds will play an increasingly important role in collection development. Currently, two endowments, the Grant Cookery and the Harrison Preservation, are fully funded. Two others, the Schmitter

Fencing and the Special Collections funds are in the process of being fully funded. An effective Library Development Office is crucial to the creation of more funds.

Sales/Duplicates. On a highly-selective basis collections and/or single books, which no longer support curriculum needs or fall outside the scope of active collecting, may be sold according to library policy and procedure. Proceeds for any item(s) will go to the Special Collections Endowment.

[drafted December 11, 1996; www.lib.msu.edu/coll/main/spec_col/about/collpol.htm]

SPECIAL COLLECTION STATEMENT FOR PUBLIC LIBRARIES

County of Los Angeles Public Library: Materials Selection Policy

A special collection is a concentration of materials in a narrowly defined subject or topical area. These collections vary in size. They may be integrated or physically separated from the host collection. The collections reflect retrospective collection building and ongoing acquisition of newly published materials.

Rose Diaz Pinan Reading Aloud Collection

After the death of Rose Diaz Pinan in September 1981, the County of Los Angeles Public Library learned that Mrs. Pinan had bequeathed funds totalling over $64,000 to the Library for the purpose of purchasing books for children. In her honor, reading aloud collections were developed to be circulated from each of the community libraries of the County of Los Angeles Public Library.

Arkel Erb Memorial Mountaineering Collection

One of the most complete mountaineering collections in the U.S. is housed at the Malibu Library branch. Collected by Ruth and Arkel Erb over a twenty-year period, the collection contains over 2,800 books, magazines, and maps. This collection includes materials on mountaineering in North America, the Andes, the Alps, Himalayas, Great Britain, New Zealand, Japan, and Africa as well as related subjects such as caving, canoeing, backpacking, cooking, and wilderness travel and survival techniques. There are also a few fiction titles relating to mountaineering subjects.

Government Publications

The County of Los Angeles Public Library maintains special collections of government publications in eight of its libraries. These collections, published by Federal and State governments and maintained by Government Services Staff at the library, contain a wealth of information on a variety of subjects in books, maps, CD-ROMs, magazines, pamphlets, microfiche, and on the Internet. These Collections are made available to the public through Federal and State Depository Library Programs.

Business Collection

This reference collection at the Norwalk Library [Los Angeles Public Library] contains current, in-depth business materials such as company directories, statistical sources, and trade journals on all aspects of business operations, import-export guides, and small business.

Californiana Collection

This reference collection about the history and culture of California contains over 15,000 books, magazines and, microfilms—as well as pamphlets, periodicals, and oral history—and is located at the Rosemead Library. This is a non-circulating resource on information about Southern California in particular and California in general. Special emphasis is given to local history materials about Los Angeles County, including individual cities and unincorporated areas. Fiction by major California writers is included as well as historical fiction about California.

Edmund D. Edelman Public Policy Collection

Established in 1994, this collection at the Norwalk Library is designed to serve the informational and educational needs of those involved in implementing public policy in local government and in the private sector. This collection has been named in honor of Supervisor Edmund D. Edelman in recognition of his more than 20 years of service to the people of Los Angeles County. Supervisor Edelman has maintained a long-held interest in public policy issues and concerns on a number of levels.

Japanese Relocation Camp Collection

This collection is located at the Gardena Mayme Dear Memorial Library [Los Angeles Public Library]. The materials are in both microfilm and paper format. There are about 100 theses and 80 newspaper and periodical titles dealing specifically with the World War II internment camp experience. In addition, there is a small collection of books, journals, and newspapers on related subjects.

Judaica Collection

Housed at the Culver City Julian Dixon Library [Los Angeles Public Library], the Judaica Collection contains materials on the history and culture of the Jewish people with a focus on the Holocaust. Many works of fiction by Jewish authors are also available. A smaller collection of materials focusing on the Jewish Holocaust is located at the Las Virgenes Library [Los Angeles Public Library]. This collection contains books on the Jewish Holocaust during World War II and includes survivor's stories in fiction and nonfiction adult and children's books.

Languages Other Than English

Most libraries have a variety of books, magazines, and other materials in many different languages such as Spanish, Japanese, Chinese, French, German, Korean, and Vietnamese. Contact your local library about the materials in other languages.

Nautical Collection

The Lloyd Taber-Marina del Rey Library [Los Angeles Public Library] houses a nautical collection that has materials on subjects such as boating, boat repair, and navigation. This special collection started when the library opened in 1976. The collection has been cited in *L.A. Weekly* as the "best nautical library." The Department of Beaches and Harbors and the Department of Regional Planning send appropriate materials to this library, anticipating demand.

Anthony Quinn Collection

This collection is housed at the Anthony Quinn Library. Donated to the Library by the world-renowned actor and artist, the collection contains over 3,000 items including photographs, memorabilia, scripts, videotape recordings of television appearances, galleys from Mr. Quinn's autobiography, *The Original Sin*, and a portion of his personal art collection.

Ron Shipton HIV Information Center

The Ron Shipton HIV (Human Immunodeficiency Virus) Information Center was established at the West Hollywood Library [Los Angeles Public Library] in 1989 as a joint venture of the County of Los Angeles Public Library and the City of West Hollywood. Its purpose is to provide accurate and accessible materials regarding education, etiology, prevention, transmission, epidemiology, treatment methods, and legal issues related to HIV-AIDS.

Services for the Visually Impaired

Most libraries have books in large print and books on tape. Contact your local library for more information.

Tony Warde Drama Collection

Located at the La Cañada Flintridge Library [Los Angeles Public Library], this memorial collection provides a broad subject coverage of books pertaining to all aspects of theatre arts such as drama education, play production, theatre history, theatre directories and who's who criticism, plays and film studies.

Topographic Maps

These maps present detailed surveys of the land with such items as contours, wells, old mines, and jeep trails. Available are maps of the United States, California, Arizona, Nevada, Oregon, Alaska, and Washington. [revised February 2001; www.colapublib.org/materials/collections/index.html]

SPECIAL COLLECTION STATEMENT FOR SPECIAL LIBRARIES AND RELATED INSTITUTIONS

The Library of Virginia: Archival Collection Development Policy

Public Records of the Commonwealth

As mandated by the *Code of Virginia*, all of the Commonwealth's public records that have historical, legal, fiscal, or administrative value will be preserved in the Library of Virginia and made accessible to the citizens of the Commonwealth and other researchers. Records in the custody of state and local agencies will be appraised following records management procedures. Those identified as having permanent value either will be transferred to the Library of Virginia, Collection Management Services Division, Description Services Branch, for archival retention on an approved records retention and disposition schedule or permanently retained in the office of origin. Records that have estrayed from public custody will be identified, and when possible, retrieved through negotiations. Reasonable fees for care and keeping may be paid to individuals or manuscript dealers who have been responsible for the maintenance and preservation of these documents. If it is impossible to obtain original public records of permanent value by transfer, gift, or purchase, the Library of Virginia will endeavor to secure alkaline photocopies or microfilm of them.

Public Records of Other Governmental Bodies

Originals or photocopies of public records of other governmental bodies whose actions relate to Virginia shall be obtained through gift, purchase, or transfer. Primary emphasis shall be placed on acquiring Virginia-related material created by the governments of the United States, United Kingdom, Confederate States, and West Virginia.

Non-Public Records

Non-public records and private papers relating to the history of the Commonwealth shall be acquired by gift, purchase, or photoduplication. Whenever possible, collections are accepted with no restrictions on access, photoduplication, or literary rights. Categories of private papers include the following:

Architectural Plans and Drawings. Architectural plans and drawings documenting the heritage of Virginia buildings, including dwellings, public, business, and religious facilities, will be acquired.

Bible Records. These include originals or photocopies of family data sheets, usually from Bibles, relating to Virginia families. Preferences will be given to records created before 1912. The Bibles are not retained, but returned to the donor after copying.

Business Records. Primary consideration will be given to business records documenting the commercial, industrial, and agricultural history of Virginia (e.g., store accounts, plantation journals, and records of railroads, canals, mills, tobacco, and retail establishments which contributed to the significant economic history of the Commonwealth). Preference will be given to records of statewide or regional importance containing significant research value and for those created in the nineteenth century or earlier.

Cemetery Records. Records of church, private, Confederate, and federal cemeteries in Virginia and compilations of burials will be acquired. Records of public cemeteries usually will be acquired according to records retention and disposition schedules.

Church Records. Manuscripts and record books documenting the colonial and antebellum religious and church history of Virginia will be acquired, especially those recording vital statistics information concerning members of churches or denominations. Preference will be given to records created before 1912 that include data concerning residents of the state during the periods when vital statistics were not recorded by the Commonwealth.

Genealogical Notes and Charts. Genealogical charts and research notes documenting the genealogy of Virginia families will be acquired. Preference is given to legible, logically arranged, and documented original research that is readily usable by researchers.

Maps. Manuscript and printed maps of Virginia and its political subdivisions will be acquired. Preference will be given to manuscript maps, first editions of printed maps, and maps that reflect the development of the Commonwealth. Maps of the southeastern and mid-Atlantic states, selected maps after 1900, U.S.G.S. topographic quadrangles of Virginia and contiguous states, and copies of unique Virginia maps from other repositories also will be collected.

Organization Records. Records of private organizations and associations with historical significance and research value to the history of the commonwealth will be acquired.

Personal Papers. Personal papers will be acquired that supplement or complement information documented in public records or provide insights about the history of the commonwealth and its inhabitants.

[last modified June 11, 2001, pp. 1–3; www.lva.lib.va.us/collect/archman/pol .htm]

LOCAL HISTORY AND GENEALOGY
FOR ACADEMIC LIBRARIES

University of Southern Mississippi Libraries: Collection Development Policy

Mississippiana

The collection includes publications about Mississippi, Mississippians, and by Mississippi authors; Mississippi state documents; materials commercially or privately published in Mississippi when they are short press runs or otherwise not widely distributed.

Formats include monographs; serials and newspapers; ephemera; microforms, 35mm films, videotapes, USM theses, and vertical file materials. The collection is primarily English, but other languages, particularly French and Spanish, are not excluded.

Materials are located in Room 302A McCain Library and Archives and the Cleanth Brooks Reading Room. Books about Mississippi published by commercial presses and widely distributed are placed in the circulating collection, Cook Library with selected duplicates housed in McCain for preservation purposes. Heavily used reference books are placed in the Reference collection, Cook Library with older editions or selected duplicates available in McCain for archival purposes. Books by Mississippi authors that have no subject connection with Mississippi are placed in the circulating collection, Cook Library if they support specific instructional needs. Audio-visual materials and microforms are placed in Cook Library.

Duplication is based on demand and availability. Donated items usually constitute duplicates. Duplication is limited to two copies, with the exception of heavily used reference materials. If the first copy is placed in Cook Library, a second copy may be added to Mississippiana. All gift books are reviewed for location placement. First copies will be placed in Mississippiana if they are autographed by a prominent author, are in poor condition, are rare or out of print, or are otherwise in need of protection and restricted use.

Selection is by the Head, Special Collections. Purchases made from library allocations to academic departments may be placed in the collection when they meet collection criteria.

Genealogy

The collection includes original historical county records and family histories, cemetery records, published church records, military and pension records, marriage and death records, wills and estate records, tax lists and census records, Revolutionary War records, and Native American materials.

The collection includes books and serials, loose materials, maps, microfilm, and privately published family histories. The collection is primarily English, with some French and Spanish, and covers primarily the southern United States from ca. 1750 to present.

Materials are located in the Cleanth Brooks Reading Room, McCain Library and Archives. Support materials for Genealogy, such as books describing how to do genealogical research or compile genealogical records, are housed in Cook Library general circulating collection. Genealogical materials are not purchased, but are accepted as gifts. There are some photocopy restrictions for fragile materials.

Duplicates for heavily used items are added to the collection. Other duplicates may be stored and used as replacements for deteriorating materials. The Director of Public Services approves the selection of materials to be added to this collection. [last modified January 24, 2001, pp. 12–13, 15; www.lib.usm .edu/policy/cdpolicy/htm]

LOCAL HISTORY AND GENEALOGY FOR PUBLIC LIBRARIES

Jackson County (Indiana) Public Library: Collection Development Policy

Indiana Collection

The Indiana Collection at the Seymour main library contains material on the history, description, and development of Seymour, Jackson County, its residents, and to an extent, the state of Indiana. Many of these materials are available only within the library with duplicate copies occasionally acquired for the branches and bookmobile. Duplicate copies are also acquired to be made available for loan. Some background histories of the surrounding area are also included in the collection, covering localities and events closely related to the development of Jackson County. Works by or about Hoosiers with limited relevance to Jackson County will be evaluated individually, and only those works that add appreciably to the knowledge of Indiana will be added to the collection.

Materials not accepted are restricted collections, undated and unidentified photographs of people, hard copy of newspapers already available in microfilm, or books by local authors that are outside the scope of the collection policy.

Local History

The Indiana Collection includes works of some Indiana and local authors. Works of local imprint are added only when they contribute directly to the social and cultural history of the region.

Family History

The library will acquire genealogical material related to Jackson County. The library attempts to include indexes to births, deaths, marriages, wills, and land records, and when possible, indexes and compilations of the records for surrounding counties. Donations of family histories are accepted if any of the ancestors or descendants had ties with Jackson County. The library purchases at least basic and current genealogical research guides and state historical society guides for states that had significant migrations to Indiana and that became destinations for groups leaving southern Indiana, and for the predominant countries of origin of the immigrants. The library purchases census microfilm for Jackson County as it becomes available. The library accepts census indexes for surrounding counties and states and, when possible, purchases censuses for years and localities for which significant local demand can be documented. [approved February 16, 1999, pp. 4–5; www.japl.lib.in.us/policies/default .asp?policy=current/CollectionDevelopment.html]

LOCAL HISTORY AND GENEALOGY FOR SPECIAL LIBRARIES AND RELATED INSTITUTIONS

Library of Michigan: Collection Development Policy: Special Areas

The Genealogy Collection, maintained at the main library, focuses on the state of Michigan and the areas from which the great majority of Michigan's early settlers emigrated. Other genealogical materials which help Michigan residents trace their family histories are also acquired. Areas of selection include the New England states, the Mid-Atlantic states, the Great Lakes states, the Southern states and the Provinces of Ontario and Quebec.

1. Geographic Area
   a. Michigan—COMPREHENSIVE (see appendixes).
   b. All the states in the northeast quadrant of the U.S. and eastern Canada—COMPREHENSIVE.
   c. Other selected states from which numbers of Michigan residents or their ancestors emigrated—SUPPORT.
   d. Other countries from which numbers of Michigan residents or their ancestors emigrated—SUPPORT.
2. Special Explanations
   a. Family histories are acquired as gifts. They are purchased only if they substantially relate to Michigan families. Michigan family biographies which do not focus on lineage are added to the Library's Michigan Collection.
   b. Genealogical reference tools (bibliographies, census indexes, periodical indexes, and guidebooks) for all geographic areas—RESEARCH.

[revised July 17, 1996; www.libofmich.lib.mi.us/collections/colldevpolicyvii .html]

RARE BOOKS FOR ACADEMIC LIBRARIES

Mount Holyoke College: Rare Book Collection Development Policy

General Purpose

The rare book program acquires, preserves, organizes, and services many of the most valuable, scarce, or important published materials in the Library's collections. The collections are kept for the use of Mount Holyoke students, faculty, staff, and outside researchers. The collections support the teaching and research activities of Mount Holyoke College students and faculty in the major areas specified in the Archives and Special Collections General Collection Boundaries.

General Collection Boundaries

The rare book collections are added to in three separate ways: a) through purchase by the Library using funds specified for this purpose, b) through donation, and c) by transfer from the Main library stacks. With the exception of materials transferred from the main library, additions to the collection must fit one of the major areas of collecting identified below:

- Americana
- Editions of Dante's *Divina commedia* (predominately illustrated)
- Renaissance science (including works from the 17th century)
- Fine press books
- Literary first editions of significant authors
- Works related to the Collège de 'pataphysique

These areas are subject to review and addition by the Director of Archives and Special Collections in consultation with the Rare Books Librarian.

Purchase of Rare Books

The Archives and Special Collections will, on occasion, purchase books that will add to the scholarly value of our existing areas of collecting. All purchases must be approved by the Director of Archives and Special Collections and the Rare Books Librarian. In cases where the cost of an individual item exceeds $5,000 a College Librarian and/or the LITS Advisory Board may also be consulted.

Donations of Rare Books

The Archives and Special Collections will accept donations of rare books if they fit into the major areas of collecting listed above. Mount Holyoke College will not accept donations of books where ownership of the books has not been transferred to the College. Mount Holyoke College reserves the right to sell or otherwise dispose of any donated materials that do not fit within our areas of collecting.

Books Transferred from the Main Library Collections

Books meeting the following criteria will be considered for transfer from the main library collections to the Archives and Special Collections:

1. All European continental imprints before 1600, including incunabula (i.e., books printed before 1500).
2. All British imprints before 1700 (books and periodicals).
3. All books from New England and other Colonial states, bearing imprints before 1830. (Pieces on religion, printed after 1799, will not be considered unless the item itself is important in the history of printing, or has some other value directly related to Mount Holyoke College.)
4. Books from states other than the 13 colonies as recommended by Library of Congress Subject Cataloging Manual: Shelflist.

5. Books from Europe, other than those printed in Great Britain, bearing an imprint prior to 1750.
6. Books from Asia or Southeast Asia bearing an imprint prior to 1900.
7. Press books (defined as books collected as examples of fine printing including, but not limited to, Golden Cockerel, Cummington, and Nonesuch Press).
8. Limited editions other than press books if the limitation is known to be 200 copies or less.
9. Books signed by persons of national or international importance.
10. Manuscript editions of published works either holographic or typed (including carbon copies).
11. Books published by Mount Holyoke College faculty.
12. Loose plates (books, portfolios, or any publications containing loose maps or plates).
13. Other unusual materials such as papyri, palm leaf manuscripts, etc.
14. Any single volume with an auction record of over $500 in the last five years.
15. Ephemera related to significant book collections including, but not limited to, medals, commemorative buttons, etc.

In addition, some books falling within the following subject boundaries that parallel materials in the archival and manuscript collections will also be considered for transfer from the main library to Archives and Special Collections.

• Materials related to missionary work
• Works by 19th-century women authors
• Works related to women in war
• Works related to women in politics
• Works related to women in science
• Works on women's suffrage
• Works related to the education of women

American imprints from states other than the 13 Colonies prior to the dates listed below should be considered for transfer from the main library. All information taken from Library of Congress Subject Cataloging Manual: Shelflist, G810, Page 1, October 1994.

Alabama, 1840	Florida, 1860
Arizona, 1890	Hawaii, 1860
Arkansas, 1870	Idaho, 1890
California, 1875	Illinois, 1850
Colorado, 1876	(except Chicago, 1871)

Indiana, 1850	North Dakota, 1890
Iowa, 1860	Ohio, 1840
Kansas, 1875	Oklahoma, 1870
Kentucky, 1830	Oregon, 1875
Michigan, 1850	Pennsylvania
Minnesota, 1860	(outside Philadelphia), 1830
Mississippi, 1840	South Dakota, 1890
Missouri, 1850	Tennessee, 1840
Montana, 1890	Texas, 1860
Nebraska, 1875	Utah, 1890
Nevada, 1890	Washington, 1875
New Mexico, 1875	West Virginia, 1830
New York State	Wisconsin, 1850
(outside New York City), 1830	Wyoming, 1890

[copyright 1997, 3 pages; www.mtholyoke.edu/offices/library/arch/rarepol.htm]

RARE BOOKS FOR PUBLIC LIBRARIES

Public Library of Charlotte & Mecklenburg County (North Carolina): Materials Selection Policy

It is not the scope of the Main Library to develop a general rare book collection. The Carolina Room at the Main Library does identify and preserve for future generations, rare and valuable materials which serve to illustrate the social, economic, and political development of the local community. The collection addresses the need for a safe and permanent repository for those local interest items considered especially valuable, either because of scarcity or exceptional quality.

As the public library for the community, the PLCMC has prime responsibility for preserving rare materials of local authors and subjects. Rare books from outside Mecklenburg County may be received as gifts if they fall within the general collection development guidelines for historical materials. [p. 5; www.plcmc.lib.nc.us/find/policy/materialselection.htm]

SUBJECT ARCHIVES FOR ACADEMIC LIBRARIES

Columbia University (New York): Oral History Research Office

Purpose and Program Description

The Columbia University Oral History Research Office is the only oral history archive in the country that is not limited by region and topic in its collection policies. In general we are guided by two differing principles. In the first case we try to collect in areas where the collection is already strong in order to enable patrons to consult as complete and complex a set of interviews as possible. Thus, since the Collection is so strong in the New Deal era, we will try to interview any New Deal participant not already in the Collection. Similarly, with the Eisenhower Administration, or New York City cultural life, we seek opportunities to do oral histories for participants.

On the other hand, we feel it vital that we build in areas where we are less strong, such as African-American history, women's history, or gay and lesbian history. In such cases, priority is given to areas where there have been major curricular developments in the University, such as the establishment of the Institute of Research on Women and Gender or the Institutes for Research in African-American Studies and African Studies. In such cases we try to work with the faculty in their areas of specialization.

Areas in which we do not collect because other institutions and projects in the New York area concentrate upon these areas are: Holocaust survivors, union histories, or certain projects in social history. Social history presents a problem because much of what would be collected is of limited use over time, but we try wherever possible to concentrate upon institutions (such as the Northside Center for Child Development), or leadership broadly defined. Outside of these areas of social history, we try to work closely with community or other projects working in those areas in the sense of giving workshops, advising on grant proposals, etc.

We also accept donated collections when they fit into our Collection, such as a recently accepted set of interviews with academics who were affected by loyalty and security policies in the 1950s, and a series of interviews on the history of heroin. In such cases, we always search for funds for processing and if such funding cannot be found, we simply store the tapes. More and more often we are being asked to house tapes produced by faculty in the process of their research which we cannot do because we do not have the storage space or resources to deal with such large collections.

General Selection Guidelines

Overall, the Libraries' existing collection, its current acquisitions commitment, based upon available resources, and its collecting goal for Oral History are all at the research level.

Specific Delimitations

Formats Collected: We collect and accept oral histories, including tapes and transcripts. We do not collect sound documents such as speeches, seminar recordings, radio programs, etc.

Imprint Dates Collected: We collect contemporary and 20th century America oral histories.

Languages Collected: We collect the English language extensively and oral histories in all other languages very selectively.

Places of Publication: We collect oral histories from North America extensively and from all other countries very selectively.

[last updated January 5, 2001; www.columbia.edu/cu/lweb/services/colldev/ oral-history.htm]

Michigan State University: Collection Development Policy Statement

Comic Art Collection

The Comic Art Collection is a research collection with a national and international patronage of scholars and publishers. The materials have proved to have incidental value to MSU curricula primarily in undergraduate studies in advertising, communication, animation, art, and English. The collection and its continuance are based on the premise that comics are an important but inadequately researched twentieth-century entertainment and communications medium.

The Comic Art Collection was begun in 1970, by Professor Russel Nye, as part of the collection now called the Russel B. Nye Popular Culture Collection. The comics are currently the largest and fastest-growing special collection at the MSU Libraries. There are currently over 100,000 cataloged items in the collection.

The four main strengths of the collection are: U.S. comic books; European comic books; U.S. newspaper strips; and history and criticism of comics. Less extensive, or sample, collections are also maintained in the following areas: African, Asian, and Latin American comics; fotonovelas; animation; cartooning; Big Little Books; comics tie-ins; other works by comic personnel; and newspaper clippings. One publisher archive, the "Eclipse Deadfiles," is maintained.

It is likely that the need for this collection will increase steadily as remote users, who already need the materials, discover that it exists. It is equally likely that local users, both students and faculty, will continue to discover or be shown potential uses for the collection. Publishing of comics and works about comics has accelerated since 1970.

Only the Library of Congress, with a reported 100,000 comic books, has a similar, publicly available collection. In our neighboring states, a major collection at Bowling Green State University numbers about 35,000 comic books, and significant, but much smaller, collections exist at Ohio State University,

Indiana University, Kent State University, Northwestern University, University of Chicago, and the State Historical Society of Wisconsin.

Newspaper comics began with the "Yellow Kid" in 1895; comic books began with *Famous Funnies No. 1* in 1934. These are the beginning points of our collection. We do not actively collect a pre-history of comics, and thus we exclude early works on caricature, illustration, or woodcut storytelling, among other examples. The emphasis is on graphic storytelling directly in the newspaper comics or newsstand comic book tradition, excluding even contemporary humorous or editorial cartooning unless done by an artist who also has a career on the comics page.

The three major and nine minor collecting areas are approached at varying intensities as listed here:

Comic Books of the United States

The American comic book collection includes 80,000 comic books of every kind, including superhero, war, underground, funny animal, new wave, and over 2,000 from the 1940s. In addition, the Library holds about 2,000 issues on black-white microfilm. Most newly published comic books are being routinely acquired through donation. It has been estimated that the U.S. has produced 100,000 comic books since 1934, and other similar estimates lead us to believe that we own more than half of what could possibly be included. As it stands, few of the longer runs are complete, and the missing issues are usually the older ones. Because of the fragility and great expense of most of these items, we are not actively purchasing originals. The limited microfilm available is being purchased instead, and donations of older comic books are regularly received. To have a comprehensive collection of U.S. comic books is not a short-term goal of the collection, although the possibility is being kept in mind against the day when microfilm or other good-quality stable formats become available. Collecting intensity: 4 (see appendixes).

European Comic Book Collection

A collection of 11,000 comic books and albums was purchased in 1995. With this addition, the Michigan State University Libraries established the most nearly comprehensive collection of European comics in any Western Hemisphere library. Continued acquisition of European comics is planned with the intent being to maintain representation of all artists and nationalities. Collecting intensity: 3 (see appendixes).

Comic Strips of the United States

The comic strip collection includes over 500 scrapbooks of clipped newspaper strips dating from the 1920s into the 1980s, plus most books that reprint comic strips. An effort is being made to purchase every book that has collected and reprinted comic strips in the English language. This collection cannot be termed comprehensive, because what is available in book form is only a small fraction, probably less than ten percent, of what has been published. We do not collect original art for comic strips. A collection of clipped comic strips is arranged by topic and keyword. Collecting intensity: 4 (see appendixes).

History and Criticism: Books and Serials about Comics

This collection includes, or intends to include, all serious or significant separately published works about comic books or strips, in whatever languages they can be obtained, with a preference for English language editions if a choice is available. This practice began in 1987 with the realization that the existing collection was already probably the best in existence. Materials that were published before 1987 and are now out-of-print are being sought. Although monographic history and criticism of comics is routinely ordered from foreign sources, serial subscriptions are entered on a sample basis only. Collecting intensity: 4 (see appendixes).

Asian, African, and Latin American Comics

Comic books from outside the U.S. and Europe are collected with the intent to represent the available body of material. Comics are rapidly developing into an international medium, so that more translations are available in English every year. Most of these translations are acquired through purchase or donation. Newsstand comic books from other countries are obtained through donations by publishers and correspondence with foreign collectors, as well as by asking staff and faculty to pick up samples when traveling. Monographic history and criticism, and occasional reprint volumes, are ordered through normal library channels. Collecting intensity: 3a (see appendixes).

Fotonovelas

Fotonovelas are a medium similar to comic books, with narratives constructed by applying word balloons to photographs. Fotonovelas are an important medium in Latin America, Southern Europe, and Northern Africa. Since there are no research collections anywhere that we know of, and since they are so similar to comic books, we have been asking travelers to bring us samples. These trickle in at the rate of about six per year, which scarcely represents a medium that must number millions of items published in several languages each year. Even at this rate, however, we are building the biggest research collection that we know of. Educational fotonovelas are a subcategory of interest that we are encouraging publishers to deposit with us. Collecting intensity: 1 (see appendixes).

Animation

Materials about animation are included in the Comic Art Collection because creative personnel and fictional characters tend to overlap between the comics and animation industries, and because books about animation tend to be attractive and are often stolen or defaced if allowed to circulate. These materials are well used by undergraduates and an effort has been made to secure the best published reference books and monographic material and sample issues of serials. Collecting intensity: 3a (see appendixes).

Cartooning

There has been an ongoing effort to collect all materials that treat cartooning in the context of comic books or strips; however, few titles of this nature exist. Books by or for editorial, magazine, or gag cartoonists are not solicited. A few examples of non-comics cartooning books are kept if they have been donated, since this is a related topic and is of interest to some users.

Comics Tie-Ins

When a comic book or strip generates a movie, there are likely to be thousands of licensed items (calendars, coloring books, posters, ink blotters, novelizations, lapel buttons, neckties, T-shirts, etc.) that are related. Even less prominent comic books and strips sometimes have success in licensing. Such items are always accepted when offered as gifts, and are purchased very selectively, in order to have available a representative selection of the kinds of objects that have been produced. Catalogs and other reference works that list these items are purchased. Collecting intensity: 2 (see appendixes).

Other Works by Comics Personnel

Comics writers, artists, editors, and publishers often work in other fields; for example, they illustrate books and write novels. Works on other media by people whose primary career identification is comics are always accepted as gifts and are purchased whenever found at unobjectionable prices. Research on any comics professional is not complete without reference to non-comics work, and bibliographies are available for very few of these people. By collecting these materials we are providing a collection that is available nowhere else. Collecting intensity: 3 (see appendixes).

Newspaper and Other Clippings Files

An extensive vertical file is kept including clippings, advertising material, greeting cards, work samples, and miscellanea relating to persons, titles, and topics. Advertising items come from local stores and publishers. Because the files are cataloged on OCLC, they are sometimes requested by remote users. Collecting intensity: 3 (see appendixes).

Eclipse Deadfiles Archive

For every comic book published by Eclipse Comics, the Library has received a large envelope typically containing one or more pre-publication forms of the work. Each envelope includes one, some, or all of the following: original and edited scripts, photocopies of the pencilled art, photocopies of the inked pages, and correspondence between the editor and other creative personnel. Many of these files illustrate in depth the process of publishing a comic book from the publisher's perspective. Although these are unique materials and there is a file for every Eclipse Comic Book, the collection level assigned was selected because some of the files are very thin and Eclipse was only one (albeit the fourth or fifth largest) of a field which includes dozens of publishers. The Deadfiles are not, therefore, comprehensive in any fashion and cannot be counted on to supply specific information about a particular comic book. They do function as support materials for research regarding the creation of comic books, Eclipse in general, or Eclipse staff. Collecting intensity: 3 (see appendixes).

All items printed on newsprint or in mimeo or ditto are kept in duplicate if second copies are donated. This reduces wear on fragile materials, and provides insurance against badly printed pages or pages with clipped coupons. We keep the comic books out of the light and away from acidic materials as much as possible, using acid-free envelopes and Mylar sleeves as appropriate. Each comic book is stamped with an ownership stamp to make recovery more possible in case of theft. We maintain a website for the collection, which includes a wantlist of out-of-print books. In the long run, we see ourselves as having a responsibility to preserve the content of our collection whether the fragile physical formats can be maintained or not. We remain committed to investigating preservation both by deacidification and by microfilming. It is our intent to support projects which will produce good-quality facsimiles, reprints, microforms, and reproductions in other formats that will help our library and other libraries to preserve comics materials. [drafted September 18, 1998; www.lib.msu/comics/ devpol.htm]

SUBJECT ARCHIVES FOR PUBLIC LIBRARIES

Canterbury Public Library: Collection Development Policy

New Zealand Collection: Haerenga Ki Aotearoa

The New Zealand Collection collects and makes available both contemporary and historical material, in a variety of formats, about New Zealand, and in particular about the Canterbury region. It is both a research and a heritage resource.

In order to fulfil these functions, no material may be borrowed from the collection.

A preservation and conservation policy aims to provide access to material in the collection both now and in the future.

In the past all material about New Zealand or written by New Zealanders was purchased regardless of quality. The volume of material now published in these categories means this is no longer possible, nor desirable, and the acquisitions policy is now more selective than in the past.

The following guidelines are used:

Books and Pamphlets

- a comprehensive collection of books about New Zealand is maintained.
- books from established New Zealand publishers with significant New Zealand content are purchased.
- most material published about or in Canterbury is collected.
- poetry from established presses is purchased. Poetry about Christchurch or written by Christchurch poets is generally purchased. Poets from other parts of New Zealand will be purchased if well reviewed.
- fiction and drama from established presses, with an emphasis on those with local content or by local writers, is purchased.
- school, church, club, society, etc., histories are comprehensively collected for the Canterbury region. For the rest of New Zealand these histories are collected if they cover 50 years or more.

The New Zealand Collection will not generally acquire:

- highly scientific or technical books.
- educational texts written in a question and answer format or those designed as teaching resource manuals.

- general cookbooks, gardening books, and sports books which do not have a distinctive New Zealand flavour.
- materials in formats which are unsuitable for library use.
- books written by New Zealanders without New Zealand content.

Duplication

Duplicates of key items will be obtained if:

- heavy use of the item is anticipated.
- replacement at some time in the future may be difficult or impossible.

One copy will be held in the New Zealand Collection for everyday use and the duplicate housed in a storage area as a preservation area. Very heavy usage and ongoing demand may occasionally justify duplicate copies held onsite in addition to the stored copy.

Special Collections

Butler Collection: A comprehensive collection of material by and about Samuel Butler is held. Material will continue to be purchased with the aim of having every published edition of Butler's works.

Newton Collection: A small collection of mountaineering books, pamphlets, and serials donated by Henry Newton. No new material is actively acquired for this collection.

Ngaio Marsh Collection: New titles will be acquired for this collection which aims to provide a comprehensive selection of works by and about Ngaio Marsh. Foreign language editions will also be held.

Pocock Collection: A very small collection of books by Lewis Greville Pocock. Other titles with specific reference to Samuel Butler are held in the Butler Collection. No new material is actively acquired for this collection.

Theses: The New Zealand Collection will acquire theses that complement and add depth to the collection. Subject areas likely to be interest are:

- history and geography topics with local content or of major importance to New Zealand.
- political topics with local content or of major movements, personalities, or organizations.
- artistic, literary, and cultural topics, including Maori material, which may have few other printed resources.
- social topics which describe major changes to the fabric or functioning of New Zealand society.
- any theses which include research conducted in Christchurch or Canterbury.

Archives

The New Zealand Collection will actively seek donations of archival materials. Donors may place limitations on access to material. An active collection or maintenance policy applies to the following areas:

Ephemera

• posters, handbills, circulars of all types.
• election material for both local body and general elections.
• art exhibition catalogues, theatre and music programmes.
• postcards and calendars.

Archives

• material relating to Canterbury Public Library.
• records of local sporting, cultural, or community institutions, clubs, and societies.
• business records (more selectively).

Manuscripts

• historical items including diaries, letters.
• fiction, drama, poetry, film scripts.
• material relating to our genealogical and local history services, e.g., church registers.

Oral History

The Library holds approximately 300 oral history tapes but does not actively record or seek oral history material.

Photographs

The New Zealand Collection will actively acquire photographs that are likely to be of historical interest. Photographs that depict the following will be included:

• Christchurch/Canterbury/South Island
• social conditions
• industry
• agriculture/farming
• transport
• sport and recreation

- domestic scenes
- major natural events
- disasters
- architecture and interior design
- fashion
- street scenes
- major social events

All time periods will be considered.

Government and Official Publications

Central Government

The New Zealand Collection seeks to hold a comprehensive range of Government and other official publications.

- Parliamentary papers and a range of publications produced by Statistics New Zealand are received under the Government's Depository Scheme.
- other official reports requiring submissions, annual reports, etc., will be actively pursued.
- arrangements have been made for the New Zealand Collection to appear on the mailing lists of as many Government organisations as possible but individual items required for permanent preservation will often need to be individually pursued.
- increasing reliance is being placed on the Internet for access to Government resources that will not be acquired as permanent additions to the collection.

Statistics

- all statistical publications produced by Statistics New Zealand are automatically received as part of the Depository Scheme.
- other Government departments such as the Department of Justice and the Department of Education regularly send statistical data.
- statistics produced by organisations such as the National Health Information Service (Ministry of Health) will be purchased as they become available.
- access to census information from 1986 onwards is available electronically via Supermap.

Local Government

Local and regional government publications, reports, district schemes, etc., are also deposited with the Library by the bodies concerned. Items are also actively pursued for this Collection. An increasing amount of local government material is also now accessed via the Internet.

District Schemes and Planning Documents

The New Zealand Collection will actively pursue and retain the following current district schemes:

- Christchurch City
- Banks Peninsula District
- Hurunui District
- Selwyn District
- Waimakariri District
- superseded copies of the schemes for these Canterbury local authorities will be retained off-site
- non-Canterbury district schemes which are donated to the Library, and for which there appears to be a demand will be held until no longer current and then discarded

Legal Resources

The New Zealand Collection will purchase:

- general legal texts and practical manuals suitable for the layperson.
- guides which assist customers to interpret and apply legislation and to understand their rights and obligations.
- subscriptions to looseleaf publications considered to have a wide general appeal.

In addition, all statutes, regulations, and bills will be held in paper form. The New Zealand Collection also provides electronic access to all current and historical legislation.

Maori Resources

The New Zealand Collection will purchase:

- material by authors who identify as Maori.
- Maori language publications.
- material about Maori subjects or which present a Maori perspective on a subject.
- material published by Ngai Tahu as Tangata Whenua.
- material relating to Ngai Tahu as Tangata Whenua.

The Maori resources held in the New Zealand Collection will complement those held in the Nga Taonga Maori Collection as well as providing long term preservation for items likely to be of enduring or increasing interest.

Maps

The New Zealand Collection will:

- collect and retain maps of Christchurch, both contemporary and historical.
- collect and retain Canterbury planning maps.
- hold only current copies of topographical maps for New Zealand.
- hold only current copies of hydrographic charts for Akaroa, Banks Peninsula, Lyttelton, and the Marlborough Sounds.

Rare or valuable maps may be photocopies for customer use and the originals stored for preservation.

Genealogy

Genealogical material in the New Zealand Collection focuses strongly on Christchurch and Canterbury. An ongoing programme exists to transcribe church records of baptisms, marriages, and burials for the region. Headstone transcripts and burial books are also held.

The New Zealand Collection holds and will continue to purchase or accept donations of:

- family histories, particularly those of Canterbury families. Preference will be given to family histories which contain extensive text, photographs, and social history rather than only genealogical charts.
- microfiche and microfilm resources which contain genealogical information about New Zealanders and people coming to New Zealand.
- publications which guide customers to genealogical sources.

Formats

Microforms. Full text items will be duplicated on microform (film or fiche) where heavy demand on the paper copy is cause for concern regarding its preservation. This policy particularly applies to newspapers. The New Zealand Collection has an ongoing microfilming programme for newspaper preservation but also purchases microform products available from other libraries and genealogical organisations.

Electronic Resources. The New Zealand Collection will seek to provide customers with access to quality educational and informational New Zealand resources in electronic formats.

Audiovisual. The New Zealand Collection will purchase items available on CD, cassette, or video that relate to Christchurch or Canterbury and are considered to be of increasing or enduring interest. One of the major factors that will be considered in retaining items is whether any other organisation in Canterbury or New Zealand will preserve the material if the New Zealand Collection does not. (pp. 33–38)

NOTES

1. Michael R. Gabriel, *Collection Development and Collection Evaluation: A Sourcebook* (Metuchen, NJ: Scarecrow, 1995), 241–242.

2. Ross Harvey, "The Preservation of Electronic Records: What Shall We Do Next?" In *Collection Management for the 21st Century: A Handbook for Librarians*, edited by G. E. Gorman and Ruth H. Miller (Westport, Conn.: Greenwood, 1997), 175.

3. Graham P. Cornish, "Electronic Document Delivery Services and Their Impact on Collection Management." In *Collection Management for the 21st Century: A Handbook for Librarians*, edited by G. E. Gorman and Ruth H. Miller (Westport, Conn.: Greenwood, 1997), 171.

Chapter Thirteen

Resource Sharing
Statements in Policies

Resource sharing encompasses cooperative collection development and the delivery of documents and information through coordinated interlibrary efforts. Formal cooperative networks—both same type and multitype—have been facilitated in recent years by means of enhanced online capabilities and the development of faster and more efficient borrowing and lending systems. The American Library Association's *Guide to Cooperative Collection Development* cites the following benefits of library cooperation in collection building:

1. Promotion of more systematic collection development planning to permit calculated responses when library income becomes flat or decreases.
2. Elimination of undesirable redundancy in development of collections of the future of distribution of responsibility for certain subject areas or material formats.
3. Ability of some libraries to exercise greater selectivity in some areas and the consequent acquisition of fewer non-core titles because of the knowledge that these titles will be available through resource sharing.
4. Coordination of retention policies for little-used materials, last copy, serial backfiles, etc.
5. Coordination of preservation among libraries to reduce redundancy of expensive preservation activities.
6. Improved staff knowledge, ability, and skills for local collection development, especially when a cooperative program includes a strong training component and there is frequent communication among staff of the cooperating libraries. (1)

A resource sharing statement within the written policy typically describes one or more of the activities at the core of the cooperative arrangements between libraries. Typical programs include:

- shared purchase of particular kinds of items;
- distributed collection development responsibilities;
- cooperative retention;
- cooperation to complete a single project (e.g., a serials union list, storage project, weeding project); and
- cooperation in areas associated with collection development (e.g., cataloging, preservation projects, automation programs, special interlibrary loan agreements). (2)

It is imperative that cooperative collection development agreements be described in the written policy, whether in the community background statement, the appendixes, or a separate section. Elizabeth Futas provides a rationale for including the text (or at least a summary) of such contracts:

> Some materials are not purchased because a member of the consortia already has them or has promised to purchase them, and the library must purchase some materials because it has commitments to the consortia. Library patrons have the right to know what effects such arrangements have on them and the use of their library and any member library's collections. (3)

The policy excerpts included here all effectively reflect the particular programs of and nature of agreement between cooperating institutions. These libraries all outline the existing formal agreements to which they presently subscribe. Stockwell-Mudd Libraries is perhaps most explicit in pointing out that research sharing arrangements are "not limited to" such legal contracts.

RESOURCE SHARING STATEMENTS
FOR ACADEMIC LIBRARIES

Albion College, Stockwell-Mudd Libraries: Collection Development Policy

Stockwell-Mudd Libraries actively pursues cooperative arrangements and consortial arrangements with other libraries and library organizations to enhance the collection and to improve access to information resources.

The Interlibrary Loan Program of Stockwell-Mudd Libraries is a cooperative program with other libraries that extends access for faculty, students, and staff to the rich resources of other libraries around the world and encourages the cooperative use of expensive acquisitions. The library maintains a number of special arrangements with other libraries and organizations to expedite this sharing of resources.

In addition, Stockwell-Mudd Libraries participates with other libraries in numerous cooperative purchasing agreements including, but not limited to, AccessMichigan, AICUM (Association of Independent Colleges and Universities in Michigan), Oberlin Group, Michigan Oberlin Group, the Michigan Library Consortium, and the Albion Public Library. Each of the agreements aids in the sharing of materials to the advantage of faculty, students, and staff. In the selection of expensive library materials, consideration is given to their accessibility through interlibrary loan agreements and through networking.

Decisions regarding the disposition of gifts, the initiation of new periodical subscriptions or the cancellation of existing subscriptions, and the purchase of expensive sets may include consideration of resources available at other libraries. [approved March 14, 2000, p. 5; www.albion.edu/library/collect2.htm]

Indiana University–Purdue University, Fort Wayne, Walter E. Helmke Library: Collection Development Policy

The library will supplement its collection through resource sharing, document delivery services, and cooperative collection development.

Resource sharing encourages free exchange of materials among the participating libraries for the mutual benefit of all parties. Helmke Library is part of several local, state, and regional resource-sharing networks. They include the Local Area Academic Libraries Reciprocal Borrowing Program, the Northeast Indiana Health Science Libraries Consortium, the Northwest Indiana Health Science Library Consortium, the Indiana University Libraries System, the Indiana Academic Resource Libraries network, the Committee on Institutional Cooperation (CIC) Reciprocal Borrowing Program, and the OCLC Reciprocal Faculty Borrowing Program.

In addition, each year the Library appropriates money from the materials budget to pay for document delivery of items not available through established resource-sharing networks. The library also dedicates the resources necessary to provide high-quality, timely document delivery.

The Library takes into consideration its resource-sharing networks in making collection development decisions. Likewise, the library works with its resource-sharing partners to establish cooperative collection development programs that will benefit all libraries involved. Cooperative collection development programs take advantage of strengths of the participants to enhance resource sharing and to improve access to research materials. [last modified June 27, 2001, p. 16; www.lib.ipfw.edu/library_info/ collections/collection_development_policy/]

RESOURCE SHARING STATEMENT FOR COMMUNITY COLLEGES

Lake-Sumter Community College: Collection Development Policy

Due to libraries' limited budgets and diminishing ability to physically collect even a small percentage of the world's information, access rather than ownership has become the reality of collection development. Increasing numbers of information resources are available only in online electronic formats. The worldwide development of electronic information systems such as online library catalogs, abstracting, and full-text databases have made it possible for libraries to direct users to vast quantities of information resources. While the libraries cannot keep all of the material relevant to the users in their collections, they can provide access to the vast amount of information available for use in other collections. This type of access requires that libraries engage in cooperative collection development, resource sharing, and document delivery systems. When it is determined that access on demand is more economically feasible in terms of storage, project use, and cost, this option can enhance the libraries' abilities to expand the information base available to their primary users.

Every possible effort will be made to cooperate with Lake County Library System, the Sumter County Library system, regional and statewide organizations, particularly the Central Florida Library Cooperative, the College Center for Library Automation, and the Florida State Community College Library Standing Committee to share resources and engage in cooperative acquisitions projects. [copyright 1997–2000, last revised April 16, 2001, pp. 14–15; http://lscc.cc.fl.us/library/coldev.htm]

RESOURCE SHARING STATEMENTS FOR PUBLIC LIBRARIES

Kitsap (Washington) Regional Library: Collection Development Policy

Kitsap Regional Library recognizes that it cannot provide everything that its customers request within its own collection of resources. Therefore, the Library is committed to the cooperation and sharing of resources among libraries and other agencies that acquire, house, and make information and materials accessible. The Library supports:

- cooperative use agreements that cross library district and agency lines, thus allowing users access to the broadest array of resources and information;
- cooperative collection development among agencies as a means to avoid unnecessary duplication and provide the most access to the most information for the most people; and
- interlibrary loan as a means of providing access to specialized, out-of-print, and other materials the Library does not acquire.

Kitsap Regional Library makes every effort to satisfy the needs of its customers through the Library's own collection or through other local resources. All requests for materials not in the Library's collection are considered for purchase first and will be purchased rather than borrowed whenever possible. The Library is committed to building a collection of resources that responds to and is capable of filling most of its customers' needs. The courtesy of resource sharing is called upon only when the Library cannot satisfy the request with its resources. The decision to purchase or borrow an item is made by the Collection Manager and delegated staff.

Because interlibrary loan is costly in terms of staff time for both borrowing and lending libraries, the Library may limit the number of requests an individual may make at a given time or per year. The Library may levy a surcharge for requests that exceed a given number per year for an individual and for rush treatment of requests.

Although the Library absorbs most of the internal costs of interlibrary loan, including most database searches and the cost of staff time involved in the process, it may pass on to the requestor any charges assesssed by the lending library. Such charges include:

- loan and photocopy charges,
- postage and handling fees, and
- lost, damaged, or overdue fees.

[approved May 19, 1998, pp. 23–24; www.krl.org/administration/policies/colldev.html]

Manitowoc (Wisconsin) Public Library: Policies & Procedures, Collection Development

Manitowoc Public Library is the headquarters and resource library for the Manitowoc-Calumet Library System, and is therefore responsible for serving the System's broader needs. Its selection policy recognizes a responsibility to meet those broader needs. Manitowoc Public Library is also able to borrow materials from other libraries for its own patrons. Such borrowing should be limited to items which Manitowoc might not be expected to own. Interlibrary loan does not relieve the library of any responsibility for developing its own collection. [adopted March 28, 1988, p. 3; www.manitowoc.lib.wi.us/Collectiondevelopment.htm]

NOTES

1. *Guide to Cooperative Collection Development*, edited by Bart Harloe (Chicago: American Library Association, 1994), 3–4.

2. *Guide to Cooperative Collection Development*, edited by Bart Harloe, 7.

3. Elizabeth Futas, ed., *Collection Development Policies and Procedures*, 3rd ed. (Phoenix, Ariz.: Oryx, 1995), 253.

Chapter Fourteen

Services Identified in Policies

Although not directly concerned with collection building functions (e.g., the evaluation of materials, weeding), many library services influence the character of library holdings. Collection development statements generally omit descriptions of these services. However, some institutions choose to include either a general inventory of services or describe in greater detail those programs placing noteworthy demands on library holdings. An increasing number of libraries are posting their policies on institutional websites along with hyperlinks to sections describing organizational services. While it might be argued that these service statements were not envisioned as part of the core written policy, the very presence of hyperlinks makes clear the intended connection.

The following policy excerpts reflect the wide array of library services tied in with collection building. Whereas the County of Henrico (Virginia) Public Library concisely outlines the full range of services based of collections use, institutions such as the Walter E. Helmke Library (IPFW) and Tufts University Health Sciences Library provide a more in-depth focus on specific services.

GENERAL SERVICES FOR PUBLIC LIBRARIES

County of Henrico (Virginia) Public Library: Collection Development Plan

Libraries reflect the diversity and character of the communities they serve. Excellence in library service is defined by the fit between the library's service roles and the needs and expectations of the community it serves. The service roles assigned to the branch and area libraries identify the perimeters of each type of collection. Those roles articulate the type of service that those libraries seek to offer their communities, and, as such, are key to building and maintaining those collections. The application of these roles must underlie every collection management decision, from the initial recommendation of a title, to its consideration for branch or area library placement, to its selection and incorporation into the collection, to its de-selection, or weeding, from the collection.

Two of the service roles, community referral and community activities center, are not specifically tied to the collection. There may be some implications for the collections at the area libraries because of their involvement in these roles. However, it is the other four roles that have the most impact on the collections. This document will define and explicate the effect of the specific roles on the area and branch libraries and will address the differences in the application of the shared roles at each.

The area and branch libraries share three roles or service responses:

- Children's door to learning
- Current topics and titles
- General information

The area libraries alone carry the additional roles of:

- Lifelong learning
- Community referral
- Community activities center

Children's Door to Learning

The Library encourages children to develop an interest in reading and learning through services for children, and for parents and children together. The Library promotes early reading and acceptance of reading, factors contributing to successful performance in formal schooling for the community. Branch and area library collections will have a variety of materials and formats for children, with popular titles available in multiple copies. Area libraries will adopt a broader approach, incorporating titles useful to adults working with children, addressing educational issues, and incorporating a wider variety of programs for adults and children.

Current Topics and Titles

Branch and area libraries will offer current, high-demand, high-interest materials in a variety of formats for persons of all ages. There will be an emphasis in both types of libraries on purchasing an adequate number of copies to reasonably meet the demand of customers. A broader approach to currently popular subjects and titles will be taken at the area libraries. Due to larger space and circulation, the area libraries will by definition have more of these materials in greater depth, but customers should expect a generous selection of bestseller titles and materials about topics of current interest in both area and branch libraries.

General Information

The library actively provides timely, accurate, and useful information for community residents at both area and branch libraries. The Library promotes on-site, remote, and telephone reference/information services to aid users in locating needed information primarily at area libraries, which will have greater depth and variety in their collections. While branch libraries will address individual needs, area library collections will include materials incorporating informational materials to support individual, business, government, and community interests.

Lifelong Learning

The Library supports individuals of all ages pursuing a sustained program of learning independent of any educational provider. Users can pursue self-determined and self-paced study on various subjects. Independent learners can use the resources of the library to "get ahead," to do better in their work, to learn something new, or to adjust to changes in life and work. The collection has a wide range of circulating subject materials relevant to the interests of independent learners of all ages. The materials are in a variety of formats and geared to varying levels of ability.

Community Referral

The Library is a clearinghouse for current information on community organizations, issues, and services. The Library maintains a high profile as a source of information about community services. The collection, in addition to regular reference materials, contains locally developed files with data on community agencies, clubs, and interest groups.

Community Activities Center

The Library is a central focus point for community activities, meetings, and services. It works closely with other community groups and organizations to provide a coordinated program of social, cultural, and recreational activities. Community members have opportunities to explore and discuss their divergent views on issues and current topics, and receive some social services at the library. This role emphasizes use of the facility, rather than the collection. [updated October 2000, pp. 2–4; www.co.henrico.va.us/library/colldev2000 .html]

DOCUMENT DELIVERY FOR ACADEMIC LIBRARIES

Indiana University–Purdue University, Fort Wayne, Walter E. Helmke Library: Document Delivery Services at IPFW

IPFW's Document Delivery Services policies are governed by the American Library Association's National Interlibrary Loan Code and by the policies of state and local cooperatives of which IPFW is a part. In addition, Document Delivery Services complies fully with provisions of the Copyright Revision Act of 1976 (PL 94-553) and its amendments in the processing of its requests.

The primary goal of the Document Delivery Services (DDS) at IPFW's Helmke Library is to obtain materials not owned at the Library but needed to fill the research needs of its faculty, students, and staff. DDS is also offered to non-IPFW patrons for a fee. The goal is to obtain these materials in the most cost-effective means possible. In an effort to achieve this goal DDS uses whatever means necessary, including traditional ILL, fee-based services, tele-facsimile, and Ariel to acquire items requested.

Although faculty, students, staff, and Alumni Association members are not charged for document delivery, these materials, labor, and postage are paid by the IPFW Helmke Library. The most recent Association of Research Libraries study (1993) calculated that the average cost of document delivery is $30.00 per item. Please order prudently; order what you need for research. Refer others who are not entitled to the University library subsidized document delivery service to the Document Delivery office for information on its fee-based service. [approved November 10, 1997, last modified June 25, 2001; www.lib .ipfw.edu/library_info/dds/]

RESERVES FOR ACADEMIC LIBRARIES

Indiana University–Purdue University, Fort Wayne, Walter E. Helmke Library: Collection Development Policy

Instructors choose the materials for course reserves and the loan period for student use. Formats can include, but are not limited to, books, photocopies of journal articles and class notes, slides, video and audio tapes, and CDs. Individual reserves are limited to 25 items. Items may be from the library collection or be the instructor's personal property. Reference books are put on reserve only with the permission of the subject librarian of the relevant area.

Fair use is observed in the photocopying of copyrighted material. In general, this means one copy of an article, a book chapter, a short story or poem, or a map or chart. The library will copy materials for reserves free of charge. Each instructor is responsible for obtaining copyright permission for multiple copies and for retaining photocopied copyrighted material on reserve for more than one semester.

When possible, the library will purchase copies of books, videos, or CDs instead of borrowing items from other libraries. Required textbooks are not purchased or borrowed via Document Delivery Services. Subject librarians are consulted about purchasing copies of material that faculty have put on reserve from their private collections. The library is not responsible for loss or damage to personal property placed on reserve. Students can be billed only for lost/damaged library property. [approved November 10, 1997, last modified June 27, 2001, p. 12; www.lib.ipfw.edu/library_info/index.html]

Tufts University Health Sciences Library: Collection Development Policy

Certain types of materials are placed in the Reserve Collection, which serves to hold them together in a convenient location, to better control their availability and to provide access to the largest number of library users. Reserve materials can be moved from other parts of the library's collections, be provided by faculty, or belong permanently to the Reserve Collection. Reserve books include:

- Materials placed on course reserve for teaching purposes based upon faculty request
- Board reviews and study guides
- Heavy demand/high loss books

In general, the library will keep 2 copies of clinical texts and 4 copies of preclinical texts on Reserve, although additional copies may be purchased when there is very high demand. Reserve materials are moved to the General Collection when new editions are received. [copyright 1997, latest version November 13, 2000, p. 2; www.library.tufts.edu/hsl/colldevelopment.htm]

Chapter Fifteen

Selection Aids
Identified in Policies

Selection aids function as a guide for librarians in deciding which resources to add to the collection. G. E. Gorman and B. R. Howes state that an effective selection tool should do either or both of two things:

1. It must identify the item, and provide the selector with enough information to determine what the item is; i.e., it must act as an "alerting device."
2. It must evaluate the item, or tell the selector whether the item is any good for its stated purpose, and if it is not, in what particulars it fails; i.e., it must act as an "evaluating device." (1)

Although not always listed in written policies, libraries rely most heavily on the following types of selection aids:

- Evaluative Bibliographies
  - subject bibliographies (total coverage and selective)
  - standard lists (current, retrospective, and out-of-print lists)
  - guides to the literature
  - library catalogs
- Alerting Bibliographies
  - national bibliographies
  - trade bibliographies
- Reviews (Guides)
  - digests
  - indexes
- Reviews (Journals)
  - general
  - subject specialist journals

- ○ library journals
- ○ specialist book selection journals
- ○ newspapers
- Advertising (Display)
- Advertising (Direct Mail)
- Advertising (Advance Notices) (2)

The arguments for including a section on selection resources within the collection development statement include:

- The section establishes a benchmark for consistency in the use of these tools;
- it assists new staff in adapting to a library's established selection procedures; and
- it communicates the level of professionalism involved in the evaluation process to the community at large.

In addition to listing useful published resources, some policies note the more specialized strategies employed by collection developers; e.g., contracts with rare book agents, consideration of purchase requests from library clientele.

The contrast in approaches—between merely citing selection tools and a more comprehensive approach, including procedures and the roles of particular departments and staff positions—is apparent in the following policy excerpts. The Acquisitions chapter also covers selection tools—both in the introduction and sample policies—at length.

SELECTION AID CHECKLIST FOR ACADEMIC LIBRARIES

The Nueva School Library: Selection Policy

The following lists and tools shall be consulted in the selection of materials, but resources are not limited to these listings:

1. Bibliographies, using the latest editions and supplements:
   - ○ *American Historical Fiction*
   - ○ *Basic Book Collection for Elementary Grades*
   - ○ *The Best in Children's Books*
   - ○ *The Bookfinder*
   - ○ *Children and Books*
   - ○ *Children's Catalog*
   - ○ *Elementary School Library Collection*

- ○ *European Historical Fiction and Biography*
- ○ *From A to Zoo*
- ○ *Guide to Sources in Educational Media*
- ○ *Junior High School Catalog*
- ○ *Reference Books for School Libraries*
- ○ *Senior High School Catalog*
- ○ *Subject Guide to Children's Books in Print*
- ○ *Subject Index to Books for Immediate Grades*
- ○ *Subject Index to Books for Primary Grades*
- ○ special bibliographies prepared by educational organizations for particular subject matter areas

2. Current reviewing media:
   - ○ *AAAS Science Books and Films*
   - ○ *ACL Review*
   - ○ *American Film & Video Association Evaluations*
   - ○ *Book Links*
   - ○ *Booklist*
   - ○ *Bulletin of the Center for Children's Books*
   - ○ *CD-ROM World*
   - ○ *English Journal*
   - ○ *Gifted Child Quarterly*
   - ○ *Horn Book*
   - ○ *Kliatt*
   - ○ *Language Arts*
   - ○ *Library Journal*
   - ○ *Reading Teacher*
   - ○ *Roeper Review*
   - ○ *School Library Journal*

[approved by the Board of the Nueva School, February 2, 1994]

NOTES

1. G. E. Gorman and B. R. Howes, *Collection Development for Libraries*, (London: Bowker-Saur, 1990), 249.

2. G. E. Gorman and B. R. Howes, *Collection Development for Libraries*, 248.

Chapter Sixteen

Copyright Statements in Policies

Although directly applicable to collection building and the dissemination of information, copyright and other intellectual property concerns are rarely addressed in written policies. Probable reasons for this include the absence of legal precedents to assist in interpreting specific copyright applications as well as librarians' general lack of knowledge regarding such issues.

Those policies that do mention copyright tend to focus on the institution's commitment to following legal directives. Other possible concerns to be addressed within a copyright policy include:

- discussion of individual library activities and services involving some form of copyright compliance (e.g., photoduplication, interlibrary loan, document delivery, public presentations, licensing of computer software);
- reference to key documents guiding copyright-related decisions such as sections 107 and 108 of the 1978 U.S. Copyright Act, the Digital Millennium Copyright Act (1998), the Copyright Term Extension Act (1998), and notable federal court decision and copyright policy committee guidelines (e.g., *Guidelines for Classroom Copying in Not-for-Profit Educational Institutions*); and
- procedures for educating the library's staff and constituency (e.g., posting guidelines near copy machines).

The incorporation of copyright information in collection development statements is likely to increase as libraries become more committed to digital technologies and are, therefore, forced to address property rights relating to the storage, manipulation, and transfer of electronic information. Legal advisers are insisting that libraries keep relevant copyright statutes close at hand, if not actually citing them in policies or, better still, reproducing the text of the documents in the appendixes.

The various copyright concerns of representative library institutions are outlined in the policy excerpts below. Whereas the Babson Library and Santa Fe Community College Library emphasize compliance with the U.S. Copyright Law, the North Vancouver District Public Library concentrates largely on procedural considerations.

COPYRIGHT STATEMENT FOR ACADEMIC LIBRARIES

Springfield College, Babson Library: Collection Development Policy

Babson Library adheres to all provisions of the U.S. Copyright Law (17 U.S.C.). The library actively promotes compliance by the college community. Reference librarians and Patron Services staff produce guidelines and other literature to aid college students, faculty, and staff in following the changes in Fair Use guidelines. [copyright 1997, last modified October 26, 2000, p. 25; www.spfldcol.edu/homepage.nsf)

COPYRIGHT STATEMENT FOR COMMUNITY COLLEGES

Santa Fe Community College Library (Florida): Collection Management Policy

The Santa Fe Community College Library complies fully with all of the provisions of the U.S. Copyright Law (17 U.S.C.) and its amendments. The Library supports the Fair Use section of the Copyright Law (17 U.S.C. 107) which permits and protects citizens' rights to reproduce and make other uses of copyrighted works for the purposes of teaching, scholarship, and research. [drafted January 18, 2001, pp. 7–8; http://cisit.santafe.cc.fl.us/~library/col_policy.htm]

COPYRIGHT STATEMENTS FOR PUBLIC LIBRARIES

North Vancouver District Public Library: Audio-Visual Collection Development Policy

The Library does not make any attempt to arrange Canadian Public Performance Licensing agreements on any videos. All videos are purchased for HOME USE ONLY, and loaned to library users for this purpose alone.

Occasionally the packaging on a video purchased by the Library is marked as being licensed for public performance. Even if a video IS marked with a PPR statement, if it was purchased outside Canada, it has not necessarily been licensed for public performance in this country. If a video is not marked in any way to indicate it is licensed for public performance, it MUST be assumed it is intended for home use only.

Exhibiting North Vancouver District Public Library videos can be a copyright violation, regardless of whether or not admission is charged. A performance which is not given in a private home may be considered a public performance. Showings in offices, clubs, hospitals, nursing homes, libraries, schools, colleges, and universities are public performances and, therefore, subject to copyright control.

Duplication of any video borrowed from this Library is a violation of copyright.

[Notices are placed in all branches to inform the public that VIDEOS ARE FOR HOME USE ONLY.] [approved August 17, 1995, last updated January 31, 2001, pp. 3–4; www.nvdpl.north-van.bc.ca/about/policies_2000/av_coll_pol.htm]

Chapter Seventeen

Intellectual Freedom Statements in Policies

The very existence of this book presumes the importance of a written collection development policy, produced in a collaborative manner and authorized by administrative units such as a library board, local government officials, a university board of regents, a college Vice President for Academic Affairs, or a corporate Officer of Information Resources. However, more than three decades of observing and discussing the phenomenon of library censorship has convinced us that the presence of an official collection development document tends to possess limited value as a deterrent to the attempted suppression of books and other materials. Administrators—who can legitimately argue that the final responsibility for decisions relating to the acquisition of library resources, as well as patron access to these resources, rests in their hands—are hesitant to delegate decision-making to subordinates (no matter how qualified and well informed) such as the Head Librarian. In cases where the Librarian acts as a conduit for simply passing on recommendations to the governing official, the latter is somewhat defensive about appearing to override or contradict such advice. Whether motivated by public intimidation, a desire to effectively dispatch a public relations headache, or a clear-cut sense of the ethical issues involved, administrators tend to rationalize that they are best situated to understand the bigger picture. They argue that if the constitutional underpinnings of American citizenship "take a hit," then so be it. After all, they ask, is one problematical decision likely to have a long-term impact on the integrity of American democracy? In their minds, it is far easier to resolve the immediate crisis. Such conflicts have the potential to threaten institutional credibility, job security, and the cohesiveness of the community at large.

Schools—both public and private—and public libraries are generally most vulnerable to arbitrary decision-making on the part of upper-level governance. Administrators representing these institutions are most likely to submit to community demands due to a direct dependence on local funding and administrative oversight.

In part due to their placement within a more decentralized environment, academic and special librarians often possess greater autonomy in deciding intellectual freedom matters. Furthermore, academic librarians are insulated by a number of principles residing at the fundamental core defining institutions of higher learning: (1) the library is the center of the institution's teaching and research activities, (2) academic freedom is essential to the integrity of the educative process, and (3) administrators within academia tend to have been educators themselves; even regents are usually well-educated products of this system.

Due to the diversity of their respective work environments (e.g., corporations, small businesses, governmental agencies, law offices, health care facilities, mass media entities) special librarians are somewhat harder to assess. However, the narrow focus of the organizations they serve (often staffed by highly trained professionals) and non-controversial nature of the information typically acquired, organized, and disseminated by the library confers secondary status upon intellectual freedom concerns.

The key factor determining the degree to which librarians are permitted input into decisions regarding intellectual freedom appears to rest more on professional intangibles than whether or not a written policy is in place. The opinions of a librarian possessing both a proven track record in executing library functions and a collegial relationship with administrators and staff possess the best chance of influencing administrative decision-making. Above all, administrators are concerned with facilitating effective organizational operations and minimizing criticism from within and without the institution. Librarians who are able to assist in achieving these goals will be valued members of any administrator's inner circle.

As part of its overall recommendation that the facets of the Collection Building Program be documented in a written policy, the American Library Association (ALA) identifies two sections relating specifically to intellectual freedom. These are outlined in the following manner within the Fifth Edition of the *Intellectual Freedom Manual* (Chicago: Office for Intellectual Freedom, ALA, 1996):

Policy on Controversial Materials (section V within Part 1, Selection of Library Materials):
   A. General Statement
   B. Library Bill of Rights
   C. Freedom to Read

Procedures for Dealing with Challenged Materials:
  A. Request for Review
  B. The Review Committee
  C. Resolution and Appeal

The *Intellectual Freedom Manual* advises that the collection development policy "address problems associated with the acquisition of controversial materials." The General Statement should set the tone for these sections, noting the relevance of intellectual freedom to librarianship. Those libraries attempting to provide a philosophical stance on this matter generally include an affirmation of the Library Bill of Rights. While some institutions may consider reference to additional documents to be redundant, others may incorporate resources which either reinforce intellectual freedom principles or focus on particular issues. Frequently employed materials include The Freedom to Read statement, ALA's "Policy on Confidentiality of Library Records," and the text of the First Amendment to the U.S. Constitution.

Since the Library's Bill of Rights was approved by the ALA Council at the 1939 Annual Conference in San Francisco, ALA has on occasion received requests from within the profession for further clarification of its stance regarding intellectual freedom. In response to such concerns, ALA's Intellectual Freedom Committee has drafted many additional documents aimed at providing additional guidance to librarians confronted with censorship issues. Among the more notable (and still useful) of these documents are:

- Access to Electronic Information, Services, and Networks (adopted January 24, 1996);
- Access to Library Resources and Services Regardless of Gender or Sexual Orientation (adopted June 30, 1993);
- Challenged Materials (adopted June 25, 1971; last amended January 10, 1990);
- Diversity in Collection Development (adopted July 14, 1982; amended January 10, 1990)
- Economic Barriers to Information Access (adopted June 30, 1993);
- Evaluating Library Collections (adopted February 2, 1973; amended July 1, 1981);
- Exhibit Spaces and Bulletin Boards; Meeting Rooms (adopted July 2, 1991);
- Expurgation of Library Materials (adopted February 2, 1973; last amended January 10, 1990);
- Free Access to Libraries for Minors (adopted June 30, 1972; last amended July 3, 1991);
- Library-Initiated Programs as a Resource (adopted January 27, 1982; amended June 26, 1990)

- Restricted Access to Library Materials (adopted February 2, 1973; last amended July 3, 1991);
- Statement on Labeling (adopted July 13, 1951; last amended June 26, 1990); and
- Universal Right to Free Expression (adopted January 16, 1991).

ALA encourages libraries to incorporate these policy statements into their respective philosophies of library service as needed. (They can be found at the ALA website, www.ala.org).

ALA has also formulated a series of intellectual freedom documents which address collection building and user access with broader brush strokes. They include the Policy concerning Confidentiality of Personally Identifiable Information about Library Users; Policy on Governmental Intimidation; Resolution on Access to the Use of Libraries and Information by Individuals with Physical or Mental Impairment; Guidelines for the Development and Implementation of Policies, Regulations and Procedures Affecting Access to Library Materials, Services and Facilities; Guidelines for the Development of Policies and Procedures regarding User Behavior and Library Usage; and Dealing with Concerns about Library Resources. As is the case with the policy statements cited above, the *Intellectual Freedom Manual* provides in-depth information regarding the historical background and application of these documents.

A survey of existing library collection development policies indicates that most institutions have either developed their own clearly worded philosophical stance with respect to intellectual freedom or adopted documents promulgated by professional organizations such as ALA, an applicable state library association, and/or various educational agencies. However, many of these same policies do not include a set of procedural guidelines and lines for handling complaints or other efforts at suppressing library materials and programs. Written (and formally approved) procedures serve as a public relations tool clarifying library actions in addition to ensuring consistent library responses to public complaints.

The *Intellectual Freedom Manual* addresses procedural matters in two sections: "Dealing with Concerns about Library Resources: Procedural Statement" (Part II, Chapter 8) and "Before the Censor Comes: Essential Preparations" (Part III). Three key features—all of which could be integrated into the collection development policy in some manner—are discussed at length in the ALA publication: (1) implementation of an intellectual freedom defense strategy prior to receiving any complaints, (2) reacting to particular censoring attempts, and (3) making available a complaint form to be filled out by the complainant.

The first two points are succinctly covered in "Dealing with Concerns about Library Resources: Procedural Statement." The complete text of this document reads as follows:

As with any public service, libraries receive complaints and expressions of concern. One of the librarian's responsibilities is to handle these complaints in a respectful and fair manner. The complaints that librarians often worry about most are those dealing with library resources or free access policies. The key to successfully handling these complaints is to be sure the library staff and governing authorities are all knowledgeable about the complaint procedures and their implementation. As normal operating procedure each library should:

1. Maintain a materials selection policy. It should be in written form and approved by the appropriate governing authority. It should apply to all library materials equally.
2. Maintain a library service policy. This should cover registration policies, programming, and services in the library that involve access issues.
3. Maintain a clearly defined method for handling complaints. The complaint must be filed in writing and the complainant must be properly identified before action is taken. A decision should be deferred until fully considered by appropriate administrative authority. The process should be followed, whether the complaint originates internally or externally.
4. Maintain in-service training. Conduct periodic in-service training to acquaint staff, administration, and the governing authority with the materials selection policy and library service policy, and procedures for handling complaints.
5. Maintain lines of communication with civic, religious, educational, and political bodies of the community. Library board and staff participation in local civic organizations and presentations to these organizations should emphasize the library's selection process and intellectual freedom principles.
6. Maintain a vigorous public information program on behalf of intellectual freedom. Newspapers, radio, and television should be informed of policies governing resource selection and use, and of any special activities pertaining to intellectual freedom.
7. Maintain familiarity with any local municipal and state legislation pertaining to intellectual freedom and First Amendment rights.

Following these practices will not preclude receiving complaints from pressure groups or individuals but should provide a base from which to operate when these concerns are expressed. When a complaint is made, follow one or more of the steps listed below:

1. Listen calmly and courteously to the complaint. Remember the person has a right to express a concern. Use of good communication skills helps many people understand the need for diversity in library collections and the use of library resources. In the event the person is not satisfied, advise the complainant of the library policy and procedures for handling library resource statements of concern. If a person does fill out a form about their concern, make sure a prompt written reply related to the concern is sent.
2. It is essential to notify the administration and/or the governing authority (library board, etc.) of the complaint and assure them that the library's procedures are being followed. Present full, written information giving the nature of the complaint and indentifying the source.
3. When appropriate, seek the support of the local media. Freedom to read and freedom of the press go hand in hand.
4. When appropriate, inform local civic organizations of the facts and enlist their support. Meet negative pressure with positive pressure.
5. Assert the principles of the Library Bill of Rights as a professional responsibility. Laws governing obscenity, subversive material, and other questionable matter are subject to interpretation by courts. Library materials found to meet the standards set in the materials selection policy should not be removed from public access until after an adversary hearing resulting in a final judicial determination.
6. Contact the ALA Office for Intellectual Freedom and your state intellectual freedom committee to inform them of the complaint and enlist their support and the assistance of other agencies.

The principles and procedures discussed above apply to all kinds of resource related complaints or attempts to censor and are supported by groups such as the National Education Association, the American Civil Liberties Union, and the National Council of Teachers of English, as well as the American Library Association. While the practices provide positive means for preparing for and meeting pressure group complaints, they serve the more general purpose of supporting the *Library Bill of Rights*, particularly Article III, which states that "Libraries should challenge censorship in the fulfillment of the responsibility to provide information and enlightenment." (pp. 187–189)

The *Intellectual Freedom Manual* also includes a sample complaint form, titled Request for Reconsideration of Library Resources (revised by the Intellectual Freedom Committee June 27, 1995). The work recommends that libraries and librarians consider using it as a model; ALA also encourages modifications of the form "to reflect the specifics of a given library situation." (p. 210)

A wealth of resource material relating to intellectual freedom is available on ALA's Office for Intellectual Freedom website. Links are arranged under the following headings: Advocates; Documents; Intellectual Freedom in Action; Who We Are and How to Contact us; Organizations; References; What You Can Do to Oppose Censorship; and Mail Comments. The address is: www.ala.org/alaorg/oif.

It should be noted that the Library Bill of Rights and all other ALA intellectual freedom documents do not provide any form of legal protection for libraries. These safeguards are limited to the freedom-of-speech provisions falling within the United States Constitution. However, the ALA policy statements have, in G. Edward Evans' words, "helped librarians recommit themselves to a philosophy of service based on the premise that users of libraries should have access to information on all sides of all issues." (1)

Intellectual freedom issues are extremely complex, encompassing a wide range of social, political, legal, religious, and aesthetic considerations. The personal belief systems and professional ethics of library staff are tempered by outside factors such as institutional governance, job security, and community tolerance. The intellectual freedom section of a materials selection policy should be a product of the in-depth thinking and research that is required during the planning stages of a collection building program.

The samples provided below represent only those portions of each institution's collection development policy directly concerned with intellectual freedom. Peripheral issues (e.g., user access to collections, copyright, media formats falling within the collection's scope) will be addressed in other portions of the books. Policies included vary greatly—even within specific library category— regarding coverage of intellectual freedom issues. Differences in physical layout are further influenced by mode of presentation, most notably, traditional print versus Internet home pages (website addresses have been included where applicable). The University of Oregon policy illustrates how one particular institution utilizes a web-based approach with multiple links to the appropriate guidelines. It would appear these variations reflect the distinctive characteristics and concerns of the institutions combined with the respective visions of library staff. Intellectual freedom statements have been reproduced in the Appendixes section of the book.

INTELLECTUAL FREEDOM STATEMENTS FOR ACADEMIC LIBRARIES

University of Oregon Library System: Collection Development

American Library Association's Library Bill of Rights, First Amendment
   Guidelines
Intellectual Freedom Principles for Academic Libraries: An Interpretation of
   the Library Bill of Rights—Click here to read the American Library Asso-

ciation's Guidelines for the Development and Implementation of Policies, Regulations, and Procedures Affecting Access to Library Materials, Services, and Facilities.

Interpretations of ALA's Library Bill of Rights—Click here to read the full-text interpretations of ALA's Library Bill of Rights on the following subjects:

- FINAL, APPROVED: Access to Electronic Information, Services, and Networks
- DRAFT v. 2—Access to Electronic Information, Services, and Networks (12/26/95)
- DRAFT v. 1.4—Access to Electronic Information, Services, and Networks (6/25/95)
- Access for Children to Videotapes
- Challenged Materials
- Policy on Confidentiality of Library Records
- Diversity in Collection Development
- Economic Barriers to Information Access
- Evaluating Library Collections
- Exhibit Spaces and Bulletin Boards
- Expurgation of Library Materials
- Free Access to Libraries for Minors
- The Freedom to Read
- Guidelines on User Behavior and Library Usage
- Library Initiated Programs as a Resource
- Meeting Rooms
- Restricted Access to Library Materials
- Access Regardless of Gender or Sexual Orientation
- Confidentiality of Library Users
- Statement on Labeling
- The Universal Right to Free Expression

[*Collection Development Policies*, updated December 12, 2000; http://libweb .uoregon.edu/colldev/public_policies/intfree.html]

Springfield College, Babson Library

Reconsideration of Materials

Babson Library supports the principle stated in the Library Bill of Rights (see below). Babson Library will challenge censorship in the fulfillment of its responsibility to provide information and enlightenment. Should a library user encounter material he or she feels is objectionable, he/she has the right to inform any Library Supervisor. If the matter cannot be resolved informally at that time, the matter should be referred to the Senior Reference Librarian or the Director. The Director, in consultation with other Library staff, makes the final decision concerning the request for reconsideration and notifies the complainant of the decision explaining the procedure and justifying the final decision.

Library Bill of Rights

See Appendix B.

Freedom to Read

See Appendix B. [*Collection Development Policy*, copyright 1997, revised September 2000, pp. 23–25; www.spfldcol.edu/homepage.nsf]

West Chester University, Francis Harvey Green Library

Academic Freedom

The Library rejects censorship as an infringement on the freedom to read and respects the student's right to think independently. The Library recognizes an obligation to provide representation for *all* sides of a controversial issue, as well as minority opinion and unpopular views. In this context, the primary test for controversial items is their relevancy to the college's academic programs. These principles will also apply to all public access electronic tools or resources and other media materials.

Censorship

What is censorship? How informed is the liberally educated person? Does erotic literature have any importance in life? How much diversity in opinion and what standards of morality is the community willing to tolerate? The very essence of the questions is a basic difference in philosophy, making it extremely difficult to answer any one of them precisely. Censorship by definition is "any action by officials of government, church, or other organizations, or by private individuals, which, by legal action, coercion, threat or persuasion prevents expression or communication" (Castagna, Edwin. "Censorship, Intellectual Freedom and Libraries," *Advances in Librarianship*. New York: Seminar, 1971. pp. 215–251).

Should someone suggest censorship of selection, the following steps one through three are recommended initially. If ineffective, the remaining steps should be utilized until the situation is resolved.

1. The librarian receiving the complaint shall remain calm, courteous, and respectful of the person's basic right to question.
2. The librarian shall ask for the complaint in writing.
3. The librarian shall refer the written statement to the Director of Library Services.
4. The Director shall inform the Vice-President of Academic Affairs, and through this office the President and the Board of Trustees are notified.
5. The President or his representative shall advise the Intellectual Freedom Committee of ALA and follow its advice.

Library Bill of Rights

The Francis Harvey Green Library subscribes to the principles and guidelines set forth in the American Library Association Bill of Rights, 1996 [see Appendix B]. The Library Bill of Rights shall be interpreted to apply to all materials, electronic tools, and media of communication used or collected by libraries. [*Collection Development Policy*, February 23, 2000, draft, pp. 5–7]

University of Wyoming Libraries: Intellectual Freedom Policy and Procedure

Intellectual Freedom Policy

The concept of intellectual freedom maintains that all persons have the right to hold whatever beliefs they desire on all subjects and to express these beliefs or ideas in whatever way they desire. A second aspect to intellectual freedom is that all persons have a right to unrestricted access to ideas and beliefs regardless of the communication medium used. The UW Libraries have several stakes in intellectual freedom. Academic freedom, as endorsed by the University's Board of Trustees, asserts that teaching and research cannot occur without freedom of inquiry in all areas of knowledge. The library community has adopted various documents defining aspects of intellectual freedom [hyperlink provided], since libraries are the primary source for recorded ideas and creative expression. These documents are the foundations for the principles listed below and are specifically endorsed by the Libraries. Both academic and intellectual freedom are grounded in the Constitutional assumption that citizens in a free society must have available to them a wide range of ideas so that they may choose from among them what is important or beautiful. This freedom of access is one of the major distinctions between democratic and totalitarian societies.

Intellectual Freedom Principles

Dangers to intellectual freedom come from two sources. Pressures from the outside may develop to censor or otherwise limit access to works that some consider to be subversive, slanted, unpopular, or provocative. Perhaps the greater danger to intellectual freedom is self-censorship by library staff members attempting to anticipate problems with particular works or groups of works. If a work clearly fits existing collection development policies in terms of format and subject matter, it should be added to the Libraries' collections. To deal with these pressures, the following principles are provided.

1. The Libraries will make available materials and information presenting all significant points of view and modes of expression on current and historical issues within its primary areas of collecting, including those which may be considered strange, unorthodox, or unpopular.
2. The Libraries do not endorse the ideas or presentations contained in the material that is made available; agreement with ideas expressed is not a condition for acquisition of an item.
3. The Libraries believe the personal history or political affiliation of authors or publishers is irrelevant to the acceptance and distribution of any factual or creative work.
4. The Libraries will challenge laws or governmental action restricting or prohibiting the publication of certain materials or limiting free access to such materials with every available legal means.
5. The Libraries will oppose labeling any creative work or its authors as subversive, dangerous, or otherwise undesirable.
6. The Libraries will not remove from circulation any challenged material acquired under present selection policies until a formal review (process described below) mandates such action.

Review of Challenged Material Procedures

In the event that some materials selected for the UW Libraries are challenged, the following procedures will be followed. Until mandated at some stage of the review process, the challenged work will remain available for patron use.

1. Any library user may complain in writing about a specific work to the Collection Development Officer. The complaint should indicate the specific materials considered objectionable, provided the complainant has read, viewed, or audited the entire work being challenged. No complaint against passages taken out of context or based on partial examination of a work will be considered.
2. The work in question will be analyzed by the Collection Development Officer in terms of the policy on intellectual freedom and current collection development policies. The results of this review will be provided to the complainant in an attempt to resolve the matter.

3. If the complaint is not resolved at this point, the Director of Libraries may review available documentation and render a decision or convene an ad hoc committee to review the work in question. The committee will consist of 1) the Collection Development Officer, 2) faculty member(s) representing the subject area most closely related to the work in question, and 3) student representatives.
4. The committee will review the complaint in an open meeting, making the decision by simple majority. A formal report of the decision will be supplied to the complainant and a copy will be filed in the Director of Libraries' office.

[Collection Development Office—*Policies and Procedures*, updated August 19, 1998; http://www-lib.uwyo.edu/cdo/cd_pol.htm]

INTELLECTUAL FREEDOM STATEMENTS
FOR COMMUNITY COLLEGES

Finger Lakes Community College, Charles J. Meder Library: Collection Development Policy

Library Bill of Rights

See Appendix B.

Freedom to Read

See Appendix B.

Freedom to View

See Appendix B. [adopted August 1998; http://library.fingerlakes.edu/colldev .htm]

Oakton Community College: Library Policies

Library Bill of Rights

See Appendix B.

Freedom to Read Statement

See Appendix B.

Controversial Materials (In Library Materials Selection Policy)

The Oakton Community College recognizes its responsibility to make available a representative selection of materials of interest to its users, including materials on various sides of controversial issues. The Library subscribes to the philosophy stated in the American Library Association's Library Bill of Rights and Freedom to Read Statement. [*Oakton Community College Library Policies*, pp. 1–4, adopted September 1995; http://serverec.oakton.edu/~wittman/find/policies.htm]

INTELLECTUAL FREEDOM STATEMENTS
FOR PUBLIC LIBRARIES

Berkshire Athenaeum, Pittsfield (Massachusetts) Library: Procedures for Handling Collection Complaints

The Berkshire Athenaeum is willing to re-examine its position on any item in the library's collections. These procedures have been established to deal with objections to materials owned by the Library. No item shall be removed or restricted because of a complaint except in accordance with this procedure.

Initial Complaint

Complainants who come in person, or submit complaints by telephone or by letter should be offered a copy of the "Request for Consideration of Library Materials" form [appended in original document] on which their formal complaint may be submitted. To activate the reconsideration procedures, a complaint must be in writing on the approved forms. Anonymous telephone calls, rumors, and voiced concerns are not sufficient to initiate action. Action occurs only when the Request for Reconsideration" form is returned. Complainants should also be offered a copy of the Berkshire Athenaeum Collection Development/Maintenance Policy to review.

Preliminary Review

As soon as a complaint has been filed, the objections should be reviewed by the person(s) that selected the item or is responsible for that part of the collection. The item should be read, viewed, or listened to in its entirety by the selector, the original reasons for purchase should be evaluated, and objections should be considered in terms of the Library's materials selection policy, the principles of the Library Bill of Rights, and the opinions of the various reviewing sources used in materials selection.

Preliminary Response

The objections and the preliminary response should be forwarded to the Library Director, who should review the response and either add relevant comments or return the response to the individual selector for further clarification, following which the selector should make a written response to the complainant.

It is critical that the review process be as objective as possible. If the challenged item does not meet the Library's selection criteria, then the Library should be ready to acknowledge that the material is unsuitable and withdraw it from the collection. If, on the other hand, the material does meet the selection criteria and is deemed suitable for the collection, the Library should respond to the complainant clearly and precisely. The response should also inform the complainant how to pursue the matter further.

Alert the Trustees

Simultaneously with the preliminary review and the formulation of a preliminary response, the Library Director should routinely notify the Trustees that a formal complaint has been made.

First Appeal

If the complainant is not satisfied with the preliminary response, the Library Director is the person to whom an initial appeal is made. The complainant should be contacted promptly by the Director, the library's decision should be explained, and further discussions welcomed.

Second Appeal

If the complainant still feels that the problem has been dealt with inadequately, a final appeal to the Trustees of the Berkshire Athenaeum can be made. The appeal should be submitted in writing and will be placed on the agenda of the next regularly scheduled Trustees meeting, at which time the Board will conduct a challenge hearing to provide the forum for the complainant to air objections to the title in the collection and the recommendation of the Library Director. It should be announced at the beginning of the hearing that the Board will issue its decision at the following regularly scheduled meeting, and that the hearing is simply to hear all sides of the issue. [*Berkshire Athenaeum Collection Development/Maintenance Policy*, December 1, 1998; www.berkshire.net/PittsfieldLibrary/requests.html]

Bettendorf (Iowa) Public Library: Collection Development Policies

General Collection Development Principles

The Bettendorf Public Library Information Center is a public forum; a place where ideas and information are freely communicated, where a broad spectrum of opinion and a variety of viewpoints are presented in its collection, displays, programs, and services and where all of these reflect both majority and minority cultures, the work of men and women, respect for young and old, and the various lifestyles and abilities and diverse aspects of our society. The library strives to present materials representing all sides of an issue in a neutral, unbiased manner. The existence of a particular viewpoint in the collection is an expression of the library's policy of intellectual freedom, not an endorsement of the particular point of view.

The Bettendorf Public Library Information Center endorses the Library Bill of Rights of the American Library Association (see Appendix B).

Controversial Materials

The Board of the Bettendorf Public Library Information Center endorses the Freedom to Read Statement and its interpretations. Materials selected under the Collection Development Policy are considered protected under the First Amendment of the United States Constitution.

Public libraries preserve and enhance the people's right to a broader range of ideas than those held by any one librarian, publisher, or government. On occasion, there can be diverse opinions by individuals or groups as to what is acceptable or appropriate for the collection. Library collections are not limited to only those ideas and information one person or group believes to be true, good, and proper.

The Board of Trustees believes that anyone is free to reject for himself/herself library materials of which he or she does not approve. However, the individual cannot restrict the freedom of others to read, view, or hear.

Parents or legal guardians have the responsibility to guide and direct the reading, viewing, or listening of their own minor children. The library does not take the place of the parent or guardian.

Patrons who initiate comments or complaints will receive copies of the Library Bill of Rights, the Freedom to Read, and the Collection Development Policy and the form, Statement of Concern About Library Materials. The Library Director will go over these materials with the patron. It is important to understand that concerns call into question selection decisions that have been made according to policy. The process of registering complaints is designed to make sure the selection was appropriate and results in informing the patron about the philosophy and criteria used. Patrons whose concerns are not satisfied by staff are invited to the next meeting of the Board of Trustees. Their decision will be final. [*Policies—Collection Development*, revised April 1999, pp. 3–4, 9–10; www.rbls.lib.il.us/bpl/policies/collect.htm]

Richland (Washington) Public Library: Washington Library Association Intellectual Freedom in Libraries

The Association believes that every library, in order to strengthen its own selection process and provide an objective basis for the evaluation of that process, should develop an official statement of policy for the selection of library materials.

The Committee is instructed to study existing policies from all types of libraries, to promote their development and official adoption by libraries not yet having them, and to develop sample prototypes of selection policies for the guidance of librarians writing such policies.

The Association is concerned with effecting liaison between itself and other groups and organizations who support the "Freedom to Read" statement as approved by the Washington Library Association.

The Committee is instructed, when appropriate, to advise these organizations of the Association's position, to request relevant support from them, and to offer the Association's support for their programs in this area.

The Association is concerned with the continuing education of librarians and the general public in understanding and fully accepting the philosophy inherent in the Library Bill of Rights and the WLA Freedom to Read Statement.

The Committee is instructed, when practicable, to develop an educational program for librarians, library trustees, and for the general public on the freedom of communication and inquiry.

The Committee is further instructed to develop sample prototypes and encourage all libraries to adopt statements of principles concerning censorship, the freedom to read, book selection, and the confidentiality of borrowers' records. [*Library Information*, revised November 22, 1999, 2 pp.; www.richland.lib.wa.us/wlaintel.html]

NOTE

1. G. Edward Evans, *Developing Library Collections* (Englewood, Colo.: Libraries Unlimited, 1972), 302.

Chapter Eighteen

Acquisition Methods Identified in Policies

Acquisitions is concerned with locating and obtaining those materials determined to be desirable additions to a library collection. A substantial number of written policies do not include a separate acquisitions section. One perspective holds that the process is not directly concerned with collection building; rather, it is a business-oriented support function better placed in the library's procedure manual. Others advocate a more holistic view. G. Edward Evans argues,

> Collection development and acquisitions have always been closely coordinated, if not integrated, in libraries and information centers with successful programs. In today's increasingly electronic environment, that coordination/integration becomes vital. (1)

Few professionals acquainted with the intricacies of acquisitions work would question its importance to a sound collection management program. According to Joyce Ogburn, acquisitions personnel are best qualified to

> [assess] the risk and feasibility of acquisition, the availability of the resources, and the chances of success; control the system and methods needed, the choice of the source, the supporting services, and the resources themselves; and quantify the resources, work, and costs involved to conduct the business of acquisitions and measures of success. (2)

The basic functions of the acquisition process include document requests, bibliographic verification, order preparation, allocation and encumbrance of funds, vendor purchase orders, outstanding order files, processing of invoices, adjustment of fund accounts, processing of incoming materials, and forwarding materials to cataloging department. (3) Those libraries addressing some aspect of acquisitions in their written policies tend to focus on order sources or vendor relationships (e.g., type of buying plans employed). Perhaps due to its perception as a support service, acquisitions functions—if covered—are often outlined within other sections of the policy, most notably Evaluative Criteria, Selection Aids, Funding, and Formats.

The differing approaches taken by libraries within this portion of the policy are immediately evident below. For example, the Fitchburg State College policy exemplifies the tendency of some libraries to incorporate evaluative principles, whereas other institutions—e.g., West Chester University—focus on specific acquisitions issues.

ACQUISITION STATEMENTS FOR ACADEMIC LIBRARIES

Fitchburg State College (Massachusetts): Collection Development Policies

The Reference Librarians have primary responsibility for pursuing a systematic program for developing the Reference Collection. However, all librarians will be responsible for selecting titles in their assigned subject areas. The following principles will be applied in selecting a title:

1. Strength and weakness of the existing subject area collection.
2. Judged usefulness of the work.
3. Favorable reviews of the works.
4. Credibility of the author.
5. Adherence to the collection development codes.

The librarians search relevant professional literature to ensure that important works of each academic subject area are included in the Collection:

1. Securing reference review from the following journals, including
   - *Booklist*
   - *College & Research Libraries*
   - *Choice*
   - *Journal of Academic Librarianship*
   - *RQ*
   - *Reference Service Review*
2. Examining publishers' pamphlets.
3. Reviewing annual lists.
4. Checking the subject guides to the literature.
5. Checking Balay's *Guide To Reference Books* and Wolford's *Guide To Reference Materials*.
6. Appropriate subject journals.

[revised April 5, 2001, pp. 10–11; http://raven.fsc.edu/library/development
.htm]

West Chester University, Francis Harvey Green Library: Collection Development Policy Statements

Order Processing

The Acquisitions Department assumes responsibility for processing all requests for monographs that are purchased through the book budget. This includes books for the general collection, reference, and standing orders. Thus
Acquisitions plays an essential role in supporting the processing of all material orders. In addition, Serials, IMC, Music, Special Collections, and Government Documents may order directly from operating funds. The department is
responsible for all aspects of the pre-order and post-order process including:
searching the vendor database (Baker & Taylor), searching titles in OCLC for
appropriate records and transferring them into the on-line system [thus creating temporary catalog records], inputting purchase order and invoice information in the online system, preparing Agency Purchase Requests (APRs), receiving shipments and paying invoices. Upon delivery materials are checked
in and the order status of the temporary record is updated. Coordinators are notified when books have been catalogued. Duplication of materials is safe-
guarded by this centralized procedure. The Acquisitions staff plays a major
role in record keeping and tracking of order status and updating the public catalog. The Acquisitions Department is the main liaison with the University
business office and is responsible for handling vendor invoices for payment.

Budget Allocations

The Library Director will determine the funds available for library materials
in each academic year. The Acquisition Librarian will be informed of this
amount and proceed to prepare a book fund allocation for each academic department using the recently revised formula, as follows:

$B + 2L + 3U + 5G + 10F$ = total number of points
B = Book cost, average by discipline as published in *Choice* annually
L = Lower division credit hours $\times$ 2, from MIS previous year
U = Upper division credit hours $\times$ 3
G = Graduate credit hours $\times$ 5
F = Faculty, number in dept. $\times$ 10

All factors are added to give a point total, then percentages are calculated.
The allocation is made on the basis of the total funds available times the per-

centage from the formula. The revised formula uses departmental data from the University's management information system and is weighted by level of students and faculty. The Library Advisory Committee approved this revision in 1996 and it was first used in academic year 1998–1999.

Standing Orders

The Acquisitions Department maintains records of standing orders by departments. Standing order costs are deducted from the final book allocation funds at the start of the new budget cycle. Historically anything published annually or less frequently is ordered by Acquisitions. Annual titles are usually hardbound. After being checked in by Acquisitions they are classified by Cataloging and put into the general book collection. Acquisitions staff also advise coordinators of price changes and provide opportunity for review and revision of standing orders.

Acquisitions Policies

- The library will purchase paperback editions if the hardback is more than $10.00 above the paperback price. Binding will not usually be done.
- The Acquisitions Department will work in close conjunction with the Serials Department to avoid duplication of significant series and collections on standing order.
- The Acquisitions Department will try to locate and purchase out-of-print books deemed essential by the requester listed in a major bibliography, giving priority to available paperbound and photocopies before resorting to an exhaustive search for a rare item.

[submitted for approval February 23, 2000, pp. 14–15]

Potomac State College, West Virginia University, Mary F. Shipper Library: Library Collection Development Policy

Materials will be acquired for the Library in the most cost-effective process.

Purchase by Request

Faculty requests receive priority attention when selecting within respective curriculum areas. Faculty are experts in their subject areas and are qualified to select and suggest materials for acquisition. Requests are taken to the Acquisitions Librarian for consideration and purchase.

Staff of the college, students, and community members may also suggest materials for purchase. These suggested resources must support the curriculum and the collection development policy. All requests are given to the Acquisitions Librarian for consideration.

Each library staff member has his/her own area of expertise and can advise in the selection of resources for this subject area. Library tools are used for materials suitable for inclusion in the collection. All requests are given to the Acquisitions Librarian for consideration.

Purchases by Acquisitions Librarian and Director

Purchases in this manner are made by using academic library reference tools for selection to ensure that the mission and the purpose of this library are upheld. Several of these tools are *Choice Magazine* reviews, Balay's *Guide to Reference Books*, Wynar's *Recommended Reference Books*, *American Reference Books Annual* (ARBA), *Magazines for Libraries* (edited by Bill and Linda Katz), *Ulrich's International Periodicals Directory*, and other sources as needed.

Gifts

Ultimate purchase decision rests with the Director and the Acquisitions Librarian. All purchased materials must uphold the mission and purpose of the Library, the curriculum and the Collection Development Policy. [copyright 1997, last updated November 1, 1997, pp. 1–2; http://psc.wvnet.edu/~library/collect.html]

ACQUISITION STATEMENTS FOR COMMUNITY COLLEGES

Central Piedmont Community College (North Carolina): Collection Development Policy

Collection Development Committee

The Collection Development Committee submits approved requests for purchase of library materials to the acquisitions area of Technical Services. The Committee, which is chaired by the Acquisitions Manager, also includes the Director of Library Services and the Collection Development Librarians.

The Committee meets on a regular basis for discussion and decisions on library material purchases. Collection Development Librarians present recommendations for purchase after consultation with faculty in their assigned program areas. In addition, the Committee monitors expenditures for library materials, renders decisions on costly items and non-program specific materials, and sets direction for the overall development of the collection. The final decision in selection of all materials rests with the Library Director.

Materials Budget and the Allocation of Funds

Using a library materials allocation formula developed in consultation with Collection Development Librarians and the Director of Library Services, the Acquisitions Manager allocates available funds, monitors allocations and expenditures, and prepares reports on the status of allocations and expenditures for the use of the Collection Development Committee. In addition, she keeps Collection Development Librarians informed of payment schedules for continuations and renewals.

Library Materials Allocation Formula

Monies budgeted for library materials are allocated in the following manner:

50% General fund allocation: This includes current periodical subscriptions, microforms, electronic databases, general standing orders and materials for the Campuses and Centers.

30% Program allocation: These funds are divided among all the programs of the College according to a program profile developed by the Collection Development Librarians.

20% Discretionary allocation: Discretionary funds are used for programs which have special needs, are up for accreditation, or which are clearly underfunded by the program allocation formula. When planning for new courses or programs, faculty members should consult with the appropriate Collection Development Librarian to discuss the need for additional library resources. Collection Development Librarians submit requests for discretionary funds to the Collection Development Committee for approval.

Program Profile Formula

The following data are considered in devising a formula for the allocation of funds to program:

- number of students enrolled in a program
- size of Library's current collection (books, AV, periodicals, electronic formats) in program area
- actual use of library materials
- cost of materials, using average prices calculated by Bowker, EBSCO, and Department of Community Colleges Institutional Services
- library dependency of program, determined by Collection Development Librarians
- format dependency of program, determined by Collection Development Librarians
- special needs of program

Collection Development Librarians construct and apply the program profile formula to divide the 30% of the library materials budget designated for program allocation.

Special Funds

If a Library receives other monies for the purchase of library materials, Collection Development Librarians will allocate expenditures in accordance with any restrictions imposed in accepting these funds.

Ordering Library Materials

Library materials are ordered and received and invoices are approved for payment by acquisitions staff in Technical Services. On-order files, records of orders, vendor information, etc., are located in Technical Services.

Ordering Books

Whenever possible, books are ordered from a book jobber. The Acquisitions Manager selects the appropriate jobber. Books that cannot be supplied by a book jobber are ordered directly from the publisher. Book jobbers are evaluated periodically for quality of service and for availability and amount of discounts.

All books, added volumes, added copies, and rush materials are shipped directly to the Library. Acquisitions staff check invoices against book shipments and approve invoices for payment.

Ordering Audiovisual Materials

Audiovisual titles are purchased from a commercial or educational distributor or licensed to be copied off-air when such licensing is available. Materials (greater than $100.00) are ordered when possible, on a preview basis prior to purchase. Materials that cannot be previewed are ordered on approval when possible. Materials are ordered with the understanding that the Library has public performance rights. The Library requests materials that meet the requirements of the Americans with Disabilities Act (ADA), when available.

Ordering Periodicals

Periodicals are ordered from EBSCO Subscription Services, whenever possible. Periodicals which cannot be supplied by EBSCO are ordered directly from the publisher.

Because of the College's technical and vocational programs, the Library subscribes, free of charge, to a number of technical and professional periodicals unavailable through traditional vendors. For some of these, the Library established eligibility by completing questionnaires detailing applicable technical educational programs. Others are acquired through faculty whose membership in professional organizations entitles them to receive professional publications.

Other Methods of Acquiring Library Materials

Continuations. Some materials which are frequently updated are designated as continuations to be purchased when published or on a schedule determined by Collection Development Librarians. Considerations in designating continuations include:

- importance of timely receipt of material
- importance of materials to the curriculum
- importance of continuity of materials
- impact on the materials budget

Approval Plans. In certain subject areas, the Library may choose to receive materials on approval and make decisions for purchase on the basis of the examination of the material. Criteria for electing to receive material on approval include:

- need to examine materials in order to evaluate them for purchase
- need for direct faculty involvement in examination and selection of materials
- need for latest available material in program area
- cost of material

In addition to these special considerations, on-approval materials recommended for purchase must meet established selection criteria. Collection Development Librarians, in consultation with faculty, review materials and make recommendations for purchase.

Gifts and Exchanges. Collection Development Librarians assess all potential gifts to the Library. Gifts are accepted by the Library in any format with the understanding that the Library may utilize and/or dispose of these materials as it sees fit. For inclusion in the permanent collection, gifts must meet the established selection criteria. All gifts are officially accepted and acknowledged by the Central Piedmont Community College Foundation. The Library makes no attempt to render a tax statement or monetary evaluation of gifts.

Contracts and Licensing Agreements. When applicable, Collection Development Librarians research and submit to the Collection Development

Committee for approval possible contract and licensing agreement options for requested library materials. The final decision on such contracts or agreements rests with the Library Director. The Acquisitions Manager acts as the Library's agent in finalizing contract licensing agreements. Records of these agreements are maintained in Technical Services.

Out-of-Print Books. The Library generally does not attempt to purchase material through the out-of-print marketplace. Exceptions may be made for an item which is clearly identified as classic and for which there is a compelling reason for owning it.

Resource Sharing. The Library will consider participating in shared purchasing to enhance access to resources beyond the Library's collection. A decision to participate depends on the obligations and restrictions of the cooperative venture. The Collection Development Committee will present recommendations to the Library Director who will pursue participation based on available funds and college policies concerning cooperative ventures.

Grants. The Library encourages College faculty and staff who are seeking grants to include funding for purchase of resource materials to support their project when writing the grant proposal. Collection Development Librarians will advise on such materials during the proposal-writing stage and will assist in selecting and acquiring appropriate resource materials if funding is approved. Collection Development Librarians will make decisions regarding including these materials in the Library's permanent collection based on established selection criteria and/or restrictions of the grant. [last modified May 5, 1999, pp. 27–30; www.cpcc.cc.nc.us/library/general/policy/cd.htm]

Lakeland Community College: Library Collection Development Procedure

A. Materials will be purchased by the acquisitions librarian/clerk using the practices and procedures established by the college's Purchasing Department.
B. Jobbers will be used for both books and periodicals to obtain the maximum discounts and the best service and to handle the large volume of materials acquired.
C. Standing orders are used for sets, monographs, loose-leaf services, etc., which are published over an extended period of time or on a recurring basis (i.e., annually). Publishers often give discounts when material is purchased as a standing order.

[approved October 6, 1998, copyright 2000, p. 4; http://lakepac.lakeland.cc .oh.us/screens/colldev/htm]

Oakton Community College: Library Selection Policy

Orders are ordinarily placed through a book jobber to ensure the greatest price discount. When appropriate or when required, some items are ordered directly. Ordering is not done through local bookstores or through the Oakton College Bookstore. Out-of-print titles are not normally searched. Budget considerations enter into all decisions. [adopted September 1995, p. 6; http://servercc.oakton.edu/~wittman/find/policies.htm]

ACQUISITION STATEMENTS FOR PUBLIC LIBRARIES

Morton Grove Public Library: Collection Development and Materials Selection Policy

Multiple Copies

While the Library does not have the budgetary resources to buy multiple copies of every title it owns, it does buy multiple copies of titles that have high patron demand. Titles with reserves or titles with broad popular appeal are generally ordered in duplicate. For titles with many reserves, one book is purchased for every five patron reserves. An annual leasing agreement with McNaughton Books Service provides access to multiple copies of high-demand titles at a manageable cost. In subject areas such as résumés and travel books where patron demand is extremely high, the Library prefers to buy one copy of several different titles instead of buying numerous copies of one title. More variety and depth in the collection can be achieved through this approach.

Standing Orders

Titles on standing order have two characteristics in common: they are seldom reviewed in the professional reviewing journals, and/or they are important enough to the collection that receiving them automatically without evaluating individual volumes is better than missing them. The majority of these are reference materials, but travel books, college guides, test review books, and other annual series are also put on continuation for the circulating collection. Many standing order and subscription titles are placed directly with the publisher/vendor, but the majority of Library continuation titles are placed with Baker and Taylor.

Large print format titles are on standing order with Thorndike to ensure ready availability of new titles. The Library also has a standing order with Doubleday for genre fiction – mysteries, westerns, and science fiction titles.

The standing order and automatic continuation titles are re-evaluated annually by the Reference Coordinator and the Head of Public Services; titles may be cancelled, new titles added, or the number of copies adjusted to accommodate patron interest and demand. [Web version published January 26, 1998, last updated August 2, 2000, pp. 5–6; www.webrary.org/inside/colldevselproc.htm]

Queens Borough Public Library: Collection Development Policy

Material Selection

In addition to examining materials that come to the Library through publisher and vendor approval and Greenaway plans, the following are among the review sources regularly consulted as part of the materials selection process: *Kirkus*, *Publisher's Weekly*, *Library Journal*, *School Library Journal*, *New York Times Book Review*, *Multimedia World*, *Multicultural Review*, *Black Books Bulletin*, *Quarterly Black Review*, the *Lambda Book Report*, *Choice*, *World Literature Today*, *Video Source Book*, *Video Librarians*, *Stereo Review*, and sources available through the Internet.

Central Selection and Purchase

In order to ensure the efficient purchase and timely acquisition of important new titles in our circulating and reference collections, the following categories of books are centrally selected and purchased 4–6 weeks in advance of publication.

Fiction. Titles by best-selling adult authors who have proven to be popular and in high demand by our customers, new authors who are likely to gain media attention, as well as the work of award-winning J and YA authors.

Non-Fiction. New books by or about high-profile personalities, by authors respected in their profession, and which—because of the publicity they receive—are in high demand by our customers.

Reference Material. Titles which, because of their subject treatment, have relevance to all agency collections.

Titles are selected by Collection Development Division staff and appropriate age level coordinators and are purchased with a special system-wide fund monitored in Collection Development Division. Central Purchase is intended to augment and give direction to, but not replace, new title selection and purchase in purchase service agencies. It is the responsibility of branch and Central Library division managers to add to the number of centrally purchased titles to meet local needs and interests.

Drop Shipment

Mass market paperback material is acquired through orders from vendor catalogs that agency managers send directly to wholesalers. Material is then drop shipped to the ordering agency where it is linked to collections. [copyright 2001, last updated March 22, 2001, pp. 3–5; www.queenslibrary.org/books/cdpol.asp]

ACQUISITION STATEMENT FOR SPECIAL LIBRARIES AND RELATED INSTITUTIONS

State Library of Victoria: Collection Development Policy

Although the collections of the State Library of Victoria are substantially built up and maintained by purchase of materials, other methods of acquisition have always played a very important part in collection development and continue to do so. These methods include legal and government deposit, donation, exchange, and creation of material (such as the creation of microfilm).

As a general rule the same principles are applied to all materials considered for acquisition. Shortage of funds may result in collection development goals not being met through purchase. Where purchasing is restricted through fund shortages, donated material is still acquired at the level set out in this policy. It is recognised that the acquisition of material by any means involves an initial and ongoing cost, in particular staff and storage costs.

The Library is entitled to receive, under the legal deposit provisions of the *Libraries Act*, 1988, one copy of every item published in Victoria. Material published by the Victorian Government and its instrumentalities is deposited with the Library under the terms of the Premier's Department Circular 85/5 and its predecessors. These form the basis of the Victorian research collections of the Library.

A number of other deposit arrangements also exist for government publications, such as those of the United States, the United Kingdom, and Canada, as well as arrangements with the Australian Government Publishing Service and with many international organisations. Economic conditions in the other countries may affect supply. In view of its central position within the State's library system, it is an appropriate role of the State Library of Victoria to act as a deposit library for governments and other bodies. These deposit collections involve the addition of material according to source rather than subject matter, and therefore the subject range of such collections is wider than that of the general collections.

The State Library receives a very large number of donations from individuals and organizations within Victoria and elsewhere. Because of its public accessibility and central role, it is widely seen as an appropriate repository to collections and items which donors wish to make generally available. Donation of material under the terms of the Taxation Incentives for the Arts Scheme is promoted. The State Library of Victoria also encourages public and other libraries in Victoria to transfer materials that are no longer useful to those libraries, but which have an enduring value and are appropriate in terms of the State Library's Collection Development Policy. In the case of significant private collections being offered to the Library which fall outside the current collecting guidelines, the collection may be accepted at the discretion of the Selection Committee. This may lead to the revision of collection guidelines to enable the Library to add to the Collection.

Where material is unlikely to be obtained in other ways the Library may obtain it from time to time on exchange. Because it is the principal library maintained by the Victorian Government, the State Library of Victoria maintains agreements with state and national libraries in Australia and overseas, as well as with other institutions such as galleries.

The State Library of Victoria also creates materials for the collection by producing microform copies or photocopies of important materials, and by commissioning photography or oral history recordings. [adopted June 1996, pp. 4–5; www.slv.vic.gov.au/slv/cdplcdppo.htm]

NOTES

1. G. Edward Evans, *Developing Library and Information Center Collections*, 4th ed. (Englewood, Colo.: Libraries Unlimited, 2000), 314.

2. Joyce L. Ogburn, "T2: Theory in Acquisition Revisited," *Library Acquisitions Practice and Theory*. 21 (Summer 1997) 168.

3. G. Edward Evans and Sandra M. Heft, *Introduction to Technical Services*, 6th ed. (Englewood, Colo.: Libraries Unlimited, 1994), 23. Also reproduced as a figure in G. Edward Evans' *Developing Library and Information Center Collections*, 4th ed. (Englewood, Colo.: Libraries Unlimited, 2000), 318.

Chapter Nineteen

Gift and Exchange
Statements in Policies

Many libraries are far too disposed to accept donated resources, relaxing the evaluative criteria as applied to traditional library purchases. They generally do so either to please would-be donors or to compensate for budgetary shortfalls. This practice opens the floodgates for patrons and others to demand the inclusion of additional materials of poor quality, albeit often at considerable cost.

Even when gifts are added to the collection according to the same standards applied to purchased items, accepting gifts poses myriad problems:

- Free items are not really free in that they require investments of time and money to process.
- Donations often come with strings attached; for example, libraries may be required to take an entire collection (rather than being allowed title-by-title discretion) or house it in a special facility. A particularly strong collection typically commits the institution to future acquisitions.
- Even where gifts meet evaluative criteria, the donation of large numbers of titles within a relatively narrow subject area often results in an unbalanced collection.
- Donors might well be offended if the library refuses their gift or, worse yet, disposes of the material in a manner they don't approve of (e.g., book sale, public giveaway, incineration).
- Some libraries choose to refuse all gifts rather than inherit any of these problems.

Other institutions opt to limit gifts to financial endowments. In this manner, the library enjoys greater control over the particular acquisitions to its collection. Name plates within individual books, honorary plaques, and the naming of libraries and special collections represent strategies employed by librarians to encourage monetary gifts.

Whatever choices the library makes, it is imperative that they be codified in a written policy statement. The statement ought to incorporate clear-cut evaluative criteria, or allude to a listing elsewhere in the policy. Step-by-step procedures for handling gifts should also be included along with a mechanism for contacting donors about materials that the library declines to place in the collection. Libraries should spell out the way by which unacceptable materials are disposed of; such actions will only take place with the prior understanding — and granted permission — of the donor. This agreement is most effectively secured by means of a donor agreement form to be read and signed prior to the actual delivery of the gift.

A truly thorough gifts policy will also note target audiences likely to provide the most valuable donations (including collection building monies) along with strategies for reaching them. A periodic newsletter (print or online) represents a useful public relations tool that can stimulate focused gift-giving (i.e., geared to perceived institutional needs) through announcements of recent donations or by profiling the library's special collections and services.

An aggressive program such as this necessitates having a plan for dealing with the donor's attaching "strings" to the giving process. Consultation with the library's body or chief administrators is an important preparatory step in drafting a consistent set of guidelines for addressing donor wishes. Satisfied donors serve as one of the strongest inducements for acquiring valuable gifts in the future. Serious collectors almost always belong to a network of like-minded individuals; news spreads quickly regarding institutions providing the most appealing amenities: an attractive and suitably located facility; a service-oriented staff; strong security measures and established procedures for handling valuable resources with care; and some degree of recognition for the donor and/or collection.

While a separate section within the overall policy helps focus attention on the process of handling gifts, it is important to include provisions within the other collection development components that are also affected by this program. Acquisitions is the sector perhaps most directly involved in terms of the expenditure of staff time and effort. The receipt of donations often entails the maintenance of an active exchange program administered by the department (or staff) charged with processing incoming material.

Two types of exchanges are typically employed by libraries to dispose of unwanted items. One consists of preparing a list of unwanted titles and sending it to exchange departments in other libraries (usually via e-mail). Libraries can either trade materials, or the institution requesting a particular item is generally assessed the shipping cost. The other method involves selling titles to a dealer in rare and out-of-print books. The transaction usually involves the dealer issuing an agreed-upon amount of credit to the library that the latter can apply to later purchases.

The following policy excerpts offer the full range of approaches employed by libraries, including materials accepted, relevant procedures, and applicable forms.

GIFT AND EXCHANGE STATEMENTS
FOR ACADEMIC LIBRARIES

College of St. Benedict and St. John's University, Alcuin and Clemens Libraries: Collection Development Policies

Gift Policy

While nearly any gift books are accepted, whenever possible the libraries ask that the books be given with no strings attached. If they are given to one library, but that library already owns a copy, we ask that the gift be placed at the other library, if we believe we can use two copies within the system. Some kinds of books are placed only at one or the other library; e.g., juvenile books are only at the College of St. Benedict, certain theology books are only at St. John's University.

The library welcomes gifts of books and other library materials which will enhance our collections. Ordinarily such works fall into one of the following categories:

- Recently published works of scholarly value.
- All works by or about Benedictines.
- Substantial works in the areas of medieval and monastic history, Biblical studies, and Catholic theology.
- Works in the area of Women's Studies.
- Critical editions of literary works.
- First editions of well-known authors.
- Other standard works.
- European books published before 1800 and American books published before 1850.
- Fine or special editions of any period, including facsimile editions.
- Journal issues in consultation with the library staff.

For reasons of space and in keeping with the character of the collection, the library cannot ordinarily accept textbooks, non-scholarly paperback books,

books that are heavily marked or annotated, books that are in poor condition (mildewed, with yellowed pages, broken spines, etc.), or gifts with special conditions attached. Such works, as well as those that are not germane to the collection, will be returned to the donor, or with the permission of the donor, *sold* or otherwise disposed of. Proceeds from the sale of gifts will be used for the purchase of library materials.

In cases of doubt as to the suitability of a proposed gift to the library, the Collection Development Librarian would be pleased to consult with the donor.

Gift Procedures

1. Gift books come to the Collection Development Office, unless they are rare or special collection books.
2. Books are stored in the cage or in the Collection Development Office, depending on available space, and are checked against the libraries' holdings as time is available.
3. Decisions on the books are made by Collection Development (or Rare Books) and, when appropriate, with the advice of faculty members or other librarians.
4. When appropriate (when the gift is major or significant), the development office of the campus receiving the books is notified so that appropriate acknowledgment may be made.
5. Books accepted for the collections, with a card saying GIFT—SJU or GIFT—CSB, are brought to Acquisitions where cataloging records are searched for before the books are passed on to Tech Services for cataloging.
6. Books not accepted for inclusion in the collections and not returned to donor are disposed of in any of several ways:
   a. sale to patrons;
   b. sale to book buyer;
   c. gift to a more appropriate library;
   d. disposal.

Policy on Unsolicited Gifts

Unsolicited materials received in the mail are, according to the U.S. Post Office, to be considered as gifts—we have no responsibility to return them.

Unsolicited material received in the mail will be given to the Collection Development Librarian. That librarian will determine in whatever way is appropriate whether or not the material would be a valuable addition to the collection. If the unsolicited material is added to the collection, any accompanying invoice will be paid. If the material is not deemed appropriate to our collection, the material will be stored for 30 days. If the sender requests the materials be returned and furnishes postage in that time period, the material will be returned. After 30 days, the material will be discarded. [Last updated December 14, 2000; www.csbsju.edu/library/about/policies/colldev/gifts.htm]

Dalhousie University Libraries: Collection Development Policy Statement

The Killam Library welcomes gifts of books, manuscripts, and other "gifts-in-kind" which enhance existing collections and support the major instructional and research programmes of the University, or deserve special consideration because of uniqueness, importance, or value. All gifts must meet the guidelines of the Libraries' collection policies. The Libraries also welcome donations for the purchase of such materials.

The Library retains the right to accept or reject gifts-in-kind. Gifts are accepted with the understanding that once received, such materials are owned by the University. The Libraries maintain the right to determine the disposition of gifts in the most appropriate manner. Duplicate material may be sold in the Library's book sale where prices are set to enable students and faculty to build their own collections. Income from book sales is used to purchase needed items to enhance the Libraries' collections or services.

An appraisal of the fair market value and corresponding receipt for income tax purposes may be arranged with the Library. Such appraisals are carried out only for materials that are being added to the collection. Large collections of gifts-in-kind require specialized handling and should be discussed with the Assistant University Librarian, Collections & Development.

The Libraries regard monetary gifts and grants as essential components of the collection building process. Individual, corporate, and foundation funding is actively sought for the acquisition of collection materials that allow the Libraries to fully serve the needs of Dalhousie's students, faculty, and staff. A receipt for income tax purposes is provided. [2nd edition, revised January 20, 2000, p. 9; www.library.dal.ca/collections/policy.htm]

West Chester University, Francis Harvey Green Library

The FHGL reserves the right to reject gift books and to handle them in a manner it deems most appropriate. Gifts will not be evaluated for tax or other reasons. The Subject Coordinators will make final decisions on what materials are acceptable to add to the library's collection. Gifts are acknowledged by letter and records kept. Gifts not added to the collection may be set aside for the annual book sale. The steps in handling gifts received are as follows:

The Acquisitions Librarian or the Collection Development Librarian will make the first cut in deciding if materials donated should:

• Be considered by subject coordinators for decision on adding to the collection.
• Be held for book sale. [Special prices may be assigned by the archives/history coordinator.]
• Be discarded.

Statistics are kept on the number of gift books added. Periodical gifts go to the Serials staff who will evaluate as follows:

• Keep if we own but need added volume or replacement.
• Decide to add new title.
• Put in book sale or discard if out of scope items.

[*Collection Development Policy*, February 23, 2000 draft, p. 11]

GIFT AND EXCHANGE STATEMENTS
FOR COMMUNITY COLLEGES

Finger Lakes Community College, Charles J. Meder Library:
College Development Policy

The Charles J. Meder Library welcomes gifts of books, journals, and items in other formats, as well as gifts of money for the purchase of library materials. Gifts are generally expected to supplement existing collections in support of the College's programs and teaching, or to provide the Library with a core of materials of interest to the college community or to other library patrons. To be accepted, all gifts must fall within guidelines of the Library's collection development policies.

Before accepting any gift, Library staff will carefully review the material in order to determine its suitability for the Library's collections. If a gift is declined, staff will suggest potential alternative institutions or collections.

Once a gift has been accepted, it becomes the property of the Library. Items may be added to the collection, or offered to other libraries through the Gifts & Exchange program, or otherwise disposed of. In general, duplicates or items in poor condition are not retained. Donors may not impose restrictions on use of their gifts.

Internal Revenue Service Regulations prohibit the Library from appraising gifts. [approved August 1998, p. 4; http://library.fingerlakes.edu/colldev.htm]

North Harris Montgomery Community College District, Learning Resources Center: Collection Development Policy

The libraries accept donations of monetary gifts and library resources. All gifts must be accompanied by a completed gift form signed by the donor (see Appendix C below). The director and/or reference librarians will work with donors of monetary gifts to select materials useful to the collection. The library accepts gift materials with the understanding that the librarians and library director reserve the right to catalog, discard, locate, and display gifts in the best interests of the collection. If adequate storage space and/or processing time are not available, the library director may decline the gifts.

Upon receipt of gift materials or monetary donations, the donor will receive an acknowledgment letter signed by the director. A notification of a gift purchase will be sent to a family or individual who has been honored or memorialized. A gift plate will be placed inside materials purchased with gift funds. All other gift materials will not receive a gift plate unless requested by the donor. All gifts become the property of NHMCCD. Appraisals of gift materials cannot be made by library personnel.

Appendix C: Library Gifts and Donations

The library accepts donations of monetary gifts and research materials. All gifts must be accompanied by a completed gift form signed by the donor. The library director and/or librarians will work with donors of monetary gifts to select materials useful to the collection. The library director and librarians reserve the right to retain or discard gift materials in accordance with the District selection criteria.

All gifts become the property of NHMCCD. Appraisals of gift materials for tax or inheritance purposes cannot be made by library personnel.

Upon acceptance of gift materials or monetary donations, the donor will receive an acknowledgment letter signed by the library director. A notification of a gift purchase will be sent to a family or individual who has been honored or memorialized. A gift plate will be placed inside donated materials at the request of the donor. See figure 19.1.

Appendix D: Learning Resources Center Program,
Donated Materials Memorandum

See figure 19.2. [approved March 27, 2000, pp. 3, 8–9]

As a donor, I have read, understood, and accepted the provisions of this policy.

_____	_____
Donor's name	Library Director
_____	_____
Street address	College
_____	_____
City, state, zip code	Date
_____	Gift plate requested:
Telephone number	_____ Yes _____ No

Figure 19.1   Donor Form.

GIFT AND EXCHANGE STATEMENTS FOR PUBLIC LIBRARIES

Bettendorf (Iowa) Public Library: Collection Development Policies

Gifts are accepted but must undergo the same scrutiny and meet the same standards as the materials purchased for the collection. Donated periodical subscriptions for which there is no indexing and which have limited appeal are marked "Complimentary" and no back files are kept. The library reserves the right to refuse any donations of materials. Donations not added to the collection are given to the Friends of the Bettendorf Public Library for their sales. [revision approved by the Library Board of Trustees, April 1999; www .rbls.lib.is.us/bpl/policies/collect.htm]

The Newark Public Library: Collection Development Policy

Gifts of materials are accepted with the understanding that they will be subject to the same criteria for inclusion in the collection as purchased materials. The Library reserves the right to not add gift materials to the collection and to sell or dispose of them as deemed appropriate. [adopted by the Board of Trustees, September 24, 1997; www.npl.org/Pages/AboutLibrary/collections devpol.html]

To:
From: College:
Date:

_____

The following materials were donated to the LRC:

By: _____   Phone: _____

Address:

_____

Title, author, or   Consultant's recommendation,
volumes, date(s)   justification

_____

_____

_____

Attached sheet:

_____

_____

Comments:

_____

_____

_____
College LRC Director's Approval

Figure 19.2   Donated Materials Memorandum.

GIFT AND EXCHANGE STATEMENT FOR SPECIAL LIBRARIES AND RELATED INSTITUTIONS

Fermilab IRD: Library Collection Development Policy

The Library reserves the right to refuse gifts and donations that do not conform to this policy. All gifts and donations become the property of the Fermilab Library, which has the right to use or dispose of them in any way it sees fit.

Donations to Fermilab are tax-deductible. Donors must include a list of all materials. When notified by the Library, the Accounting Department Office can provide a letter acknowledging receipt of the donation.

The Library may donate materials to other institutions in accordance with DOE policies and procedures. Requests for approval of donations are submitted to the DOE Fermi Group. [approved by the Fermilab Library Advisory Committee October 2, 1998, expanded June 25, 1999; http://fnalpubs.fnal .gov/library/cdpolicy.html]

Chapter Twenty

Collection Maintenance
Identified in Policies

Collection maintenance—which includes binding, disaster preparedness, preservation, replacement, and weeding—has received increased attention in recent years. This can be attributed largely to advances in knowledge regarding media care and renewed emphasis on protecting library resources in the face of exploding costs for both new technology and traditional materials. Binding procedures, disaster plans, preservation programs, and the like have been utilized by large public libraries and many academic institutions for some time; however, they were rarely included in collection development statements. Perhaps due to concerns regarding stylistic flow, some libraries have chosen to include these materials within the appendixes rather than as part of the text. Institutions opting to keep such documentation separate from the written policy altogether would be advised to note its existence somewhere within the text. In such cases, the cited documents should be readily accessible if requested by staff, administrators, or clientele.

Many libraries incorporate their weeding policies into the overall collection maintenance portion of the policy. The sample policy excerpts included below are concerned with other aspects of collection maintenance, whereas weeding statement examples are located in the next chapter.

COLLECTION MAINTENANCE STATEMENT
FOR ACADEMIC LIBRARIES

Columbia University Libraries: Collection Development Policy

The responsibility to build research collections carries with it the obligation to ensure that these collections are permanently accessible. The Columbia

University Library is committed to the preservation of its collections. Preservation is the action taken to prevent, stop, or retard deterioration of all library materials in all media; to prevent their theft or loss; where possible to improve their condition; and, as necessary and appropriate, to change their format in order to preserve their intellectual content.

The comprehensive approach to preservation entails choosing the most appropriate method of preservation for every item. This is accomplished through storage of materials in proper conditions, through careful handling and housing, through use of security systems designed to eliminate mutilation and theft, through refreshment and migration of electronic files, and through repair or replacement of damaged materials. Materials of unique aesthetic or historical value should be preserved in their original form. There are many other materials whose value lies primarily, or only, in the information they contain. When repair of such materials becomes impossible or prohibitively expensive, their content may be preserved through reformatting into other media. The indefinite storage of unusable materials within the Libraries cannot be justified.

Columbia, as a research library, selects most materials for permanent value. Some materials, however, may not be a permanent part of the collection because they are of only short-term interest to scholars. Department and distinctive collection librarians and selection officers are responsible for developing and maintaining a collection which meets the needs of their library users. Therefore, preservation decisions for materials in the collections is best determined by these officers in consultation with each other, the Preservation Division, reference staff, and others including the faculty when necessary. Preservation decisions must always be made within the context of overall collection policy, balancing the constraints of cost, historical and aesthetic and scholarly value, and user accessibility. [last updated January 4, 2001; www.columbia.edu/cu/lweb/services/colldev/preservation-policy.htm]

COLLECTION MAINTENANCE STATEMENT FOR COMMUNITY COLLEGES

Lake-Sumter Community College Libraries: Collection Development Policy

Preservation of Materials

Library materials are expensive to purchase, process, and house. The Lake-Sumter Community College libraries acknowledge the necessity of preserving all holdings.

- Library employees and library users will be informed of the proper care and handling of library materials.
- Temperature and humidity controls are essential for maintenance of library materials.
- Book repair is provided for damaged materials.
- Binding is used to preserve periodicals and other materials as needed. Print periodicals and journals are bound or replaced by microfilm on a regular basis. Titles will not be bound or replaced by microfilm if only the current two to three years are retained.
- Newly acquired paperbound books are not rebound. Exceptions may be made when heavy use is anticipated.

Replacement of Materials

Decisions must be made regarding the replacement of lost, damaged, missing, or worn-out materials, based on the following criteria:

- Does the material being replaced meet the general library collection policy?
- Does the frequency of use justify replacement?
- Is the item used for class reserve reading or is it on a faculty recommended reading list?
- Is the item listed in *Books for College Libraries* or other recommended book list?
- Is an electronic version available that would provide remote access for users?

[revised April 2001, p. 13; http://lscc.cc.fl.us/library/coldev.htm]

COLLECTION MAINTENANCE STATEMENT
FOR PUBLIC LIBRARIES

Kitsap (Washington) Regional Library: Collection Development Policy

The Library's collection of resources, regardless of format, is continually and systematically reviewed and evaluated in light of how well individual titles and the collection as a whole are meeting the expectations and needs of the Library's customers. Under the direction of the Collection Manager, delegated staff are responsible for determining which resources no longer belong in the collection as well as which ones will be mended, rebound, updated, or replaced. Factors considered in the collection review process are:

1. obsolescence of information,
2. number of copies in the collection,

3. circulation of reference use over the last 2 to 3 years,
4. adequacy of other resources in the subject area to meet customer needs,
5. ease of replacement by purchasing another copy or a similar resource,
6. availability of the resource or information outside the Library, including whether it can be accessed, checked out, or rented locally, through interlibrary loan, or on-line.

The library very selectively mends materials that are in poor physical shape. To be considered for mending, an item is expected to have been checked out or been used in the library at least five times during the last year. Items that are not mended are removed from the collection and may be replaced with a new copy or a similar resource.

A very small number of resources are sent to a professional bindery or microfilmed.

Duplicate copies of titles are removed from individual branch collections and from the collection as a whole when they are no longer being frequently used.

Resources that are not being frequently used at one branch may be reassigned to another branch.

Items that have gained historical significance, assumed reference value, or increased dramatically in monetary value may be considered for inclusion in special collections.

Resources that no longer meet expectations for the collection are discarded and the record for them deleted from the Library's catalog. They may then be declared surplus by the Board of Trustees and:

- given to other libraries.
- given to governmental offices or community agencies.
- sold.
- destroyed or recycled if dilapidated, outdated, misleading, or not otherwise disposable.

(third edition, adopted May 19, 1998, pp. 21–22; www.krl.org/administration/policies/colldev.html]

Chapter Twenty-One

Weeding Statements in Policies

Weeding—sometimes referred to as de-selection or negative selection by library professionals—has traditionally been one of the most overlooked components of the collection management process. For a variety of reasons—most notably, time limitations, the tendency to place a higher priority on other activities, a personal distaste for disposing of information sources (particularly books), and the fear of offending patrons and administrators—cause librarians to avoid (or at least put off) this function. Therefore, it is essential that collection developers have access to written weeding guidelines.

Above all, the weeding section should emphasize policy rather than procedures. Rose Mary Magrill and John Corbin address the differences between these two concepts in their work, *Acquisition Management and Collection Development in Libraries*:

> The ideal . . . policy clearly indicates the general intent of the library administration with regard to the collection and is both generally applicable and adequately flexible. Policies are sometimes confused with procedures, which are entirely different. A procedure statement documents the best way to carry out a specific activity, giving detailed, step-by-step instructions. While procedures leave little room for individual judgment, policies spell out limits of acceptable action and grant freedom to exercise professional judgment within those limits. (1)

From this perspective, an effective weeding document sets forth a philosophical stance based on the library's mission and goals as well as documented client needs. Although many libraries include various procedures within the collection development policy, there appears to be widespread agreement that the weeding statement should be much more than a listing of steps or directives. Some institutions, in fact, include weeding procedures in a separate document utilized primarily by library staff. In such cases, a copy of these procedures—in addition to any other guidelines dictating collection building practices—should be retained in a readily accessible place, particularly when cited in the policy.

Libraries lacking useful weeding procedures can consult a wide array of professional sources such as *The CREW Method: Expanded Guidelines for Collection Evaluation and Weeding for Small and Medium-Sized Libraries* (1995), published by the Texas State Library and Archives Commission. Vital procedures should include checking the circulation record of an item in order to determine how often and how recently it has been used, noting copyright dates for currency in subject areas where this is an issue, consulting tables of contents or indexes for relevance, checking statements of fact for accuracy, assessing physical condition, and ascertaining whether other materials on the subject are available in the holdings. Procedures often include directions for the consideration of special formats.

Providing a rationale for weeding which itemizes the advantages associated with the process should prove useful in securing staff support while neutralizing outside criticism. Both librarians and their clientele tend to forget that few libraries possess the space or resources to engage in comprehensive collection building. Once institutional limitations have been acknowledged, it is imperative to construct an effective decision-making model for weeding.

Content criteria guidelines constitute the core of a weeding policy. These guidelines will mirror to a considerable extent the evaluation criteria outlined in the selection process. Therefore, to achieve the best results, librarians involved in selection should also be responsible for weeding. Acknowledging that specificity can be important to understanding, weeding criteria should nevertheless be general enough to provide librarians some degree of latitude in the decision-making process.

A structured, periodic review process is essential to the weeding process and should be documented in writing. For libraries possessing limited slow periods, the weeding schedule must be adapted to the library routine. The key is not to approach the process as an unimportant, last-minute, addition to the overall collection building plan.

The weeding policy should also consider options to outright discarding, whereby references to the material are removed from library records, and the material itself is destroyed. These alternatives include:

- relegation, in which the material is removed from the open shelves, or from easy access, and stored in stacks, or at some remote location;
- transference of the material to group storage, in which case there could be common ownership of the material and access to it, or else the library could

retain ownership, even though there might be some form of common storage; and
- transference of the ownership, in which case access could be possible if the material is transferred to another library, but difficult or impossible if it is transferred to private ownership, by sale to the public. (2)

The above introduction to "Weeding" was written by Debbie Cox, Reference Librarian/Collection Developer, Montgomery College, The Woodlands.

The following policy excerpts reflect the various approaches to weeding employed by libraries. They also illustrate the issues (e.g., evaluative criteria, procedures) of greatest concern to these institutions.

WEEDING STATEMENTS FOR ACADEMIC LIBRARIES

College of St. Benedict and St. John's University, Alcuin and Clemens Libraries

The following is our joint library weeding policy for the monograph collections in our libraries. In order to make room for new acquisitions and to keep our collections current, worn-out and dated materials are removed from the collections of the joint libraries on a regular basis. The following procedures are followed:

- If subject collections are to be extensively weeded, faculty members from the appropriate departments are recruited to identify obsolete materials. Librarians may also perform this function in their subject areas.
- A librarian will review the books selected for weeding and will identify the appropriate means of disposal. Some books are put up for sale to members of the academic community, others are sent to MLAC (Minnesota Library Access Center). The library may discard books with no long-term value.
- Every attempt is made in the weeding process to consider current needs of the CSB/SJU curriculum and to retain works of outstanding historical value, particularly to the individual institutions.
- In all cases the library staff retains the final responsibility for weeding decisions. In the case of theology materials an exception is made because with this material weeding does not take place on an ongoing basis. When theological materials appear to need weeding, whether for reasons of condition, use, datedness, or whatever, the Collection Development librarian will make the appropriate decision in consultation with a theology faculty member in whose area of expertise the material belongs.

[*Collection Development Policies*, last updated December 14, 2000; www
.csbsju.edu/library/about/policies/colldev/index.htm]

West Chester (Pennsylvania) University, Francis Harvey Green Library

De-Selection and Collection Maintenance

The activities of keeping the collection current and in good repair are constant. De-selection should be completed for every subject area at least once every ten years. Librarians should rotate between all subjects for which they are responsible and seek input from faculty familiar with the subject. This should result in a part of the collection being reviewed every year, so that the process is perpetual and by the end of a ten-year cycle the entire collection will have been examined closely by the coordinator.

The following criteria or guidelines should be used in deciding which titles to withdraw. Following major withdrawals a concerted effort should be made to re-build the collection for the topic.

De-Selection Criteria

- Last date and/or frequency of circulation.
- Physical condition of volume.
- Need and/or demand for subject matter.
- Multiple copies of subjects no longer in demand.
- Older editions replaced by later editions.
- Give special consideration to out of print works.
- Inclusion on a basic bibliography related to discipline.
- Historical interest.
- Suitability in content and vocabulary.
- Is work indexed to provide adequate access?
- Fair picture of the subject.

Withdrawal Process

In order to avoid mass dislocation problems and backlog of books waiting for withdrawal processing, the following steps should be taken:

1. Using the library shelflist, a black striped catalog card overlay will be placed on cards/items to be withdrawn.
2. Books will be withdrawn as part of the routine work of the cataloging staff.

[*Collection Development Policy Statements*, approved February 23, 2000, p. 10]

WEEDING STATEMENTS FOR COMMUNITY COLLEGES

Central Piedmont Community College (North Carolina): Library Collection Development Policy

General Policies on Preservation, Replacement, and Duplication of Library Materials

The Library attempts to purchase materials of a quality which will withstand expected use. In addition, the Library encourages proper handling of materials and takes preventive measures in the physical processing of materials to enhance longevity of use. When items become worn or damaged, steps may be taken to repair, mend, or bind materials to extend their useful life. If items must be discarded or have been lost, replacement or updating is considered.

Collection Development Librarians, in consultation with cataloging staff, make decisions on preservation, duplication, or replacement based on general selection criteria.

Replacement of Materials

The Library will not automatically replace all materials withdrawn because of loss, damage, or wear. Factors considered include:

- number of duplicate copies
- extent of adequate coverage of the field in the collection
- importance to collection
- usage
- availability of material for purchase
- availability of more up-to-date material or alternate format
- cost of replacement

Final decisions concerning replacement copies rest with the Collection Development Librarians.

Multiple or Duplicate Copies

In order to maintain basic library service, the purchase of multiple copies may be necessary due to high demand, deterioration, theft, or mutilation. In addition, duplicate copies of materials may be purchased for additional campuses and centers. A decision to purchase duplicate materials for campuses and centers is determined by:

- curriculum offerings
- demand for material at both Central Campus and other locations

- availability of funds
- accreditation requirements

The Library considers microform and electronic format alternatives to paper duplications of both books and periodicals. Decisions to purchase multiple or duplicate copies of an item are made by Collection Development Librarians based on an analysis of usage patterns.

De-Selection (Removal of Irrelevant, Outdated, or Superceded Material)

In order to provide an active up-to-date collection, the Library systematically removes obsolete, damaged, and little used materials from the collection. De-selection is the responsibility of all Collection Development Librarians in consultation with teaching faculty.

General Criteria for De-Selecting Materials

The following criteria are considered when discarding materials:

- obsolescence
- physical condition
- significance
- usage
- faculty recommendation
- duplication
- inclusion in standard bibliographies
- program profiles
- accreditation requirements
- availability of updated materials

Disposition of Excess Library Materials

North Carolina Administrative Code 2C.0403 allows disposition of excess books and book-like materials through the following methods:

1. Local sale of books at predetermined prices.
2. Donation to non-profit, tax-exempt organizations and other state agencies.
3. Public bid sales through State Surplus Property Services.

Books may be sold to individuals by single volumes or in large quantities at a price determined by the college. Discarded books that are not useable may be destroyed locally.

Magazines may be disposed of through donation or local sales. They may also be transferred to other departments within the college for use by students. If materials remain after these procedures are followed, they may be destroyed locally. AV materials that have value to others may be disposed of through donations or sales. When deciding the usability of AV materials, consider the total unit. For example, a 16mm film may be of no value, but the reels and canisters may be sold through public bid sale. Those that are not usable by others may be destroyed locally.

The librarian must use his/her own judgment in determining what is useable. Local sales do not have to be advertised. [last modified, May 5, 1999, pp. 10–11; www.cpcc.cc.nc.us/Library/general/policy/cd/htm]

North Harris Montgomery Community College District: Library Program

Weeding/Withdrawal of Materials

In order to maintain a collection of optimal usefulness, and to assure the best utilization of library space, librarians will engage in a continual evaluation of materials in all formats. Those materials that are no longer appropriate to the collection will be removed, with the final approval of the director. Criteria for withdrawal are listed at the conclusion of this document.

Criteria for Withdrawal of Materials

The following criteria are used when removing resources from the collection:

- Materials which are obsolete or which contain inaccurate data.
- Materials in formats which require equipment that is obsolete.
- Superseded editions.
- Incomplete sets of which the individual volumes do not meet selection criteria or are no longer available.
- Incomplete holdings of periodicals.
- Multiple copies of titles for which there is not adequate justification.
- Worn, badly marked, or severely damaged materials.
- Lack of use.
- Appropriateness of the subject matter to the current collection or changes in the college curriculum.
- Expense of continuing subscriptions/continuations.
- Replacement by comparable product or material.

[*Collection Development Policy*, pp. 3, 5; last update March 27, 2000]

WEEDING STATEMENTS FOR PUBLIC LIBRARIES

Middleton (Wisconsin) Public Library: Collection Development Policy

A. Weeding is necessary to maintain a vital, useful, and up-to-date collection. This task takes skill, care, time, and knowledge of the materials to do a competent job.

B. Selection of materials for weeding is based on the following criteria:
   1. Materials worn out through use.
   2. Ephemeral materials which are no longer timely.
   3. Materials no longer considered accurate or factual.
   4. Materials which have had little recent use and are of questionable value.
   5. Excess copies of a title no longer in demand.

C. Replacement of materials that are withdrawn is not automatic. The need for replacement is based on the following criteria:
   1. Number of duplicate copies.
   2. Existence of adequate coverage of the subject.
   3. Demand for the specific title or for material in that subject area.

D. Disposal of materials weeded from the collection is accomplished according to the following priorities:
   1. Materials which can be used by another tax-supported library are made available to the library with all responsibility for transfer assumed by the receiving library.
   2. Materials which can be used by another tax-supported institution, not a library, are made available to that institution with all responsibility for transfer assumed by the receiving institution.
   3. Materials which are of no interest to other libraries or other tax-supported institutions but which are judged by the Library Director to have possible resale value are kept for the Friends of the Library book sale, where they are offered on a first-come, first-served basis. No weeded or donated materials may be sold by library staff.
   4. Materials unsuitable for transfer or sale are discarded.

E. The Library will not accept requests to hold weeded materials for individuals.

[adopted May 14, 1981, last updated October 16, 1997, p. 9; www.scls.lib.wi
.us/middleton/policies/midpolcol.htm]

Westerville (Ohio) Public Library: Collection Development Policy of Adult Services, Youth, and Audio/Visual Departments

The Westerville Public Library weeds its collection on a regular basis to keep the collection current and as a timely resource for the community. The library staff will generally follow the principles established in *The Crew Manual* for detailed procedures for weeding. [last revision: August 2000, pp. 2–3; http://winslo.state.oh.us/publib/wplcldpl.html]

WEEDING STATEMENT FOR SPECIAL LIBRARIES AND RELATED INSTITUTIONS

Medical College of Georgia, Greenblatt Library Services: Collection Development Policies

Weeding Criteria

- Reference Collection weeding is based on the need for the newest information to be in a small, current, easy-to-use collection and does not mean that all weeded items are discarded; rather, many will be relocated to the circulating collection or Special Collections.
- Audiovisual Collection weeding is based on evolving curriculum needs and the aging of materials and equipment.
- Circulation Collection has been the repository of older materials not fitting into Special Collections and criteria for weeding must be set for consistent decision-making.

Book Collection Weeding

Decisions to weed book titles will be based on factors such as:

- Lack of recent circulation;
- Older date of publication superseded by newer editions;
- Out of current scope;
- Duplicate copies of older materials.

Journal Collection Weeding

Decisions to weed journal titles may be taken when:

- There are only a few volumes or issues of a title;
- The journal publication has been discontinued; or
- The journal no longer shows value to the institution's mission.

Cooperative collection development for the University System of Georgia encourages preservation and retention of materials that are unique; therefore, weeded titles may be:

- Checked against the University System of Georgia library holdings.
- Offered to the University of Georgia Libraries when no other library in the University System of Georgia owns another copy.

Discarding of State Property Surplusing of library-owned discarded materials will follow:

- Institutional guidelines;
- Library practice.

[copyright 1998, last updated October 2000; www.mcg.edu/library/services/collectionpolicy/weeding.htm]

NOTES

1. Rose Mary Magrill and John Corbin, *Acquisitions Management and Collection Development in Libraries*, 2nd ed. (Chicago: American Library Association, 1989).
2. G. E. Gorman and B. R. Howes, *Collection Development for Libraries* (London: Bowker-Saur, 1990), 324–325.

Chapter Twenty-Two

Collection Evaluation
Sections in Policies

The evaluation of library holdings is currently recognized as one of the most important collection management functions. (1) This process, while hardly a recent development, has gained importance due to general reduction of acquisition budgets beginning in the 1980s and the expansion of cooperative planning among libraries. (2) In a seminal article published in the January 1974 issue of Library Trends, George Bonn identified five distinct methods of evaluating library collections:

1. Compiling statistics on holdings, use, and expenditures.
2. Checking lists, catalogs, and bibliographies.
3. Obtaining opinions from regular users.
4. Examining the collection directly.
5. Applying standards, plus testing the library's document delivery capability and noting the relative use of several libraries by a particular group. (3)

All of these techniques remain useful to the present day, although it could be argued that a combination of two or more types would provide a greater likelihood of obtaining an accurate indicator of collection strength. Faced with the considerable time and resource (staff, funding) demands typifying a collection assessment program, a number of scaled-down methodologies have appeared in the literature in recent years, most of which claim to sacrifice little in the way of reliability. (4)

It is imperative that libraries of all types implement a sound collection assessment strategy as a precondition for achieving service excellence. Given the wide array of options available, the collection development policy's evaluation section serves to delineate the process adopted by the library.

While the Walter E. Helmke Library (IPFW) and Dalhousie University Libraries both appear to actively practice collection assessment, they take divergent paths in documenting this commitment. IPFW simply underscores the importance of the evaluation process, whereas Dalhousie attempts to delineate—in some detail—the techniques they actually employ.

COLLECTION EVALUATION SECTIONS
FOR ACADEMIC LIBRARIES

Indiana University–Purdue University, Fort Wayne, Walter E. Helmke Library: Collection Development Policy

The continual review of library materials is necessary as a means of maintaining an active library collection of current interest to users. Evaluations will be made to determine whether the collection is meeting its objectives, how well it is serving its users, in which ways it is deficient, and what remains to be done to develop the collection. This process requires the same attention to quality and authority as the original selection of materials.

Helmke librarians will evaluate portions of the collection on a regular basis, using a combination of standard qualitative and quantitative methods. [approved November 10, 1997, last modified June 27, 2001, p. 15; www.lib .ipfw.edu/library_info/collections/collection_development_policy/]

Dalhousie University Libraries: Collection Development Policy Statement

Guidelines for the Assessment of Library Support for Proposed New Courses and Programs

Library collections and services are established and maintained to support the teaching, research, and community service objectives of the University. Library assessments are undertaken by Dalhousie University Libraries' staff to determine how well existing collections and services meet new academic objectives as outlined in course and program proposals.

The Libraries make every effort to respond quickly to requests for information on the available support for proposed new graduate/undergraduate courses, graduate cross-listing of undergraduate courses and proposed new programs. However, a lead time of three weeks is required for library subject selectors to complete such as assessment. The following guidelines outline the general procedures followed.

Purpose

The Library assessment attempts to present an objective evaluation by the Libraries of how well present collections and services will support a proposed new course or program and what additional resources, if any, will be required.

Means of Evaluating the Collection

While different subjects may require different methods of assessment, some if not all of the following will be used is assessing support for new courses and programs:

Checking course reading lists and syllabi. Depending on the course content, the Libraries' subject selector may search headings in: Novanet, bibliographic databases (e.g., Global Books In Print, Medline), and other works as required. By these means, relevant works are identified: primary and secondary authors, reference works, and frequently cited current journals. If course or program information provided is insufficient or unclear, the subject selector will consult with the faculty member(s).

Checking standard subject lists. The Libraries' subject selector will check holdings against standard lists of recommended titles, if available for the subject area (e.g., Brandon-Hill lists in medicine).

Supplemental holdings. While the most important collection support will be provided by Dalhousie Libraries, the subject selector may also determine if other local libraries/institutions' holdings will supplement the course or program.

Examining the collection directly. By this procedure appropriate Libraries staff will review the materials available, both print and electronic. The examination can reveal size, scope, depth, and significance of collection; currency of material; and physical condition. (however, it is important to keep in mind that print items may be circulating.) The subject selector may enlist faculty opinions regarding the status of the collection.

Assessment Report

The Library Assessment Report includes a brief description of the evaluation methods and sources used, results of bibliographical checking, a summary of the major available resources in the Dalhousie Libraries and other local collections and an itemization of significant needs, if any, which will require an additional allocation of financial resources. Significant needs are not limited to acquisition of library materials. For example, the needs of distant students may need to be met through electronic delivery of articles from secondary journals and, for programs with small enrollments (under 15 per year), high cost primary journals may be preferred to print or electronic subscriptions.

Dalhousie Libraries reserve funds from their collections budgets to support resource needs associated with new courses and programs. However, substantial new program requirements must be met from external one-time or base transfers to the Libraries budget. The Libraries' subject specialists work with faculty to determine the necessary level of funding support for new courses and programs.

Significant new resource needs are itemized in the assessment as follows: new print sources; additional, or changes in access to existing electronic sources; and anticipated significant document delivery demand, if appropriate. If the libraries cannot meet these resource needs from within the existing budget, the type of external budget support requested will be specified:

1. Base funding: annual, ongoing support. A base transfer from a faculty or other budget envelope to Library collections will not only support the course or program on an ongoing basis, but the amount transferred will also be protected from cuts and increased by the C.P.I. each year as long as the University protects the collections base budget in this manner. Annual transfers from a faculty or other budget envelope are not protected and are only appropriate for programs with a specified, finite lifespan.
2. One-time funding: a specific grant for one-time expenditures. Normally this type of funding builds the retrospective collection in a specific subject area (e.g., back files of journals), or provides electronic systems support (e.g., extra RAM). It may also be needed to supplement base funding.

Because an assessment can take considerable library staff time and should include sufficient consultation with the academic department submitting a proposal, the Libraries must be involved early in the proposal process. The course proposal including course outline, assignment and reading lists should be sent to the most appropriate of the Libraries' collections coordinators. [1984 edition, last revised January 11, 2000, pp. 11–14; www.library.dal.ca/collections/policy.htm]

COLLECTION EVALUATION SECTIONS
FOR PUBLIC LIBRARIES

Eugene (Oregon) Public Library: Collection Development Policy

The Eugene Public Library materials collection will be evaluated on the basis of the following criteria:

- # items per capita
- $ spent per capita

- # magazine subscriptions per capita
- % holdings in non-print formats
- % annual growth or decline in total holdings
- document delivery rate

All individual subject areas will be assessed according to one or more of the following criteria:

- % holdings in a particular subject area compared to % of circulation from that area
- comparison to standard lists
- proportion of subject area in circulation at any given time
- median age of publication
- representation of diverse viewpoints
- completeness of sets or series
- # of interlibrary loan requests
- # of reserves placed
- % annual growth/decline

[adopted September 2, 1992, updated November 2000, pp. 10–11; www.ci .eugene.or.us/Library/hour...tions_cards/collection_development.htm]

NOTES

1. Michael R. Gabriel. *Collection Development and Collection Evaluation: A Sourcebook*. Metuchen, NJ: Scarecrow, 1995. p. 77.

2. Eugene Wiemers, et al. "Collection Evaluation: A Practical Guide to the Literature," *Library Acquisitions Practice and Theory*. 8:1 (1984) 65–78.

3. George Boon. "Evaluation of the Collection," *Library Trends*. 22 (January 1974) 265–304.

4. Among the collection assessment tools developed in recent years, those outlined in the following sources place a premium on the minimal expenditure of time and resources:

Loertscher, David V. "Collection Mapping—An Evaluation Strategy for Collection Development," *Drexel Library Quarterly*. (Spring 1985) 9–39.

Lopez, M.D. "Lopez or Citation Technique of In-Depth Collection Evaluation Explicated," *College and Research Libraries*. (May 1983) 251–255.

Sandler, M. "Quantitative Approaches to Qualitative Collection Assessment," *Collection Building*. 4 (1987) 12–17.

White, Howard D. *Brief Tests of Collection Strength: A Methodology for All Types of Libraries*. Westport, CT: Greenwood, 1995.

Chapter Twenty-Three

Policy Revision
Statements in Policies

Advocates of written policy statements agree that the document must be updated frequently to reflect the continuously evolving landscape in collection development. According to G. E. Gorman and B. R. Howes,

> Once formulated a policy must never be regarded as fixed for eternity. If collections are to grow and change in response to a host of factors, then their policies must be flexible enough to guide them. Therefore, while the policy forms a basic framework for projected growth, it must also be reviewed at regular intervals to ensure that it continues to provide an acceptable and viable pattern for effective collection building. (1)

Because some policies limit coverage to a specific time frame, they presume the need for periodic revisions. A representative example, the Santa Cruz City County Library System's *Collection Development Plan 1990–1995* (published August 1990), includes the statement, "The Collection Development Plan should be reviewed by the Library Oversight Committee no less than once every five years." (2)

The Santa Cruz statement is tacked on, apparently as an afterthought, to a section entitled "Evaluation of Standards." Many policies append a comparable message to the end of the policy. A lesser number of libraries announce plans for policy updates in a separate section, perhaps to focus attention on this commitment. These institutions tend to include a brief reference to the revision process itself.

The institutions represented in the examples provided here are in a distinct minority as relatively few libraries seem to include a direct reference to the revision process.

POLICY REVISION STATEMENT FOR ACADEMIC LIBRARIES

Indiana University–Purdue University, Fort Wayne, Walter E. Helmke Library: Collection Development Policy

The Collection Development Policy will be reviewed periodically by the Helmke Library Collection Development Coordinator. Any changes in policy will be submitted to the Library Council and the IPFW Senate Library Subcommittee for approval. [approved November 10, 1997, last modified June 27, 2001; www.lib.ipfw.edu/library_into/collections/collection_development_policy/]

POLICY REVISION STATEMENTS FOR COMMUNITY COLLEGES

Clatsop Community College (Oregon): Library Collection Development Policy

Due to the rapidity of electronic growth and changes of formats the collection development policy must be considered a means of communication for the staff and a means of yearly evaluation of practices and workflow by the professional library staff. [revised October 31, 2000, p. 5; http://library.clatsop.cc.or.us/cd00-01.htm]

Sheridan College, Griffith Memorial Library: Collection Development Policy for Federal Government Publications

Because of constant change in the needs of the college and of the community, this policy should serve only as a guideline for decision-making. It should be reviewed annually by the library staff and then forwarded for review with advisory groups as appropriate and revised as necessary. [The balance of this section is deleted because it does not relate to policy revision.]

As mentioned in the introduction [above], this policy should be reviewed by library staff annually and forwarded to advisory committees for approval when changes are considered. Computers and other electronic formats are changing the way we organize and provide access to information. [adopted by the Sheridan Campus Instructional Resources Committee, May 4, 2001, pp. 8, 13; www.sc.whecn.edu/library/services/scgml_colldev.html]

POLICY REVISION STATEMENT FOR PUBLIC LIBRARIES

Granby (Connecticut) Public Library: Collection Development Policy

This policy will be revised no less frequently than every three years by the Director of Library Services and staff members as assigned. Recommendations for revision will be brought to the Granby Library Board. [revised December 21, 1992, p. 12; www.cslib.org/cdpgra.htm]

NOTES

1. G. E. Gorman and B. R. Howes, *Collection Development for Libraries* (London: Bowker-Saur, 1990), 7.
2. Elizabeth Futas, ed., *Collection Development Policies and Procedures* (Phoenix, Ariz.: Oryx, 1995), 154.

Chapter Twenty-Four

Definition of Terms and Glossaries in Policies

Some terms or phrases used in collection development policies may be unfamiliar to the reader. In other cases, words possess a variety of meanings; individuals consulting the policy often lack sufficient professional background or expertise to ascertain the appropriate definition based only upon textual context. For example, "material" has a wide range of meanings, including legal and philosophical applications (adjectival) and—as a noun—referring to the constituent parts of an object, data, a type of cloth or fabric, tools for performing an operation (e.g., a pen for writing), etc. While these meanings may be foremost in the minds of the general public, librarians tend to employ the term to denote information sources such as books, audiovisual titles, and computer software comprising library collections. As a result, many libraries include a section within their policies devoted to clarifying key terms.

Rather than providing a broad-based glossary of applicable terms, libraries inserting definitions tend to concentrate on a particular area of concern. The majority of institutions emphasize terminology referring to library resources; however, some focus on the *process* of collection building or special collections.

The focus on process terms is represented by both the University of North Texas and Cumberland County Public Library policies. Special collections may include materials that are sufficiently unique to require clarification of a related group of concepts. Accordingly, the National Library of Canada's policy attempts to provide a foundation for the understanding of Canadiana.

DEFINITION OF TERMS OR GLOSSARY
FOR ACADEMIC LIBRARIES

University of North Texas Libraries: Collection Development Policy

Collection Librarian: a librarian who works daily within a specific collection or portion of a collection and who has responsibility for developing that collection.

Library Liaison: a member of the Libraries' staff who has the responsibility for working in a partnership with one or more academic departments, schools, or colleges for developing the Libraries' collections. Guidelines and responsibilities for library liaisons are contained in the *Manual for UNT Library Liaisons.*

Departmental Library Representative: a member of the academic department who works with the library liaison in expending the departmental allocation and developing the Libraries' collections in the department's area of expertise.

General Collection: the collection that contains the majority of the materials in the areas of the humanities, social sciences, science, and technology.

Special Collection: a collection that contains resources of specialized interest due to format, subject, issuing agency, audience, and other factors as identified in specific special collections policies. Current special collections include Archives, Curriculum Materials Collection, Government Documents, Juvenile Collection, Media Library, Microforms Collection, Music Library, and Rare Books and Texana. For statements of Responsibility for Selection, Guidelines, Collection Maintenance, and Gifts, consult individual collection policies.

[revised October 12, 2000, p. 2; www.library.unt.edu/about/policies/pp16 .htm]

DEFINITION OF TERMS OR GLOSSARY
FOR COMMUNITY COLLEGES

Oakton Community College: Library Policies

Definition of Library Materials: Library materials are defined as print instructional materials including books, periodicals, pamphlets, and manuscripts. Formats include paper and microfilm. [adopted September 1995, p. 4; http://servecc.oakton.edu/~wittman/find/policies.htm]

DEFINITION OF TERMS OR GLOSSARY
FOR PUBLIC LIBRARIES

Cumberland County Public Library: Collection Development Policy Statement

"Materials" is used for all forms of media and has the widest possible inclusion. Materials may be but are not limited to: books (hardbound and paperback), maps, magazines and journals, newspapers, video cassettes, filmstrips, compact discs, audio cassettes, databases, and CD-ROM products.

"Selection" refers to the decision that must be made to add a given item to the collection. It does not refer to guidance or assisting a library user.

"Collection development" refers to the ongoing evaluative process of assessing the materials available for purchase and in making the decision, first, on their inclusion, and, second, on their retention if they are needed. [p. 2; www.cumberland.lib.nc.us/poltab2.htm]

DEFINITION OF TERMS OR GLOSSARY FOR SPECIAL
LIBRARIES AND RELATED INSTITUTIONS

National Library of Canada: Collection Management Policy

"Canadiana" is material published in Canada, and material published in another country if the creator is Canadian or the publication has a Canadian subject.

"Creator" may include the a) author (writer), b) translator, c) editor, d) compiler, e) illustrator, f) composer, g) lyricist, h) arranger, i) performer, j) producer, k) exhibition curator, l) chairperson of a committee issuing a report, m) binder, n) printer, or o) a person who has assumed another creative function.

"Canadian creator" is:

- a Canadian citizen;
- a permanent resident in Canada;
- a resident in Canada during the time that the Canadiana material was created;
- a former Canadian citizen who trained and developed professionally in Canada before taking up residence elsewhere and who is still generally recognized as being Canadian.

"Canadian subject" focuses on:

- a Canadian place, personality, group, event, policy, activity, experience, theme, or any combination of the above;

• Canadian involvement in a place, group, event, policy, activity, theme, or any combination of the above.

The definition excludes topics relating to Canada only by association or common interest. [February 1993, revised August 1999, pp. 1–2; www.nlc-bnc.ca/9/9/index-e.html]

Chapter Twenty-Five

Bibliographies in Policies

While it seems likely that the majority of collection development policies were created—and revised—with the assistance of other information sources, rarely are these materials cited either directly in document passages or in a separate bibliography. Rather than any aversion to giving credit where credit is due, policy compilers may simply feel these devices represent unnecessary scholarly trappings for what is essentially a practical manual. Nevertheless, where included, bibliographies can serve a number of very useful functions:

- They lend an aura of authority; i.e., the points made within the policy were obtained from reputable sources.
- They draw attention to the professional literature on collection development in general as well as specific issues such as intellectual freedom, weeding guidelines, and the assessment of library holdings. As a result, anyone consulting the policy would have a pathfinder for obtaining more in-depth information on a particular topic of interest.
- They provide a link to standards, forms, policies, and procedures that are germane to a library's collection building program.

Although each of the bibliographies below differs markedly from the other examples, all can be said to serve at least one of the previously noted functions. The titles listed below relate specifically to the institutions that have included them within their respective policies. Their inclusion here does not constitute a recommendation on the part of the authors of this work. Due to a variety of factors—lack of timeliness, lack of applicability to specific collection building needs, etc.—these works may not prove useful to some libraries.

BIBLIOGRAPHY FOR ACADEMIC LIBRARIES

West Chester University, Francis Harvey Green Library: Collection Development Policy Statements

Anderson, James S., ed. *Guide for Written Policy Statements.* 2nd ed. Chicago: American Library Association, Association for Library Collections and Technical Services, 1966.

Curley, Arthur, and Dorothy Broderick. *Building Library Collections.* 6th ed. Metuchen, NJ: Scarecrow, 1985.

Gabriel, Michael R. *Collection Development and Collection Evaluation: A Sourcebook.* Lanham, MD: Scarecrow, 1995.

Gillespie, John T., and Ralph J. Folcarelli. *Guides to Library Collection Development.* Englewood, CO: Libraries Unlimited, 1994.

Gorman, G. E., and B. R. Howes. *Collection Development for Libraries.* London: Bowker-Saur, 1989.

Powell, Nancy, and Mary Bushing. *WLN Collection Assessment Manual.* 4th ed. Lacey, WA: WLN, 1992.

Shapiro, Beth J., and John Whaley, eds. *Selection of Library Materials in Applied and Interdisciplinary Fields.* Chicago: American Library Association, Resource and Technical Division, Collection Management and Development Committee, 1987.

White, Howard D. *Brief Tests of Collection Strength: A Methodology for All Types of Libraries.* Westport, CT: Greenwood, 1995.

Wood, Richard J., and Frank Hoffmann. *Library Collection Development Policies: A Reference and Writers' Handbook.* Lanham, MD: Scarecrow, 1996.

[submitted for approval February 23, 2000, p. 37]

BIBLIOGRAPHY FOR COMMUNITY COLLEGES

Central Piedmont Community College (Charlotte, NC) Library: Collection Development Policy

American Library Association Publications

American Library Association. (1989). *Guide for Written Collection Policy Statements.* Collection Management and Development Guides, No. 3. Chicago: American Library Association.

American Library Association. (1987). *Guide for Writing a Bibliographer's Manual.* Collection and Development Guides, No. 1. Chicago: American Library Association.

Collection Development Policies

Collection Development Policy. (No Date). Unpublished Manuscript. University of North Carolina at Charlotte, J. Murray Atkins Library, Charlotte, N.C.

Collection Management Policy: Guidelines for the Ida Jane Dacus Library. (1986). Unpublished Manuscript. Ida Jane Dacus Library, Rock Hill, S.C.

CSUS Library Collection Development Policy. (1989). Sacramento, CA: California State University, Sacramento (ERIC Document Reproduction Service No. ED 315085).

Tubesing, R. (1989). *Library Collections Development and Maintenance Policies and Procedures Manual.* Hobbs, NM: Scarborough Memorial Library, College of the Southwest (ERIC Document Reproduction Service No. ED 309782).

Articles

Anderson, C. (1990, September). Spreadsheet Programs and Collection Development. *Wilson Library Bulletin.* p. 90.

Criteria for Not Discarding Books from a Public Library. (1991). *Unabashed Librarian.* 78, 9.

Fischer, K. (1991). *Value of Collection Assessment in a Small Academic Library.* Bend, OR: Author.

Gifts and Donations for the Library. (1986). *Unabashed Librarian.* 60, 27.

Jacob, M. (1990, September). Get It in Writing: A Collection Development Plan for the Skokie Public Library. *Library Journal.* p. 169.

Johnston, M. (1990, September). Selection Advisor: An Expert System, for Collection Development. *Information Technology and Libraries.* p. 219.

LaGuardia, C. (1992, July). Electronic Databases: Will Old Collection Development Policies Still Work? *Online.* p. 60.

Management Techniques and Service Philosophy, Their Impact on Collection Development. (1985). *Unabashed Librarian.* 56, 9.

Schwartz, C. (1993, January). Evaluating CD-ROM Products: Yet Another Checklist. *CD-ROM Professional.* p. 89.

[copyrighted 1999, last modified May 5, 1999, pp. 30–31; www.cpcc.cc.nc .us/Library/general/policy/cd.htm]

BIBLIOGRAPHY FOR PUBLIC LIBRARIES

Howell Carnegie District Library (Michigan): Collection Development Policy

American Library Association. *Guide for Written Collection Policy Statements.* Brant, Bonita, Editor. Chicago: American Library Association, 1989.

Carter, Mary Duncan, Wallace John Bonk, and Mary Rose Magrill. *Building Library Collections.* Fourth Edition. Metuchen, New Jersey: Scarecrow Press, 1974.

Gardner, Richard K. *Library Collections: Their Origin, Selection, and Development.* New York: McGraw-Hill, 1981.

[p. 7; http://hcdl.howell-carnegie.lib.mi.us/pol_collection.shtml]

BIBLIOGRAPHY FOR SPECIAL LIBRARIES
AND RELATED INSTITUTIONS

Medical College of Georgia: Collection Development Policy

Medical Library Association Courses for Continuing Education, CE 701, *Development and Assessment of Health Sciences Library Collections*, Daniel T. Richards, Collection Development Officer, National Library of Medicine, 1991.

National Library of Medicine, *Collection Development Manual of the National Library of Medicine*, 3rd ed., Duane Arenales, 1993.

Collection Management and Development Section/ALCTS, *Guide to Written Collection Policy Statements*, 2nd ed., draft, November 1994.

Collection Development Policies and Procedures, 3rd ed., by Futas, Elizabeth, Oryx Press, 1995.

[copyright 1997, last modified October 2000; www.meg.edu/library/services/ collectionpolicy/bibliog.htm]

Chapter Twenty-Six

Appendixes in Policies

Appendixes serve much the same purpose in collection development policies as in books and other formats; i.e., they supply useful supplementary material that has been deemed inappropriate for placement within the main text. There are a number of reasons that may dictate this decision, all of which are concerned with disruption in the narrative flow, or exposition of ideas:

- the material is of considerable length, and is hard to understand if presented in truncated form.
- the material, while germane to issues covered in the core policy, may include extraneous details or a somewhat different central thrust.
- the material may be organized in a completely different format; e.g., a form, legal document, chart, budget sheet, etc.

Libraries vary considerably regarding their use of appendixes; some ignore them altogether, whereas others include many entries at the end of the policy. If incorporated into collection development statements, it is imperative that all material be clearly labeled under the heading "appendixes" in the Table of Contents. Headings in the Table of Contents should match those in the actual appendixes. Continuous pagination should be employed from the beginning through to the end of the policy, including the appendixes.

APPENDIX FOR ACADEMIC LIBRARIES

West Chester University, Francis Harvey Green Library: Collection Development Policy Statements

Contents

Preface: Mission Statement
Part I: General Collection Principles and Responsibilities
Part II: Selection Guidelines for Specific Collections
Part III: Approvals & Revision Schedules
Part IV: Bibliography
Part V: Appendixes
A. Standards for College Libraries, ACRL
B. Sample WLN Conspectus Worksheets

[submitted for approval February 23, 2000, p. 2; prepared by Diana P. Thomas]

APPENDIX FOR COMMUNITY COLLEGES

Lake-Sumter Community College Libraries: Collection Development Policy (Internet home page links)

- Purpose of Collection Development
- College Mission
- Mission of College Libraries
- Purpose of Collection Development Policy
- Collection Development Responsibility
- Collection Overview
- General Criteria for Selection of Materials
- Types and Formats of Materials Collected
- Detailed Analysis of Subject Collections
- Donations
- Deselection
- Preservation of Materials
- Replacement of Materials
- Standards
- Intellectual Freedom
- Copyright
- Cooperative Collection Development
- Policy Review

- Appendix A: LSCC Libraries Mission Statement
- Appendix B: Government Documents Collection Development Policy
- Appendix C: Request for Reconsideration of Library Resources
- Appendix D: ALA Intellectual Freedom Statements

[revised April 2001, p. 1; http://lscc.cc.fl.us/library/coldev/htm]

APPENDIX FOR PUBLIC LIBRARIES

Canterbury Public Library: Collection Development Policy

Contents

1. Overview
2. Collection Management
3. General Collections
4. Special Collections
5. In House Databases
6. Future Trends

Appendixes

    I. Access to information and censorship in libraries
    II. Policies on library services to children & young people
    III. New Zealand collection preservation policy
    IV. Application for reconsideration of material
    V. Interloans
    VI. Tagging of books
    VII. Donations—individual
    VIII. Donations—collections
    IX. Guidelines for collection management
    X. Guidelines for deselection (weeding)

APPENDIX FOR SPECIAL LIBRARIES AND RELATED INSTITUTIONS

Smithsonian Institution Libraries: Collections Management Policies

Contents

    I. Introduction
    II. Acquisitions

III. Deaccessioning
IV. Access and Loan
 V. Library Materials Placed in the Custody of SIL
VI. Care and Control of Collections
VII. Insurance
VIII. Inventories

Appendixes: Branch Collection Development Policies

1. Anacostia Museum
2. Central Reference and Loan Services
3. Cooper-Hewitt Museum
4. Harvard/SI Center for Astrophysics
5. Museum Reference Center
6. Museum Support Center
7. National African Art Museum
8. National Air and Space Museum
9. National Museum of African Art
10. National Museum of American History
11. National Museum of the American Indian
12. National Museum of Natural History, including Anthropology and Botany Branches
13. The Naturalist Center
14. National Postal Museum
15. National Zoological Park
16. Horticulture Services Division
17. Smithsonian Environmental Research Center
18. Smithsonian Tropical Research Institute
19. Special Collections
20. Exposition Literature
21. Smithsoniana
22. Trade Catalogs

[SIL 87-02, revised August 10, 1992; author: Nancy E. Gwinn]

Part 2

VIRTUAL COLLECTION
DEVELOPMENT

Chapter Twenty-Seven

Introduction to Virtual Collection Development

Most libraries today manage two quite different information systems, one print and audiovisual (physical resources) and the other electronic (virtual resources). The latter increasingly means Internet accessible resources. While these two types of resources are quite different from each other, they share some similarities, particularly in terms of the components and principles that should be considered when writing and revising their collection development policies.

Traditional and virtual collection development has been becoming more centralized and technologically based in the way they provide resources and services. Client-server technology and the Internet are making digital conversion and transmission the preferred method of delivery for print and multimedia materials. In nearly all academic and large public libraries, Internet accessible databases and other electronic resources have changed the nature of library research and scholarly communication. The change, that is, involves more than format. It is changing how and where authors publish and the very control of publishing. Distribution of scholarly communication has been inalterably changed. Users of information, particularly students, who have learned how to use electronic resources demand and prefer electronic access over the print when they have a choice because electronic information systems have searching, retrieval, linking, sharing, and dissemination features the printed work cannot offer them. A requisite component of up-to-date collection development policies for libraries that do so, therefore, should cover electronic resources, including Internet accessible databases. For librarians and others in institutions considering whether to provide access to the electronic resources, this chapter should be very useful in making decisions about how, when, and why they should be provided and what priority they should have in the collection management program.

We are indebted to Jane Pearlmutter, Director of Continuing Education, School of Library and Information Studies, University of Wisconsin–Madison, for the invaluable information provided in Chapter 28 about the essential aspects of policy components for online electronic resources. Jane Pearlmutter is a nationally known authority on electronic collection development and presents papers and workshops on virtual collection development and other topics throughout the country. Contact information may be found at the end of the next chapter.

Chapter Twenty-Eight

Policy Components for Online Electronic Resources

Jane Pearlmutter

With the enormous growth of the World Wide Web, online resources have become increasingly important to libraries. Along with purchased books, journals, videos, and CD-ROMs, today's collection might include Internet resources, online or networked databases, and electronic journals. The virtual collection consists of those materials that the library provides access to without physical ownership.

In light of these changes in the nature of library collections, many librarians are writing a new information resources policy, supplementing the traditional collection development policy, to reflect the increased emphasis on access to materials rather than ownership and a place on the shelf. These policies recognize that the virtual collection needs to be developed in a way that is compatible with the print collection.

There are several benefits to having a distinct collection development policy for electronic resources. It will serve as a guide in choosing one format over another, help the selector make the best use of limited resources, and can be used to justify selections. In many library settings, it is not enough to just provide unguided and unsupervised access to the Internet. When access is provided in a more systematic way (through subject guides, links from library web pages, or cataloging), then the library is, in effect, saying that it stands behind these resources and they should, therefore, be subject to collection policies. The policy also is used to justify the selection of certain resources, particularly those which have ongoing costs or are available in multiple formats.

Most policies that have been written for online resources are limited to the ones that have fees, licenses, and access agreements—full-text databases, electronic journals, indexes, and electronic versions of reference works that are also available in print. As costs rise, a policy will help librarians find the rationale when shifting collection dollars and predicting future costs.

However, since so many libraries are providing formal access to free Internet resources, formal policy and selection guidelines for these resources are a logical next step. As in a traditional collection development policy, the document might refer to the scope of the collection, general selection principles, selection tools, provision of access, and deselection. Because there are different implications for free Internet resources and those that have a cost, the specific collection development issues will be considered separately.

ELECTRONIC RESOURCES ACQUIRED THROUGH LICENSE, PURCHASE, OR SUBSCRIPTION

One of the roles of the collection development librarian is budgeting for library materials, including justification for purchases, monitoring the spending, and projecting future costs. The same holds true for virtual collections. Among the selection criteria, the policy should include cost, including the cost difference between formats, the compatibility of the resource with existing hardware, and predictability of future costs.

In the future, delivery of information and licensing/access fees may constitute a major part of the library's non-personnel budget. Instead of paying for ownership of actual library materials, the library is paying for the right to access them electronically. The hardware and software to access the electronic resources must also be planned for. Another component may be fees for commercial document delivery. The policy may include specifics on funding these items, particularly if the subject content will determine the individual fund. As with all other formats, the collection budget may allow for expenditures outside of specific departmental funds for those titles deemed major purchases.

There are often financial benefits of consortial licensing of virtual resources such as substantial discounts, centralized negotiation and billing, and broader access. The virtual collection development policy could define the terms of participation and division of costs, and should describe a procedure for re-evaluating resources that may be dropped from a consortial agreement.

Whether the organization enters into a license individually or through a consortium, no license should be signed without scrutiny and most likely some negotiation. The policy should define the library's user population, because this will be very important when the pricing formula is examined. Will the cost be determined by actual users, potential users, number of workstations? One issue that arises in delivery of licensed electronic resources is defining who those users actually are. In a public library, users can be defined as those who hold valid library cards, but should also include patrons who walk in to use public-access terminals, whether they have library cards or not. In an academic or school library, the user population might be defined by default as current faculty and staff and all enrolled students. Even if fees are based on unlimited access, even if the information is supplied on a subscription rather than per-use basis, the user population may have to be defined and the method of delivery specified when negotiating a license for online resources. If the library offers very limited access—one or two workstations—it may be advantageous to refer to the number of simultaneous users allowed, rather than the total user population.

Other considerations that should be part of the selector and negotiator's checklists:

General

- Is this a recommendation/request from faculty/students/patrons?
- Do we have other subscriptions with this vendor?
- Is the vendor reliable? Is the product stable?
- Is there a trial period?
- Are terms of license clearly stated?
- Does the license cover the uses your patrons will expect to make of the information? (i.e., display/browse only; print for personal use; transmit and download for personal use; incorporate portions of data into new work)

Content

- Are the subjects covered wholly or in part by existing subscriptions to electronic services?
- Is the product full text? Image database? Numeric? Other?
- Does the library have a print subscription? If yes, could it be canceled?
- Are there specific value-added features in electronic version?
- Is the material timely?
- How frequently is the product updated?
- Is database information from the public domain?
- Have selection tools been consulted for reviews?
- For electronic journals, is there a peer review process? Can you identify an editor?

Format

- Is the interface easy to use?
- Is the screen layout well-organized?

- Is it easy to move from search results list to full record and back?
- Is the response time acceptable?
- Are there context-sensitive help screens?
- Is there printed documentation? Online tutorials?
- Are special viewers or other software needed? Are there audio or video clips?
- Does it offer both beginning and advanced searching options?
- Boolean search capabilities?
- Proximity search capabilities?
- Able to truncate, limit by language, etc.?
- Is there an index for browsing?
- Can searches be saved and modified?
- Can search results be downloaded, printed, e-mailed?
- Able to interact with bibliographic citation management software?
- Are full-text articles text-only?
- If pdf files, are page images legible?
- Do page images retain format of original document?
- Are there size/display options for graphics?

Access

- Does the license cover expected modes of access? (i.e., in library, on campus, remote dial-in)
- What kind of authentication is allowed/required? (IPs, passwords, etc.)
- How is remote access handled?
- Does product need to be adapted for ADA compliance?
- Is cataloging of this item recommended?
- Who is covered as an "authorized user"?
- Does the agreement restrict or limit fair use rights?
- Are interlibrary loans permitted?
- Is document delivery permitted?
- Can articles be incorporated in electronic reserves pages or distance education courseware?
- Can material be e-mailed or downloaded?
- Can material be linked to the library's catalog?
- Does vendor provide usage data?
- Does vendor provide number of turn-aways, if relevant? (e.g., requests exceed simultaneous user limit)

Archiving

- Will the library need archival rights to this material?
- Are archives and backfiles available?
- Is it covered by a document delivery service?

Duplication of Existing Print Resources

- Does the resource have significant historical value?
- Is one format unstable?
- Is there a cost benefit for purchasing multiple formats?
- Will multiple formats meet the different needs of user groups?
- Are there specific value-added features in electronic version?
- Does "full-text" include *all* material of print version?
- Pricing
- Are there options for single-station, networked, and multi-user contracts?
- Are there additional costs for upgrades?
- Are backfiles available at a one-time cost, ongoing cost, or pay-per-use?
- Is the product available as part of a bundled package? Are there economies in subscribing to a larger package?
- Is consortial pricing available?
- If print counterpart is available, how does price compare?
- Is print subscription required for electronic subscription or access to backfiles?
- Liability
- Does contract need review by legal department?
- Are there any provisions that require the library to indemnify the vendor?
- Does the contract include an indemnity from the vendor regarding intellectual property rights?
- Are there provisions that make another state's law govern the contract?
- Are there provisions regarding termination, renewal, and review of contract?

FREE INTERNET RESOURCES

While libraries are paying for an increasing number of electronic resources, much on the Internet remains free. Along with the vast number of commercial sites, there is a surprising amount of substantive material which can be a great asset to a library with a limited collection budget. For example, academic libraries, museums, the Library of Congress, and other institutions are digitizing—and mounting on the Internet—wonderful, searchable collections of primary source materials that would otherwise be unavailable to other libraries. Internet resources are a valuable way to expand the library's collection, and are often taking the place of an outdated, unwieldy pamphlet file. They should be used for material outside the scope of the library's print and AV collection, for material that will not appear in print (for example, some government information is moving to electronic format only, available via government websites), and for information that comes with a "value-added" component, such as the ability to interact with a site and search within a database.

In addition, since there are frequently-voiced concerns about letting children surf the Internet on their own, many libraries prefer to provide more formal access to Internet resources. Some simply have a flyer of recommended sites. More often, the library website features links to those recommendations, arranged by subject. Others are even including links to recommended Internet resources in their online catalogs. In such a catalog, if a search were done, for example, for information about volcanoes, it would retrieve citations not only for the books on volcanoes in that library, but also a link to *Volcano World* (http://volcano.und.nodak.edu/).

One policy, at the University of Oregon, written specifically for Internet resources points out, "while the Internet is easily accessible, the Library recognizes that careful selection of Internet resources and availability of these through the Library's catalog will accomplish several objectives:

1. increase awareness and maximize use of significant sites;
2. provide value-added access to Internet resources often absent when using various search engines to locate resources; and
3. enhance and expand the Library's collection of traditional formats.

In these situations, if librarians are putting the effort into "collecting" these resources (even though the library does not own the materials), certain selection criteria should apply. These might include:

Relevance and Use

- Does the material relate specifically to curriculum or community interests?
- Are there classes that will use it regularly?
- Does it enhance the reference collection?
- Is it valuable for the teachers' professional collection (i.e., lesson plans)?
- Is it a resource available in a language spoken in your community?
- Has this resource been around for a while?
- Duplication of existing print resources
- Is this information already in the library in another format?
- Is there a demand for multiple formats?
- Are there specific value-added features in electronic version?

Content

- Does the material meet traditional selection criteria in regard to quality, comprehensiveness, authority, and grade-level if applicable?
- Is the site updated frequently (if timeliness is a concern)?
- Are the site's links relevant?

Ease of Use

- Is the format easy to use?
- Is the screen layout well-organized?
- Is the site easily searchable?
- Is the reading level and/or intended audience appropriate?

The University of Oregon's policy goes on to state a very important issue: "select materials which meet the standards the Library expects of all materials in regard to excellence, comprehensiveness, and authoritativeness." Even without reviews, selectors make certain judgments about the reliability of print materials, based on previous knowledge of a publisher or a serial, the appearance of the book, the presence of features such as indexes, bibliographies, recent copyright dates, etc. But the Internet is primarily a world of self-publishing. Selectors need to apply additional evaluation criteria when selecting Internet resources for inclusion in the collection, whether the citations are simply added to a bookmark list or cataloged with the library's holdings. These criteria might include:

- Who is the author or producer of the information?
- What is the expertise of the page's creator?
- Is there an institution affiliated with it?
- Does the institution appear to exercise quality control over the information appearing under its name?
- Is contact information included?
- Does the site carry advertising?
- If it is a commercial site, is there significant content apart from the commercial intent?
- There are a number of evaluation checklists on the Web, which will be helpful for patrons as well as selectors (see Additional Resources).

SELECTION TOOLS

A collection development policy for online resources may also suggest consulting available reviews of Internet resources. Such reviews are still in short supply compared to reviews of print materials or even CDs. Reviews can outline how well a resource meets specific criteria and can provide further insight regarding the resource's overall quality. Subject specialists should not necessarily exclude a title because it does not meet every individual criterion. However, subject specialists should attempt to select resources that adequately meet as many of the selection criteria as is possible. In reviews of licensed products, look for dates of coverage, frequency of updates, if a demo disk is available, and which formats are available. In reviews of free Internet resources, the most useful reviews provide some idea of the content or purpose of the resource, the authority, and the level or intended audience. In addition, reviews of electronic resources should always review not only the content of the resource, but the design/user interface, and the technical merit.

The Charleston Advisor

Critical Reviews of Web Products for Information Professionals. Published quarterly online and available by subscription at http://www.charlestonco.com/.

The CHOICE Supplement

CHOICE, a review journal used primarily by academic libraries, put out a special supplement of Internet reviews in 1997, and additional supplements in 1998 and 1999. The reviews considered such criteria as content, audience, duplication of information from other formats, and made recommendations as to what type of collection or level of student would find it useful. Included with subscriptions to *CHOICE*, the supplement may also be purchased separately.

Fulltext Sources Online

Hawkins, Donald T. and Mary B. Glose. Medford, NJ: Information Today, 2001. *Fulltext Sources Online* is a directory of publications that can be found online in full text through an aggregator or content provider. *FSO* is published biannually in January and July and lists over 15,000 newspapers, journals, magazines, newsletters, and transcripts. It includes coverage dates for each listed publication, update frequency and lag times (if online lags behind print publication), and amount of coverage (when a publication is available as selected articles only, versus cover-to-cover articles).

Gale Directory of Databases

Detroit: Gale Research, 2001 (this includes about 13,000 publicly available databases)

KidsClick!

http://sunsite.berkeley.edu/KidsClick!/: An annotated list created by a group of librarians at the Ramapo Catskill Library System, *KidsClick!* is an extensive, searchable subject guide, with some very nice features, such as noting the number of illustrations and the reading level of the sites they include.

LJ Digital Web Reviews

http://www.ljdigital.com/articles/multimedia/webwatch/webwatcharchive.asp

LJ Digital Database Reviews

http://www.ljdigital.com/articles/multimedia/databasedisc/databaseanddiscindex .asp: Monthly reviews published online by *Library Journal.*

The Librarians' Index to the Internet

http://sunsite.berkeley.edu/InternetIndex/: *The Librarians' Index to the Internet* is a searchable, annotated subject directory of more than 7,300 Internet resources selected and evaluated by librarians for their usefulness to users of public libraries.

Multimedia and CD-ROM Directory

18th ed. London: TPFL Multimedia, 1997

The Scout Report

http://scout.cs.wisc.edu: *The Scout Report* is published every Friday by the Internet Scout Project. The Internet Scout Project is located in the Department of Computer Sciences at the University of Wisconsin–Madison, and is sponsored by the National Science Foundation to provide timely information to the education community about valuable Internet resources. *The Scout Report* also offers a searchable archive of over three years of the best of the resources from the Scout Report, the Scout Report for Science & Engineering, the Scout Report for Social Sciences, and the Scout Report for Business & Economics. These are fully cataloged resources that may be browsed by Library of Congress Subject Headings and Classifications and are searchable by title, author, subject, resource type, language, resource location, publisher, and URL.

PROVISION OF ACCESS

Print resources usually follow an established pattern from selection to acquisition to processing, with points of access through the library catalog as well as browsing the shelves. Because access to electronic resources does not follow this pattern, the policy may refer to provision of access specifically. For example, the library will maximize access to Internet resources through several means:

- links from subject guides on the library's website
- links from lists of databases and electronic journals on the library's website
- cataloging of electronic journals and selected Internet resources
- regular updating of records when information, particularly the site's URL, changes
- provision, maintenance, preparation, and loading of necessary software and hardware
- appropriate staff and user support and training for in-building use

Internet resources to be cataloged should be selected as carefully as any other material that is added to a collection. Because of workload considerations (the large percentage of original cataloging required, the need for more authority work and link maintenance), it is unlikely that all Internet resources selected will also be cataloged. Criteria for addition to catalog might include:

- Does the resource support the needs of institution?
- Does it contain significant full-text material?
- Is the resource considered a known and respected source?
- Is the material the same for the electronic version as the print version?
- Does a single record describe print and electronic version?
- Is cataloging data already available? If not, is bibliographic information easy to locate?

DESELECTION

Space considerations rather than collection needs are often the motivating force (although not the principle) behind the weeding of print collections. Although lack of shelf space is not a factor with online resources, ongoing deselection of Internet resources is a necessity nevertheless because of the dynamic nature of such resources. These guidelines should provide some suggestions for when to deselect a resource:

- Is this resource no longer available or maintained?
- Has the currency and reliability of the resource's information lost its value?
- Does another Internet site or resource offer more comprehensive coverage?

• Is the publication now available through another source? (For example, a paid subscription to an electronic journal may be discontinued if the journal is available through a state-funded full-text database.)

ADDITIONAL RESOURCES

ALSC Children and Technology Committee. How to Tell if You Are Looking at a Great Web Site, 1997: http://www.ala.org/parentspage/greatsites/criteria.html, 23 Jan. 2001.

Antelman, Kristin. "Web lists and the decline of the library catalog." *Library Computing*, Westport; 1999; v. 18, no. 3, pp. 187-193.

Columbia University. Collection Development Policies: Digital Libraries: http://www .columbia.edu/cu/libraries/about/colldev/digital-library.htm, 23 Jan. 2001.

Davis, Trisha L. "License Agreements in Lieu of Copyrights: Are We Signing Away Our Rights?" *Library Acquisitions: Practice and Theory*, vol. 21, no. 1, 1997. pp. 19–27.

InFoPeople Project. Evaluating Internet Resources: A checklist. Last update 8/4/00: http://www.infopeople.org/bkmk/select.html, 23 Jan. 2001.

Internet Scout Project. Scout Report Selection Criteria, 2001: http://scout.cs.wisc.edu (23 Jan. 2001).

Mazin, Beth, ed. AcqWeb's Directory of Collection Development Policies on the Web. Last updated: November 28, 2000: http://acqweb.library.vanderbilt.edu/acqweb/cd_policy.html (23 Jan. 2001).

Montgomery, Carol Hansen. "Measuring the Impact of an Electronic Journal Collection on Library Costs." *D-Lib Magazine*, Volume 6, Number 10, October 2000: http://www.dlib.org/dlib/october00/montgomery/10montgomery.html (23 Jan. 2001).

Morris, Sara E. "A great deal of time and effort: An overview of creating and maintaining Internet-based subject guides." *Library Computing*, Westport; 1999; Vol. 18, No. 3; pp. 213–216.

Morton Grove (IL) Public Library Collection Development and Materials Selection Policy. First published on the Web: 1/26/98. Last update: 1/12/2001: http://www .webrary.org/inside/colldevadultwww.html (23 Jan. 2001).

Oliver, K., Wilkinson, G., & Bennett, L. Consolidated Listing of Evaluation Criteria and Quality Indicators, 1997: http://www.edtech.vt.edu/edtech/kmoliver/webeval/criteria.html (23 Jan. 2001).

Tillman, Hope. Evaluating Quality on the Net, May 30, 2000: http://www.hopetillman .com/findqual.html (23 Jan. 2001).

University of California Libraries. Principles for Acquiring and Licensing Information in Digital Formats, May 1996: http://sunsite.berkeley.edu/Info/ principles.html (23 Jan. 2001).

University of Oregon Libraries. Collection Development Policy for Internet Resources. First published 10/2/95, update 9/14/2000: http://libweb.uoregon.edu/colldev/intres.html (23 Jan. 2001).

University of Tennessee, Knoxville Libraries. Electronic Resources Collection Development Policy. May 1998: http://toltec.lib.utk.edu/%7Ecolldev/elrescd.html (23 Jan. 2001).

University of Texas. Software and Database License Agreement Checklist. Last update 3/13/97: http://www.utsystem.edu/OGC/IntellectualProperty/ckfrm1.htm (23 Jan. 2001).

University of Texas at Austin General Libraries. Digital Library Collection Development Framework. Last Modified: March 29, 1999: http://www.lib.utexas.edu/cird/Policies/Subjects/framework.html (23 Jan. 2001).

Yale University Library. Licensing Digital Information: A Resource for Librarians. Last update 1/14/01: http://www.library.yale.edu/~llicense/index.shtml (23 Jan. 2001).

CONTACT INFORMATION:

Jane Pearlmutter, Director of Continuing Education
School of Library & Information Studies
University of Wisconsin–Madison
600 North Park Street
Madison WI 53706 USA
608-262-6398
jpearl@slis.wisc.edu

Chapter Twenty-Nine

Discussion of Recent Issues

The authors wish here to discuss recent issues of increasing importance that are not addressed above because some libraries might want to develop a policy for their collection development statements. These issues are so recent that none of the policies examined by the authors dealt with them. The issues are as follows:

- Book or electronic access?
- The "big deal"
- Publisher embargoes
- Journal content retrenchment and shifts
- Allocating funds for electronic resources
- Electronic books
- Copyright, Digital Rights Management, and Intellectual Property Rights
- The Internet, Electronic Security, and Filtering Policy
- Acceptable Use Policy

BOOK OR ELECTRONIC ACCESS?

Books are constantly being digitized by publishers and entities like netLibrary, or offered by publishers in electronic format only. A library's collection development should tell selectors and users alike when one format might be preferred over the other. Kitsap Regional Library puts it quite succinctly this way:

> Information found in electronic sources, both within the system and from outside resources, increasingly impacts the size of the print collection. As on-line alternatives become user-friendly and can be selected, cataloged, and presented

so that our customers can find them useful, or superior to the print collection, they are included in the Library's collection. On-line information will be increasingly included in the collection when it offers a wider cost-effective distribution of access throughout the County than can be achieved with print resources.

This library's vision statement for 1997–2000 dealt quite honestly and openly with the question of whether the printed will be replaced by electronic books as follows:

> The print collection will steadily begin to decrease in size over the next four years in response to more widely available and cost-efficient electronic alternatives. For example, the print collection supporting reference services may be reduced by as much as ten percent by the year 2000 as on-line alternatives become available. As sufficient display and capture devices are made available and graphical user interfaces are installed, the library staff can select, catalog, and present on-line resources in such a way that our customers will find them as useful and, in some cases, perhaps superior to the print collection.

Academic libraries that must meet the needs of distance education students and students in multiple locations might substitute the words "when it offers a wide cost-effective distribution of access to students, staff, and faculty regardless of their location." The University of Iowa Libraries' Electronic Resources Management Policy adds a few additional criteria as follows:

1. The resource offers some value-added enhancement to make it preferable over, or a significant addition to, other print or non-print equivalents. Examples of such enhancements include wider access and greater flexibility in searching.
2. If the item is an electronic version of a resource in another format, it contains or covers the equivalent information to the extent appropriate and desirable.
3. The resource meets usual and customary technical standards in the industry.
4. If currency is important, the resource is updated often enough to be useful.
5. The resource is "user friendly." Some measures of "friendliness" are:
   a. The existence of introductory screens
   b. The availability of on-screen tutorials
   c. Prompts and menus
   d. Function-specific help
   e. Novice and expert searching levels
   f. Helpful error messages
   g. Ease of exiting from one point in database to another
   h. Index browsing
   i. Software allows for both printing and downloading

6. Vendor-related issues, such as:
   a. Vendor reliability and business record suggests continued support for the product via updates or new versions.
   b. Vendor-produced documentation is thorough and clear.
   c. Customer support is available from the vendor during library working hours.
   d. Price penalties, if any, for different formats have been investigated.
7. The resource is potentially networkable.
8. Textual resources are in the most commonly used and appropriate language for the subject matter.
9. Published reviews of the resource have been taken into account.
10. A trial period is available for examining the utility and value of the resource before a final commitment is made with the vendor.
11. Access-related issues, such as:
    a. The physical location of the resource, if applicable.
    b. Vendor-required limitations to access.
    c. The resource can be made available in agreement with the Intellectual Freedom statement of the American Library Association, which the University Libraries fully support.

THE "BIG DEAL" ISSUE

Publishers such as Elsevier, Wiley, and Springer-Verlag have offered member institutions of library consortia, large library systems, or groups of libraries access to the full-text articles in their databases owned by all of the other institutions, or to all of the publisher's online titles. This "big deal" issue, as it has come to be called by many librarians, refers to the full-text article database licenses offered by publishers of electronic journals to library consortia, large university systems, or other groups of libraries. The reader interested in this topic should also see our chapter on cooperative collection development. Here, the authors wish to explore the topic as a component of a library's collection development policy.

These "big deals" have been attracting a number of libraries and consortia to participate, particularly those who may have cancelled these publishers' titles for financial reasons, or were not able to afford print subscriptions to begin with. The deals are attractive to libraries because they provide their users with web access at the article level to the publishers' journal titles held collectively by the consortia or system members. For yet a higher premium, the publishers will offer access to all of the articles in all of the titles published, regardless of whether consortia members subscribe to the print titled. In this way, a library can gain—or regain—access to many titles not currently subscribed to in print.

One of the controversial aspects of this issue has to deal with the value of the articles or journals to which a library consortia member gains access. Members gain web access to the articles in titles subscribed to in print by other members of the consortia, if not all articles in the publisher's database. In well-funded libraries, detractors might contend that their library already subscribes to the print titles that are valued by its community of users and do not need to pay a premium for web access. Instead, interlibrary loan could be used. Proponents of the big deal are likely to be from libraries that have cancelled the publisher's most expensive or little used titles through the years (and regain access to them and possibly the titles they would like to have subscribed to had their budget been sufficient. For these institutions, the real value is web access to all of the publisher's titles they are provided access to (but to which the library does not subscribe). The value in dollars is represented by the premium paid by the library to the publisher. The smaller the percentage, the greater the value. The big deal consequently favors the members of a library consortium that have the least number of print subscriptions of the particular publisher. A library's collection development policy might address this issue.

THE EMBARGO ISSUE

An "embargo" occurs when a journal publisher does not allow electronic access to the last three or more months of articles in the respective journal issues. The publisher, that is, does not provide the aggregator access to the articles in the latest issues so as to encourage print subscriptions, which are still the mainstay of these publishers. An embargo severely limits information to recent information contained in those titles, plus puts pressure on the library to subscribe to the print. While this may be the objective of the publisher, unless this practice is mentioned in the promotional literature of the publisher, it may be regarded as a deceitful practice. Most collection development policies examined by the authors do not mention this concern specifically. Rather, the issue can be addressed in the selection criteria statement. As publishers find it more profitable to eliminate print subscriptions, this scenario is likely to change. As Dartmouth College (see Chapter 30) states: "However, problems and questions continually arise as we select, acquire, process and make these resources accessible."

JOURNAL CONTENT RETRENCHMENT AND SHIFTS

Aggregators of digital collections and services such as EBSCO, Ovid, Information Access Company, and Bell & Howell (ProQuest databases) must negotiate with many journal publishers to provide content (full-text articles) to libraries and other customers. Scholarly societies, university presses, and similar non-profit entities are also packaging digitized collections; Johns Hopkins University's Project Muse is perhaps the best known example in this category. These and several other full-text article database providers offer access to aggregated electronic articles from hundreds of journals. There is a large percentage of du-plication in the aggregated journal titles list of these vendors, but libraries are forced to pay for access to the duplicated titles because the vendors also provide access to unique titles. One product alone does not meet the full-text article needs of many library users. Put another way, libraries cannot pick and choose the titles they want access to and thereby avoid paying twice or more for access to the same titles. Each vendor, that is, provides access to unique titles, so many libraries feel the need to license two or more such full-text article databases to meet the needs of their users. Complicating this situation is the fact that the list of the aggregated journals constantly shift due to publisher retrenchment. Pric-ing models also vary due to changes in demand, requests for customized pric-ing, and other variables. Some libraries want vendors to offer a pay-for-viewing pricing model, or a model based on individual library and library consortia needs and circumstances. The latter has not yet occurred.

Due to the rapidly evolving nature of the full-text article delivery business, the collection development policies of libraries examined by the authors have not spelled out detailed criteria for making decisions.

THE ALLOCATION ISSUE

Some recent questions and discussions on the collection development and other library Listservs concern allocating electronic serials and resources to departments or subject funds. This might suggest that some librarians or users believe that if book funds are allocated, electronic resources funds also should be allocated. Judging from such discussions, few libraries do so because it is increasingly frustrating and difficult to make decisions about what academic department of a large university, for example, should be assigned the partic-ular electronic resource or title. If the allocated funds belong to the library, not the college or department, why allocate? Discussions suggest that most li-braries do not allocate journal and electronic resources funds by subject, ac-ademic department, or a college because a large percentage of articles in the same journal title cross disciplinary lines. Articles about the environment, psychology, or personnel management might be read by persons of diverse academic backgrounds. Articles about environmental issues such as pollution, for instance, might have relevance to persons with academic backgrounds or interests in urban planning, sociology, or biology. A general psychology journal title might be of particular relevance to teachers or researchers in health science, nursing, medical science, or psychiatry. Whether or not a library allocates the materials budget in this fashion should be addressed in its collection development policies.

ELECTRONIC BOOKS ISSUE

Electronic books are being offered by more and more commercial publishers, and not-for-profit publishers, associations, and other entities. Twelve major university presses in 2001, for example, formed ebrary to publish electronic books and make popular content available online to the general public. Its business model resembles a virtual digital copier because readers of ebrary's freely available content will pay copy fees for each page they download or print. Ebrary is also signing agreements with for-profit companies. Although ebrary is directed to users, not libraries, it might appeal indirectly to some academic library selectors and collection development librarians because ebrary can take the pressure off spending limited materials budgets for acquiring scholarly and specialized university press titles of marginal value to the collection. Some of the same university presses who have signed with ebrary have also closed deals with Questia or netLibrary because, presumably, university presses do not know which business model will be successful. Participating university presses are likely to decide that agreeing to a variety of business models will increase the total sales of their titles. A cautionary note is in order, however, because it is too early to determine if the university presses and publishers signing-up with ebrary will offer their latest titles. Books are out-of-date upon publication, so an embargo on new titles is likely to limit ebrary's appeal to users. If this is the case, selectors should not hesitate to acquire titles offered by ebrary and other electronic book vendors.

Libraries and other entities may also sign with ebrary for materials scanned from special collections and archives, or materials in the public domain. If this practice becomes commonplace and causes libraries and archives to curtail offering such collections through the Internet, commercial electronic document providers might limit the number of important collections libraries and archives are making available for free from their Internet sites.

Electronic "libraries" of books offered by commercial companies to the public have raised many concerns among librarians, educators, and others. Commercial entities such as Questia (Houston, Texas) sell to electronic books directly to students at all levels of education subscriptions by the week, month, and year. Questia says it will provide students with information to write better papers quicker (than resorting to library resources and services). Given Questia's huge start-up costs, it is still too early to determine if the company will be financially successful any year soon, but it is giving trepidation to many librarians who fear that the company will spell the beginning of the end for book collections and collection development as they know it today. The company is even offering quantity discounts to academic departments and colleges. If this marketing scheme is successful and occurs at the expense of the academic library's materials budget, librarians do have every reason to be alarmed. While the company's marketing techniques have disturbed librarians and educators by disparaging the role of libraries and librarians, Questia's huge start-up costs are not likely to be ever recovered. The digitized books Questia currently provides access to, moreover, are not adequate to cover the diversity of required and suggested texts in many upper-division courses that require in-depth treatment of narrow topics. Even though Questia does appeal to some faculty who teach online and distance education courses, there is little likelihood of Questia meeting the information needs of the traditional students taking classes on campus. If students still need to do research at the library, why not borrow the library's books and save the fee charged by Questia? Thus far, that is, Questia poses only a theoretical threat to library collection development efforts. So, while a library's collection development policy may not need to address Questia's product per se, it might address the larger issues such as cost justifying such licenses of electronic books, and the library's priority on building a collection that meets the basic and long-term information needs of its clientele. In the final analysis, reading books or significant amounts of text entirely online appeals to very few people due to hardware, software, and telecommunication problems or limitations.

NetLibrary (Boulder, Colorado) markets its subscriptions to electronic book collections covering a wide array of subjects mostly to thousands of libraries and to an increasing number of library consortia. Subscribing libraries and library consortia can license access to all or a portion of the company's digitized books and make them available to their users through the Internet. This company has both proponents and detractors.

Proponents of netLibrary might view the company's products as being able to relieve demand for thousands of popular titles and also relieve the pressure to archive electronic texts by other means. Proponents also point to the significantly higher use of the electronic titles compared to the equivalent print titles. Detractors, on the other hand, might see such companies as a threat to the existence of libraries, or their materials budget at a minimum. If a library that relied exclusively upon netLibrary holdings must cancel the license, library users lose immediate and direct access to the titles in the database.

Detractors of netLibrary and entities like it point to the lack of acceptance of online books due to hardware, software, and telecommunication limitations. Reader software, monitors, and digitization technologies are improving all the time, but few users will read online. Detractors might also claim that the cost to the library of providing netLibrary has a negative impact on a library's collection development program if the product's cost was borne without any increase in the library's budget to cover it. Why pay for electronic access to a title the library will acquire in print format? That is, why pay for an electronic license each year for titles held in the library's book collection and already paid for? While netLibrary has not been a real financial threat to any library to date to the authors' knowledge, we suspect that the cost of the license to subscribing libraries does result in fewer purchases of traditional printed books unless the library's budget increased sufficiently to cover the license.

A library's collection development policy should address the issue of licensing electronic book services. Whether the library's policy is against or in favor of such licenses, the policy should state the policy and philosophy behind it. The authors were not able to locate examples in policies.

COPYRIGHT, DIGITAL RIGHTS MANAGEMENT, AND INTELLECTUAL PROPERTY RIGHTS

Hundreds of collection development policies were reviewed by the authors; very few policies covered the federal law per se with respect to copyright, digital rights, and intellectual property rights. Instead, most made reference to the pertinent laws or institutional policies covering such concerns. Presumably, the vast majority of libraries view these matters, and rightly so, to be wholly separate from collection development. Most colleges, universities, corporations, and large municipalities have broad policies covering how the institution manages the rights of employees or students with respect to copyright, patents, and intellectual rights, particularly when research and development of any kind is encouraged. While librarians employed by these entities would also be covered under such institutional policies, policies are unlikely to control access and usage of the types of digital material acquired, controlled, or licensed by the library if the policies were written before 1995. Suffice it to say that the chief administrative officer of the library should suggest revision of the institutional policies when access to and usage of digital materials the library acquires or licenses is necessary. The economic survival of the publishers of the commercial databases licensed by libraries, for example, depends on the enforcement of such policies. With respect to non-commercial information databases under the management of a library, librarians need to be sure institutional policies protect producers, authors, and users. While librarians would never make unauthorized reproduction of works to add to the library collection, they should work with computer systems and network personnel to help ensure that network security is sufficient to prevent violation of the terms of license or other agreements signed by the library administrator. It is advisable in collection development policies, therefore, to at least refer to the institutional policies and federal laws covering such matters. In this way, librarians can help assure database providers or owners that it takes their rights seriously. Kitsap Regional Library, for example, does so as follows:

> U.S. Copyright law (Title 17, U.S. Code) prohibits the unauthorized reproduction or distribution of copyrighted materials, except as permitted by the principles of "fair use." Any responsibility for any consequences of copyright infringement lies with the user. The Library expressly disclaims any liability or responsibility resulting from such use.

THE INTERNET, ELECTRONIC SECURITY, AND FILTERING

The Internet poses a number of concerns that acquisition of physical materials such as books, videotapes, and audiotapes do not. Academic, public, school, and other libraries can physically examine these materials and choose not to add them to the collection if their content is seen as objectionable by whatever standards are applied. Selection, cataloging, shelving, and circulation of physical library materials, therefore, may be controlled easily by library staff. Selection criteria listed in a library's collection development policy, as well as circulation and other library policies, may be applied to limit access of physical library resources. Can the same be said of electronic resources available through the Internet?

Librarians, library administrators, library boards, parents, or employers have very little control over information available freely (unlicensed) to anyone over the Internet. Librarians select "best sites" on the Internet and organize their library's home pages as reference tools so users can locate information more easily and quickly. But legally can or should librarians use commercial filtering software to block or restrict access on their libraries' Internet accessible computers on all or some public stations? Install filtering software on all Internet accessible computer but allow users to request it be turned off? Monitor use of those computer stations accessing the Internet and stop users from viewing objectionable websites?

Supreme Court decisions thus far give reasonably clear answers to these questions. Libraries that use filtering software to control any users' access to the Internet put the library at risk of facing a court case it is almost certain to lose. Use of filtering software raises questions of the constitutional rights of users. Public libraries that use such software face being sued by citizens or groups of citizens for violating their First Amendment right to receive information (Mainstream Loudoun II, 24 F. Supp. 2d, 562-63), including information accessible through the Internet (Reno v. ACLU, 521 U.S. 844, 1997) because that information is as diverse as human thought. Blocking users' access to content on the Internet, therefore, also raises constitutional issues of free speech and access to protected information.

When Congress enacted the Children's Internet Protection Act (CIPA), the American Library Association filed suit because CIPA mandated that libraries and schools install and use filtering software on computers that the students or the public had access to in order to receive federal funds. Failure to do so made those schools and libraries ineligible to receive Library Services and Technology Act funds, Elementary and Secondary Education funds, and E-rate funds. ALA's position is that First Amendment rights apply to all U.S. citizens, including children of any age. Further, policies and practices blocking Internet accessible computers in schools, school libraries, and other public libraries raises First Amendment concerns and is unconstitutional. ALA contends that educating users, including children, is the best protection. Library collection development or other policies should also do so in order to keep the library out of court, if not to protect the freedoms we enjoyed by citizens of free countries. To legally restrict or block use to web accessible sites in a public library, the library would need to demonstrate a compelling government interest and that there is not a less restrictive alternative (Perry Education Association v. Perry Local Educator's Association, 460 U.S. 37, 46, 1983, and International Society of Krishna Consciousness, Inc. v. Lee, 505 U.S 672, 678, 1992). However, schools may have a compelling interest in restricting the access of children to some materials and some Internet sites (Ginsberg v. New York 390 U.S. 629, 1968, and FCC v. Pacifica Foundation, 438 U.S. 726, 1978).

Control of the Internet, in practice, cannot be exercised by library selectors, or other individuals, associations, or governmental entities. Filtering software, in fact, is very limited in its ability to restrict content because it screens for certain words or websites. The company that develops the filtering software, not the library that buys it, controls the criteria used in blocking websites and keywords. Filtering software cannot, moreover, work on sexually explicit images; companies or others intent on sending such images to unsuspecting users through electronic mail often do so. Thus, it is a well-established fact that librarians, teachers, employers, or others who attempt to use filtering software to block content on the Internet that they define as pornographic or otherwise objectionable will not be effective. In addition, filtering software is imprecise and cannot distinguish between "good" and "bad" websites and will block access to information that the user should have, or needed, access to.

At one time, it may have been realistic to believe that only users, ultimately, could control what websites they view, but this is not the case either. Companies selling any product, pornographic materials for example, can and have been known to manipulate the technology in such a way that innocent and unsuspecting users receive unsought images. Neither the use of filtering software by libraries, nor following ethical business practices, is something such companies worry about because filtering software is simply not foolproof. Many companies with websites showing pornography, that is, have found ways to send pornographic images unwittingly to users who have no intention of viewing them. Removing patrons from the library when users are viewing a pornographic image, therefore, is a practice or policy that could bring legal charges against the library administrator or governing board.

It is irrelevant if the American Library Association, librarians, library boards, parents, or educators might all agree that particular websites are objectionable. It is irrelevant because the question that must be asked is if anyone has the right to deny library users access to any information or websites on the Internet. Clearly, to deny the right is likely to be judged a violation of a person's constitutional rights if the matter went to a court for review.

If a library assumes the responsibility to monitor Internet accessible computer in children's areas, the question of the library's legal liability becomes important. For this reason, the responsibility of monitoring young dependents who use Internet-accessible library workstations should belong to the parents or guardians of children or others in their care. Employees or teachers who bring minors to a library for a visit, tour, or class should be told that it is their responsibility to monitor all behavior of the dependents in their charge. Librarians or library administrators who want to "block" or prevent the public from seeing pornographic or other objectionable images or text on their Internet accessible computer workstations, should investigate the possibility of installing privacy devices on those stations, or positioning them in such a way that their monitors are concealed from view, especially in public libraries with a large user base of children. For the reason explained above, many public library boards or directors, for example King County Library System Board of Trustees, say something like "mandatory filters or other barriers will not be employed to restrict access on all terminals in the System. Such restriction, universally applied, is tantamount to censorship and is not consistent with the principle of free and open access so central to the mission of libraries."

The library policy goes on to address responsibility and says that "from the library's perspective, only parents or legal guardians have the authority and responsibility to decide the reading, viewing, listening or Internet use of their own minor children." This library's policy also specifies the rights of individuals, saying the following:

> The Board defends the principles of the freedom to access print, non-print and electronic information and considers that all materials selected or accessed under this policy are protected under the First Amendment of the U.S. Constitution until such time as they are determined unprotected by jurisdictional action and after appeals, if any, have been heard. Only then will the Board take action which may result in removal of materials from the collection or system-wide restrictions to electronic information resources.

With respect to security of networked PCs, users are warned when sites are not secure to use for credit cards, or to send other personal information. Most public institutions of higher education, special libraries, and large public libraries do not offer secure Internet service, nor use filtering software. These libraries take no responsibility for monitoring what users access but, rather, deal with users accessing pornography or similar material administratively. If librarians find users viewing pornography, for example, the library's policy will address the action that needs to be taken. This is not a matter for the collection development policy to address. Collection development policies might address the issues of pornography, security, and filtering as the Kitsap Regional Library sample policy does neatly in one section of its collection development policy section on the Internet as follows:

> The Internet offers access to a wealth of information that is personally, professionally, and culturally enriching. Kitsap Regional Library's home page includes links to resources on the Internet which are consistent with the Library's Collection Development Policy. However, users must be aware they can also access ideas, information, images, and commentary on the Internet that do not meet the Library's selection criteria and collection development policies.
>
> Not all the information available on the Internet is accurate, current, or complete. Users are encouraged to exercise critical judgment in evaluating the validity of information accessed via the Internet. The Library assumes no responsibility for any damages, direct or indirect, arising from its connections to the Internet.
>
> Users are cautioned that security in an electronic environment such as the Internet cannot be guaranteed. All transactions, files, and communications, e.g., credit card numbers and e-mail, are vulnerable to authorized access and use and should therefore be considered public.
>
> As with other library resources, parents and legal guardians are responsible for their minor children's use of the Internet. In order to support parents and legal guardians in their efforts to guide their minor children's use of the Internet, Kitsap Regional Library provides one or more focused terminal at each branch.

ACCEPTABLE USE POLICY

Libraries of all types have been adopting acceptable use policies as the preferred way to deal with how their users use their computer hardware, software, and telecommunications resources. Such policies address the accept-
ability to the library of their patrons using networked computers for electronic
mail, as well as accessing explicit sexual images. Oftentimes, acceptable use
policy will state that the number of such devices are very limited and the first
preference must be given to patrons who need to access licensed information
databases. If a library limits the use of electronic mail, word processing,
spreadsheet and other software, its acceptable use policy will explain the reasons for this policy. Acceptable use policy, therefore, is a management approach to the same issue, but is based on the assumption that all users have
the legal right to access information and freedoms to read, view, or listen to
materials housed in the library, or accessible electronically to users from computers housed in the library. While not a matter of collection development per
se, acceptable use policies should address the issues raised above, but from a
different perspective. Collection development policies should, therefore, at
least refer to a library's (or parent institution's) acceptable use policy and,
perhaps, include it in an appendix. Such policies, or their applicable sections,
should be posted in the library, particularly near public accessible networked
computers.

Chapter Thirty

Sample Policies

Two public libraries are included and demonstrate the effectiveness of a simpler statement meant for the general public. The entire statement covering Dartmouth College Library's policy for electronic resources is reproduced here to provide a sense of how such policies should flow from one topic to another. It should also be emphasized that the authors have found that most libraries have separate policies covering electronic media, probably because Internet accessible and other electronic information which is licensed is so fundamentally different from print and audiovisual materials which are purchased and owned. Regardless of whether a library has been licensing electronic databases for a long time, or is just beginning, a collection development policy covering electronic resources should be written and maintained as a framework or guide to librarians, library administration, and users alike. The Dartmouth College Library's policy gives a flavor for just how such a statement was written and will be revised.

COUNTY OF HENRICO PUBLIC LIBRARY: COLLECTION DEVELOPMENT PLAN

Electronic Resources: All criteria relevant to the selection of materials in traditional formats apply to electronic resources as well. However, because machine-readable formats require non-traditional means of acquisition, storage, and access, some additional criteria must be considered:

- Ease of access and number of access points
- Hardware and software requirements; networking capabilities
- Vendor support and maintenance requirements
- Ownership of product and contractual issues

- Staff training and/or client assistance requirements
- Comparison with other formats

COOK MEMORIAL PUBLIC LIBRARY DISTRICT: COLLECTION DEVELOPMENT POLICY

Computer-Based Materials

The Library purchases information products and services which may be loaded into or are accessible through computers. The general selection criteria apply to these products. Additionally, computer-based materials are judged for their compatibility with existing systems, ease of use, information retrieval power, and general usefulness. These factors, as well as cost, frequency of access, and convenience, will influence whether the library buys the product for local installation, buys a share of the product in partnership with other libraries, or pays a vendor for access to the product. The Internet is an important and dynamic information resource. Internet access and use is governed by the most recent revision of the Internet and Computer Use Policy.

DARTMOUTH COLLEGE LIBRARY: COLLECTION DEVELOPMENT POLICY, INFORMATION IN ELECTRONIC FORMAT

Contents

Introduction to the Statement
Dartmouth College Information Environment
Types and Formats of Materials
Cooperative Arrangements
Access Modes
Local Access to Resources
Remote Access to Resources
Selection Criteria
Licensing Agreements
Archival Responsibilities
Task Force Recommendations

Introduction

Information in electronic format is integral to many academic disciplines represented in the Dartmouth College Library collection. However, problems and questions continually arise as we select, acquire, process, and make these resources accessible.

The purpose of this policy is to outline the decision-making process, factors influencing the selection decision, the range of available formats, and access options in Dartmouth's information environment. This policy is a response to the growing need among bibliographers for guidelines to assist them in answering questions raised in selecting, processing, and making accessible information in electronic format.

This is a format-related guide intended as a collection management resource for bibliographers. It describes the subject's scope, Dartmouth's information environment, and the types of electronic information considered. Finally, it presents a detailed outline of considerations in the decision-making process.

The task force's goal was to develop a useful policy for bibliographers. We suggest testing the policy's usefulness by having a bibliographer consult and use it when next considering the purchase of an electronic information resource. Through this, we hope to better understand from a collection management perspective what information is most helpful to bibliographers when selecting information in electronic format.

Dartmouth College Information Environment

The annual publication *Computing and Information Technologies* summarizes the campus information environment. Dartmouth has an impressive history of computing innovations, including the BASIC computer language, and a time-sharing system that served dozens of other educational institutions at its peak. The Kiewit Computation Center, built in 1966, serves as the administrative and support center for computing activities.

In 1984 Dartmouth first recommended the purchase of Macintosh personal computers to incoming students and began the process of wiring all buildings on campus for access to the campus network. This coincided with the Library's Online Catalog being made available experimentally on the network and the development of the Dartmouth Name Directory to facilitate electronic mail.

Today, Dartmouth is primarily an Apple campus. IBM-PCs and UNIX-based workstations are used as well, particularly at the Tuck, Thayer, and Medical schools. Apple computers running DOS and Windows-based applications are available. Undergraduate students are required to purchase Macintosh personal computers.

Users of Dartmouth's computing services can access the Internet, Usenet news groups, discussion groups, the Gopher system, and other resources. Participation in electronic bulletin board services and other online forums is commonplace. Blitzmail, the College's electronic mail service, has revolutionized campus communications.

The Online Catalog is one component of the Dartmouth College Information System (DCIS), under continuous development as a joint project of the Library and Computing Services. The Public File Server is the primary mechanism for shared electronic files, documents, and programs, including KeyServer-controlled (shared) software.

Types and Formats of Materials

The types of electronic information in this policy include: bibliographic, text, numeric, graphic, and multimedia files. The formats include tape-loaded products (for mounting on the campus network), CD-ROM products (networked and stand-alone), and remotely accessible files of many types available via Internet.

The software needed to run an electronic information product is within the scope of this policy. The policy excludes general-purpose applications such as word processing or database management software; it also excludes integrated library systems such as INNOPAC.

Materials selection is an intellectual decision best made by each bibliographer for his/her own particular subject areas. Consultation with colleagues and relevant Library groups may assist the bibliographer in answering the technical questions raised by selecting and acquiring information in electronic format.

Cooperative Arrangements

Electronic information resources are often very expensive. Their acquisition may involve negotiations with publishers or vendors, particularly when networking is involved.

Cooperative development and purchase arrangements negotiated with other institutions stretch our funds and make more services available to the Dartmouth community. At this writing, cooperative projects have been done and are being planned with Middlebury College and Williams College, respectively. The Director of Collection Services helps initiate and manage such arrangements.

Access Modes

For electronic information resources, bibliographers can provide one of two modes of access to the Library's users, local or remote. This section outlines issues and considerations in both cases.

Local Access to Resources

A.1. Access via the Network. This provides the broadest access to our users. When files are mounted using the existing DCIS/DCLOS interface, it also provides a familiar method of searching. This is often the preferred method of access, but licensing fees and mainframe storage costs necessitate a discretionary selection process.

As a general rule, the Library supports network access for materials of utility to the greatest number of Dartmouth users. Interdisciplinary materials of use to a variety of users in diverse locations also receive priority treatment. Those databases which provide enhanced bibliographic access to existing library collections [i.e., Early American Imprints, Marcive, Wilson Indexes] are also appropriate for networking campus-wide.

When bibliographers wish to recommend an electronic resource be networked on DCLOS, they should discuss the feasibility of mounting the resource with the Director of Library Automation. If it is more appropriate to DCIS because of the need to use PAT or another search and retrieval software, they should discuss the proposal with the DCIS Project Director. Cost estimates for both the staff resources to mount the files and the disk space to store them should be assessed. If funding is available to support the acquisition, and the material can be networked within the Dartmouth environment, a proposal detailing costs and benefits should be submitted to the CMDC sub-committee which we propose in this document.

A.2. Access via the Fileserver. The Dartmouth Fileserver predates the existence of Gopher and other World Wide Web servers widely available today on the Internet. Computing Services have set up a Gopher and a Mosaic Home Page at Dartmouth, and the Library has experimented with their utility as document storage mechanisms and as links to other resources. For the present, resources that are useful to have on the network, but are kept as documents and are not indexed/searchable files, may be stored on the Public Fileserver/Library folder. Materials archived in this manner should be represented in the Online Catalog, with the necessary location to link the user to the resource.

B. Access via Networked CD-ROM. Resources that are of interest to a more limited clientele, or to a group of users primarily served by an individual library within the Dartmouth College Library, should be considered in a CD-ROM format. If access via one workstation is not sufficient to meet demand, or if providing ease of access to clientele linked by an existing local network is an important factor, the bibliographer should consider purchasing a license agreement to network the CD-ROM product.

C. Access via Stand-Alone Workstation. Electronic products of interest to a limited number of users, or those difficult to network due to the size of the data, restrictive licensing agreements, specialized software needed for operation, prohibitive cost, etc., should be considered for purchase in a stand-alone workstation environment.

Remote Access to Resources

Bibliographers may also provide access to and inform users about electronic information resources located outside Dartmouth. Those resources include: catalogs; bibliographic, text, numeric, sound, image, and data files; software; discussion lists, etc.

External data sources available via Telnet, Gopher, and Mosaic are selected based upon expected utility and ease of access. Proven stability of the resource, and the host institution's intention to maintain an archive, are important factors for a bibliographer to consider when deciding to provide remote access. In general, if a desired resource is maintained and made accessible at a remote host site, it is preferable to provide a pointer to it within the Dartmouth College Information System rather than store archival files on-site.

In general, the provision of full bibliographic control via the Library's Online Catalog is limited to materials that are owned and stored locally (including on the Library Fileserver). Resources that are pointed to will generally not be cataloged, unless the connection requires expenditure of materials funds.

A number of factors influence how access to external information is provided:

- means of access: Telnet, FTP, Gopher, Mosaic, Netscape, WAIS
- hardware and software requirements to get and receive files
- file characteristics: size, type (image, text, sound, data, etc.), database search capabilities, type of indexes
- expected frequency of potential use: may help bibliographers decide if the resource should be made available in the Navigator (implies frequent use) or in the Gopher (less-than-regular use)
- options for saving text, viewing, or browsing

Bibliographers should refer identified external resources available through the Internet to the Internet Resources Subcommittee of LOSC. Subscription materials available over the Internet should be processed through normal acquisitions channels.

Selection Criteria

Making the Decision to Acquire Information in Electronic Format

Selecting an electronic information resource is similar to selecting other formats for the Library's collection. Bibliographers base selection decisions, regardless of format, on relevance to Dartmouth programs, the curriculum, and faculty and student research.

Cost is always a consideration because bibliographers must fund purchases from their respective materials budget, and they must continually balance the cost of information against importance and relevance to the collection.

Several bibliographers may share the cost of a purchase when they conclude a resource is relevant yet too expensive for one bibliographer's budget. Electronic information sources are often more expensive than print and may be appropriate candidates for central funding or split funding.

Points to Consider Before Purchase

- If there is a choice of formats, consider the advantages and disadvantages to be sure the electronic form is the most useful. Frequency of updates, inclusion of additional information, ability to manipulate data, and the ability to network all add value to the product.
- Consider only fully documented products with well-known system requirements. Helpful sources in this regard: comments from relevant Listservs, vendor presence in the Library community, vendor's reputation, other products owned by the Library from the same publisher or vendor.
- Consider whether the Library has the necessary staff resources and expertise to support the hardware and software, including installation, maintenance, troubleshooting, etc.
- From a user services perspective, consider the staff time that may be needed to prepare user guides and to teach faculty and students how to use the product.
- Specify the type of hardware (Mac, IBM or compatible) and hard disk and RAM capacity required.
- Note any video or audio requirements.
- Based on any knowledge of the product gained from the literature, product reviews, conferences etc., evaluate the user interface, any additional product features (downloading, for example) and users' familiarity with the software.
- Investigate potential for saving and manipulating search results (i.e., printing, saving to a disk, to a hard disk, e-mail, or FTP). Also, can the results be imported into a word processing program?
- Check possible exposure to computer viruses resulting from a choice of media and access.
- Look at ways to access archival issues.
- Investigate ways to assure compliance (is monitoring software provided?) with license agreement or copyright requirements.

- Consider the level of access most appropriate for the product (should it be on the campus network? on a LAN? etc.) and consult appropriate people or groups.
- In the case of compact disk databases, consider possible obstacles or constrictions: network speed, CD reader speed, printing bottlenecks.
- Note stability and adequacy of hardware; for example, high-capacity disk drives will be needed to read high-density disks.
- Decide on a location and necessary furniture for optimum access and use; investigate ergonomic considerations in setting up the workspaces.
- If an electronic acquisition duplicates a print product currently received, consider whether the print subscription can be cancelled.
- If the product exists in electronic form in the library system, consider whether it could be networked instead of duplicated.

The Product

- Are product reviews available?
- Do relevant Listservs exist to query colleagues?
- Is the product user-friendly?
- Can product quality and database content be easily appraised? (can one request a demo?)
- What workspaces are necessary and appropriate?
- What is the currency of content and frequency of updating?
- Could information be supplied by other vendors? If so, what are the advantages and disadvantages of each, including cost?

The Vendor

- What is the reputation of the vendor?
- Do we have other products from the vendor and if so, what are bibliographers' impressions?
- Are terms and conditions of contracts and access arrangements negotiable enough to meet Dartmouth's needs?
- Is customer service and support available?

Necessary Equipment

- What equipment—hardware, printer(s), specialized accessories such as a math co-processor—is needed to run the product?
- Is existing hardware adequate or will new purchase(s) be necessary?
- What software is needed?
- What technical expertise and support is available?
- Is new furniture needed to adequately house the product?

Service after the Sale

- Is equipment maintenance/support/service available?
- Is vendor support available after the sale?
- What is known about hardware reliability?
- Is documentation included and is it adequate?

The Bibliographer's Communication and Decision-Making Environment

- Bibliographer and colleagues with whom he/she consults
- Bibliographer's means of learning about electronic resources: Listservs, newsgroups, product reviews, colleagues, faculty and student recommendations
- Library committees and departments: library groups (LOSC, Internet Resources Subcommittee, Automation), computing services (IBM Specialists, Academic Computing Coordinators), college attorneys

Budget

As noted previously, bibliographers fund purchases for the collection from their respective budgets. As the cost of electronic information may exceed the ability of one bibliographer to fund it, several bibliographers may collaborate on a purchase. In addition, the Director of Collection Services may be consulted to explore other funding possibilities. In the case of bibliographers working in a library associated with the professional schools, operating with acquisitions budgets separate from Arts and Sciences, these decisions rest with the Department Head, who may in turn consult with the Director of Collection Services.

Information Format and Type

1. CD-ROM Databases
   a. hardware and software requirements
   b. stand-alone systems
   c. networked for one location
   d. networked across zones
   e. terms and conditions of use, including licensing and contracts
2. Magnetic Tape Databases
   a. hardware and software requirements
   b. constituencies served
   c. terms and conditions of use, including licensing and contracts
3. Remotely Accessible Files: files are accessible using various tools, including FTP, Gopher, Mosaic, text, images, and data—software and hardware requirements at the requestor's workstation

4. Types of Information Content: bibliographic, text, numeric, graphic, and multimedia
5. Augmented Collection Services: tables of contents providers and/or document delivery services

Information Access

1. Local Access
   a. Fileserver Resources
   b. Dartmouth Gopher
   c. DCLOS, DCIS
2. Remote Access
   a. Internet-accessible resources such as newsgroups
   b. Commercial online services: pricing options (discounted for educational use, fixed-price, off-peak pricing)
   c. Access tools: FTP, Mosaic, Gopher, WAIS, WWW, Veronica, etc.
   d. Hardware and software requirements to gather and receive data

Licensing Agreements

Note: The following is derived from University of Southern California Library. Draft Collection Policy Statement #2 for Information in Electronic Formats.

1. In general, it is the responsibility of the College Librarian or her/his designee to negotiate and sign licensing agreements. In the instance of simple CD-ROM agreements this responsibility may be delegated to the Unit Head in the holding library.
2. The Director of Collection Services will maintain a file containing copies of all licensing agreements and database contracts, regardless of the original Library signatory.
3. The library unit which houses or provides access to an electronic resource is responsible for the day-to-day oversight of licensing requirements.
4. Final responsibility for compliance with licensing agreements rests with the College Librarian or her/his designee in consultation with appropriate College offices, as appropriate.

Archival Responsibilities

The Library's responsibility to preserve electronic information is equal to its responsibilities for collections of printed materials and other formats. Priority should be given to locally produced and unique resources that are irreplaceable via standard commercial means. Attention should be given to electronic information in the development of a preservation plan for the Library.

Task Force Recommendations

Recommendation 1: Because of the rapidly changing nature of electronic information relevant to the Library, this policy should be reviewed at least every two years.

Recommendation 2: We recommend that CMDC form a permanent electronic information resources sub-committee to develop a priority list of electronic resources that bibliographers want to acquire for the collection or make accessible to the Dartmouth community. The sub-committee should serve as a resource for bibliographers in answering the questions raised when electronic resources are considered for acquisition.

Recommendation 3: In light of this new collection policy statement, review the document "Bibliographic Control of Computer Files" [Appendix to the Bibliographers' Manual, Ch. IV]. Since that document covers materials processing and handling aspects of access, it should be a companion piece to this policy.

Recommendation 4: Working with bibliographers, Library Systems should provide the support necessary to mount stand-alone datafiles and CD-ROM databases. Library Systems could also be a resource for bibliographers and help them answer questions such as what hardware and software are appropriate for different products, and how networking can best be accomplished.

Chapter Thirty-One

Resource Sharing in the Digital Age
An Integrative Perspective

Libraries of all types and sizes have been sharing resources and otherwise co-operating with other libraries for decades for purposes of collection management. Libraries can overcome the political, social, economic, religious, and other barriers that governmental or other agencies often cannot or are not willing to overcome. Academic administrators often extol the benefits of library cooperation that the faculty, staff, and students of their institutions receive as a result of library cooperative agreements. Such agreements among libraries may be easier to obtain because government officials, library boards, school boards, and the chief academic officers of our universities and colleges generally accept the principle that information and literature should be disseminated and shared freely among the citizens of a democratic country, as well as the advantages of library resource sharing such as:

- No library can acquire every resource needed by its clientele,
- Resource sharing increases the diversity and number of unique items available to members of the cooperative, and
- Resource sharing is often more cost effective than acquiring, licensing, or digitizing the same item.

Despite these practical advantages of resource sharing, it does require a certain level of altruism because some members benefit more than others by interlibrary loan and cooperative collection development agreements. Some libraries need inducements or subsidies to participate. The collection development policies of libraries that have signed resource sharing or cooperative collection development agreements often address the reasons for them, as well as anticipated benefits to remind constituents why they entered into these agreements.

This chapter will deal with several complementary or related library resource sharing and cooperative programs that may be addressed in collection management polices today such as:

- interlibrary loan and document delivery
- reciprocal borrowing
- cooperative collection development
- the Conspectus
- cooperative storage
- publisher or other partnerships

We shall see that one type of program often encourages or expands into another type.

INTERLIBRARY LOAN AND DOCUMENT DELIVERY

Both interlibrary loan and document delivery programs were initiated and developed by most, if not all, individual libraries to increase access to books, journal literature, and other materials that could not be acquired due to limited financial resources. Access to, rather than ownership of, information and the world's literature is now the primary goal of most libraries, even the largest research libraries. They often have collections so scattered among departmental libraries and storage facilities, for instance, that their users must rely upon a delivery system and wait for one or more days until they obtain the item at the location of their preference. By the close of the twentieth century, the demand for costly electronic access to the journal literature, rather than subscription to or ownership of it, became the primary goal of most libraries, even the largest research libraries. Few, if any, libraries in the last decades of the twentieth century were able to avoid budget cuts and high inflation that resulted in serial cancellations. The licensing of journal article databases by libraries, however, often came at the expense of the library's monographic purchases.

Over the past few decades, interlibrary loan (ILL), or the loaning of resources held by one library to another, also became an expanding and growing service offered by most public, academic, and other libraries. Conventional ILL models based on mailing books, articles, and other materials between the borrowing and lending libraries has been giving way to a new model based in electronic technologies such as scanning and digital transmission. The number of conventional ILL transactions in more and more libraries is slowly declining as a result.

More dramatically, however, the rapid deployment since the 1990s of digitized, web accessible full-text journal articles and documents have emerged. Publishers and organizations such as the Canadian Association for Research Libraries (CARL), the Canadian Institute for Scientific and Technical Information (CISTI), and the British Library Document Supply Center that offer these document delivery services to libraries have had a significant impact on ILL and cooperative collection development programs. Moreover, the federal government and many state and municipal governments make documents available on their websites. As access to the journal literature and government publications has increased, it seems that the interest in cooperative collection development has decreased, or at least been deemphasized in favor of making digitized collections at the local level available on the World Wide Web through the Internet. While the authors applaud all efforts to digitize otherwise relatively unknown and unavailable manuscripts, archives, photographic collections, and the like, we must call attention to the need for both cooperative collection development and digitization programs. If anything, that need is stronger than ever because more books and journals are being published than ever before.

ILL and document delivery programs should complement good collection development programs. For cooperative collection development, or the Conspectus as discussed below, to be successful, the cooperating libraries must have a reliable and acceptable document delivery program in place. If such a cooperative delivery program is not fast enough to meet the needs of most users, document delivery will not be highly valued by users. A library's collection development policy should reflect when, how, and why document delivery and interlibrary loan programs are beneficial to users.

Even the largest research libraries long ago recognized that they could not acquire and store every item that a user might want someday. While limited or reduced library budgets might reinforce cooperative collection development and resource sharing efforts, they also might encourage the success or attractiveness of document delivery services. Such programs are oftentimes developed, however, at the expense of library materials budgets. Ultimately, recognition of this risk should result in libraries acquiring, digitizing, and sharing more, not fewer, unique materials. Libraries of all types and sizes, therefore, can play a part in making unique material available. Collection development policies should recognize and address this responsibility.

The following sample policy is provided as one example of a good policy that the authors believe establishes the relationship between ILL and collection development.

KITSAP (WASHINGTON) REGIONAL LIBRARY: COLLECTION DEVELOPMENT POLICY

Kitsap Regional Library views interlibrary loan as an adjunct to good collection development at the local level. It is a courtesy to be exercised responsibly to provide access to those materials that the Library does not, cannot, or will not add to its collection. Such materials include those that are:

a. out of print or very expensive
b. specialized and/or unlikely to be of general community interest
c. outside the scope of the Library's Collection Development Policy or guidelines for collection development
d. not available at nearby institutions, through purchase, or by other means in a manner or time satisfactory to the requester.

Interlibrary loan is available to any Kitsap Regional Library customer. The Library does, however, urge students enrolled in formal academic programs to go through the sponsoring institution to obtain materials connected with courses. It is the responsibility of the academic institution to provide curricular support for its students.

Comment

Presumably, due to cost, the types of materials identified above (sections a–d above) are not candidates for purchase by most public libraries even from the out-of-print book trade. Academic libraries are more likely to use antiquarian book dealers to locate out of print and very expensive materials, particularly if they will support the curriculum or research needs of the faculty.

Libraries are generally not permitted by the Interlibrary Loan Code to make certain types of materials available through interlibrary loan. Kitsap Regional Library's Collection Development Policy explicitly states which types are excluded:

a. whole issues of magazines or newspapers,
b. video and audio,
c. reference works or works in special collections,
d. books published in the last two years,
e. items that are in high demand in general or at the lending library.

Another section of the Kitsap Regional Library's policy, however, states the importance of acquiring materials that meet the needs of its users and the goal of its collection development program as follows:

> Kitsap Regional Library makes every effort to satisfy the needs of its customers through the Library's own collection or through other local resources. All requests for materials not in the Library's collection are considered for purchase first and will be purchased rather than borrowed whenever possible. The Library is committed to building a collection of resources that responds to and is capable of filling most of its customers' needs. The courtesy of resource sharing is called upon only when the Library cannot satisfy the request with its resources. The decision to purchase or borrow an item is made by the Collection Manager and delegated staff.

RECIPROCAL BORROWING

In addition to interlibrary loan, libraries can complement their own collections by making reciprocal borrowing arrangements with other libraries so that users of one library have physical access to libraries in the same community or region. While few collection development policies that we examined deal with reciprocal borrowing, the authors believe it is sometimes an outgrowth or unintended consequence of interlibrary loan, cooperative collection development, and union listing agreements. It might also occur when users of two or more libraries have easy access to the library holdings of each library, or use the same vendor's automated system. Easy access to the online catalogs of nearby libraries through the Internet encourages reciprocal borrowing, as well as proper bibliographic control of materials held by cooperating libraries. For example, Endeavor has a Universal Borrowing module that should encourage reciprocal borrowing efforts of libraries.

Geographic proximity, however, has been the most common facilitator of reciprocal borrowing. Once two libraries within a comfortable geographic range of each other see the benefits of allowing users to have access to each other's resources, attention is likely to turn to reciprocal borrowing, particularly if the libraries share the same automated system. Students and faculty who learn that the library resources they want are readily available in a nearby library are not normally bashful in requesting borrowing privileges. Also, federal and state granting sources often encourage reciprocal borrowing and other resource sharing programs.

In any geographic location, particularly large metropolitan areas, where a number of libraries in close proximity to each other agree to allow their users to use and borrow each other's circulating collections, reciprocal borrowing agreements may make economic sense.

COOPERATIVE COLLECTION DEVELOPMENT

Cooperative collection development involves the selection of materials by two or more libraries for the purpose of increasing the resources available to their users. In its broadest definition, it might also involve cooperation in licensing databases and digitizing collections.

The purpose of most cooperative development and resource sharing agreements remains to increase access to unique materials and information for the library's users. Cooperative collection development efforts of each library increase access to materials not owned by any one member. These efforts often focus on the following:

- Expensive materials
- Primary subject responsibilities or mission of each library
- Grade or age level of the library's primary user group

Schools, institutions of higher education, special libraries, and public libraries in the same geographic community or region may find it easy to establish and develop cooperative collection development agreements because their missions, primary user groups, and subject responsibilities are obvious and often unique.

Every library, on the other hand, should assure their users that every attempt will be made to acquire materials in high demand. Also, collection development policies should stress that cooperative efforts are not meant to reduce expenditures of library materials, but rather expand the resources available to users.

Because libraries of all types might own such materials, the authors have deliberately avoided reference to only one type of library. It might be particularly advantageous, for example, for public or academic libraries to cooperate with special and school libraries even though large multi-type agreements are not as common as agreements among like libraries.

Discussion here will be limited to cooperative collection development and how a library's collection development policy might address it. Further, passive strategies are not covered here. In the absence of formal agreements, individual selectors in a library make collection development decisions based on their knowledge of other libraries' policies or acquisition commitments. Making such selection decisions is legitimate, of course, but should be mentioned in the selection section of the policy because this practice falls short of being actively cooperative.

The library's collection development policy itself should at least summarize any cooperative collection development agreement that it has with other libraries, a library consortium, or a group of libraries. Unless there is an overriding reason not to do so, any written agreement should be included in the text of the policy (if it is brief), or in an appendix (if it is lengthy). The text of the policy itself should inform the reader of the essential aspects of the agreement such as:

- the name(s) of the cooperating libraries, library consortium, or group of institutions
- when the agreement was made
- the purpose and objective(s) of the agreement
- topics, subjects, formats, geographic areas it covers
- governance and other terms of the agreement

It is important for the cooperating library's collection development policy to address cooperation because the advantages it offers might not be readily apparent to users and those to whom the library administrator reports. While ownership (acquisition) is rapidly giving way to electronic access, many administrators or board members will remain apprehensive about cooperating to acquire traditional library materials and to sign consortial database licenses. Whenever city, county, state, and private entities cooperate, politics can always be an impediment to cooperation.

Collection development policies should make it clear that cooperative collection development agreements mean that the local library does not purchase or license certain types of materials or databases, but instead relies upon one or more other libraries to purchase or license the material or databases. For example, a public library may not acquire school or college level textbooks and specialized subject material that support the curriculum of the schools and colleges in the library's service area. Conversely, an academic library's collection development policy might state that it does not acquire general fiction, local history, and specialized genealogy sources because the local public library does so. This may be the case whether there is an agreement in place or not.

Passive cooperative collection building occurs when there are no formal agreements that acknowledge such selection criteria. When such criteria do apply, it is advisable to make mention of them in the library's selection criteria section of its collection development policy. The purpose here is not to elaborate on passive cooperation, but rather on active cooperative collection development as determined by formal agreements. Suffice it to say, that if there is a desire to establish a cooperative agreement among public, academic, or school libraries in a city or county, exploring such obvious or common criteria can be a logical first step in establishing a meaningful agreement.

Many academic, public, and other libraries across the United States and other countries cooperate with other libraries of all types not only in terms of interlibrary loan, but also in cooperative collective development agreements. Most public and academic library materials budgets over the past two or more decades have not kept pace with inflation, and libraries have faced growing demand for new formats, particularly electronic. As a result, most public and academic libraries have cooperative arrangements of some type with other libraries. Acquiring expensive items, particularly among libraries in a geographic area, is often a common reason for cooperating. Many libraries use the Conspectus, discussed later in this chapter, as a framework for cooperative collection development efforts. The Conspectus offers a way to assign primary subject collecting responsibility among cooperating libraries.

Major publishers such as Elsevier and Wiley since the late 1990s have given libraries an impetus to cooperate in terms of electronic licenses. Elsevier, for example, has been marketing its Science Direct product since about 1998 to library consortia and groups of libraries in a state or region. Elsevier's Science Direct license encourages libraries to sign multi-library agreements by allowing all cooperating library members to have web access to the articles in Elsevier titles held by all other members for a percentage charge above and beyond each library's print subscriptions to Elsevier titles. For a greater premium, members can have access to all the articles available through its Science Direct product, which in 2001 included over 1,100 journals.

These types of license agreements allow even the smallest members of a library consortium to have the same access to these publishers' journals as the largest university libraries. Local print collections of even the largest research level libraries, thus, are losing their supremacy in an increasingly global and digital environment. While this "homogenization" of libraries might seem to work against cooperation, libraries that have not cooperated with others in terms of print resources are now finding it very profitable to cooperate with libraries across a state or region in order to reduce the costs of such licenses, as well as to increase the web access to the journal literature they can offer their users. Access through the Internet from the local library is, therefore, becoming the focus of cooperative collection development and also spelling changes in bibliographic control. Libraries want their users to know they have access to the articles available through aggregators such as EBSCO, Elsevier, Wiley, etc., so collection development policies might include the library's policy with respect to bibliographic control over the respective web accessible titles.

Dartmouth College Library policy says: "Cooperative development and purchase arrangements negotiated with other institutions stretch our funds and make more services available to the Dartmouth community. At this writing, cooperative projects have been done and are being planned with Middlebury College and Williams College, respectively. The Director of Collection Services helps initiate and manage such arrangements."

Critics of cooperative collection development contend that when a library lacks financial resources to acquire the materials needed to develop the local collection, cooperative efforts that assign primary collecting responsibilities, for example, are doomed to be disappointing, if not fail. Naysayers argue that there is little reason for libraries to cooperate in subject areas of low interest and that in subject areas of high interest or need at the local level, users will expect such materials to be on the shelf. It makes little sense to be a primary collector in an area of low interest and low need. Nevertheless, when libraries can cooperate by assigning primary collecting responsibilities, we suggest that readers review the chapter on Resource Sharing in Part 1, as this concept is discussed there, and also in the section in this chapter about the Conspectus. Bibliographers who work in individual academic libraries, for example, often make basic assumptions about what subjects are emphasized in selection by bibliographers in other academic libraries in the consortium. Bibliographers in an essentially undergraduate level institution of higher education will assume that bibliographers in a nearby university library, for instance, will acquire research level materials for subjects when the institution offers a doctoral degree program. Such an assumption is likely to result in those bibliographers minimizing acquisitions in the areas they believe a cooperating library should have subject collection strengths. Using a device, such as the Conspectus, to test such assumptions and to formally determine the primary collecting responsibilities of each member library will give selectors the guidance that is needed both in hard and ample financial times.

SAMPLE POLICIES FOR RESOURCE SHARING

The two sample policies—one public and one national library—provide readers with the rationale and the language that might be adapted for any library with a mission of sharing or providing access to their collections, particularly outside of its broader geographic setting. Although few libraries are national libraries, the National Library of Canada example provides the language that may be adapted by state, county, or large urban libraries, as well as the smaller libraries that digitize materials that have national heritage interest.

Kitsap (Washington) Regional Library: Resource Sharing Policy

Kitsap Regional Library recognizes that it cannot provide everything that its customers request within its own collection of resources. Therefore, the Library is committed to the cooperation and sharing of resources among libraries and other agencies that acquire, house, and make information and materials accessible. The Library supports:

- cooperative use agreements which cross library district and agency lines, thus allowing users access to the broadest array of resources and information;
- cooperative collection development among agencies as a means to avoid unnecessary duplication and provide the most access to the most people;
- interlibrary loan as a means of providing access to specialized, out-of-print, and other materials the Library does not acquire.

National Library of Canada: Collection Management Policy

Resource Sharing

Both Canadiana (service collection) and non-Canadiana acquired to support heritage and library development are available for resource-sharing purposes. In addition, the Library role in resource sharing is supported by the following collection.

National Resource Collections

Within Canada, the national collection available for resource sharing is the sum of many parts—the collections of individual libraries. Within these collections there are national or regional resource strengths, which other libraries have come to rely on. Although developed primarily in support of the heritage role, the National Library collection areas are seen as national resources and will continue to be developed in response to resource sharing needs, both for reference and lending.

THE CONSPECTUS

The Conspectus is a collection assessment tool or framework used by individual and cooperating libraries as a basis for collection assessment and development. This tool is discussed here because Conspectus methodologies will allow selectors to systematically map the strengths and weaknesses of their respective collections at narrow subject or topical levels and to communicate with each other much like photographs or snapshots. The Conspectus allows the selectors to continue to acquire the material that is most critical at the local level, but strengthen the collections that are collectively available to all members.

As a cooperative collection assessment and development tool developed initially by members of the Research Libraries Group (RLG) when they realized none of them alone had the financial means to acquire all the materials their constituents needed, the RLG Conspectus became an effective way for RLG institutions to assign primary collecting responsibilities to each member. The RLG Conspectus became a valuable tool both in the United States and many other countries because it provided a useful and easily understood structure and nomenclature for cooperative collection assessment and development.

It is important to realize that the RLG Conspectus developed beyond research level libraries because smaller academic, public, and other types of libraries needed a nomenclature and structures for collection assessment and development that could be adapted for their own individual and collective use. Throughout the 1980s and 1990s, non-research level libraries adapted the RLG Conspectus. This development was particularly evident among libraries in the Pacific Northwest where the Library and Information Resources for the Northwest (LIRN) modified the RLG Conspectus and in 1984 gained copyright of the Conspectus structure. The Washington Libraries Network (WLN), a non-profit bibliographic utility, became the copyright owner of the Conspectus in 1990. WLN by default gained total management of the Conspectus by RLG's decision in 1997 to no longer support the RLG Conspectus due to lack of interest and support by members.

Long before then, however, the member libraries of LIRM and WLN had modified the RLG Conspectus coding structure in such a way that differentiations could be made among collections serving undergraduate and graduate programs, or those serving a very basic or introductory information need such as the need for students writing compositions. Once adapted in this way, public library selectors found the new Conspectus methodologies and structure useful for their own libraries, as well as for the collective purposes of the group of libraries to which they belonged. WLN developed and sold manuals and other products or services to libraries throughout the world. Some librarians might contend, therefore, that the Conspectus is a communication tool for several reasons:

- It allows librarians in a given library or consortium using it to understand the collection as a whole.
- It conveys the anticipated strengths and weaknesses of library collections.
- The fertile literature about the Conspectus and its common nomenclature allow new librarians to learn it quickly and experienced selectors to train new selectors to use it profitably.
- The literature on the Conspectus also allows for easy communication with the library's primary users and gains their participation when needed.

- All of its advantages make it easier for library administration to communicate the need for additional financial resources to those making such decisions.
- Conspectus results should be communicated in a published or web accessible report that consists of the following:
    - A description of the subject or topics being assessed and appropriate mission and goal statements. In academic libraries, this focuses on the curriculum and the goals of the academic departments.
    - Conspectus results and analysis. This will include the bibliographies and catalogs checked against holdings and results, as well as results of other methodologies.
    - Recommendations and conclusions. This always entails a discussion of collection strengths, weaknesses, and gaps. Recommendations should suggest appropriate priorities and strategies for filling gaps in the collection, or otherwise providing access to the subject literature.
    - Appendixes: worksheets, statistics, relevant courses offered, relevant collection development policies, and the like.

The Conspectus is based on the assumption that to improve collection development within a library, library system, or group of libraries, it is necessary to assess each library's collection strengths, weaknesses, desired collecting level or goals, and acquisition commitment. When subject bibliographers in each library know explicitly what subjects or topics (by call number ranges) are the primary collecting responsibilities of their own library and other member libraries, there is a comprehensive framework to assign responsibilities. These responsibilities should then be implemented through the allocation structure of the materials budget. In most academic libraries, as an example, all of the academic departments are allocated a percentage of the total materials budget for monographic purchases, and within that budget, each college or each academic department and program is in turn allocated a portion. In most public libraries, the total materials budget is allocated in such a way that the main library, branch libraries, fiction, non-fiction, children's literature, young adult literature, and other specialized user needs are met. Budget allocations are designed, therefore, to match user needs with available financial resources. The library's policy statement needs to define the allocation structure.

SAMPLE POLICIES FOR THE CONSPECTUS

A library's policy statement might briefly describe what the Conspectus is and why it is used as did a New Zealand public library (Canterbury Public Library) policy below. Throughout the Fairbanks North Star Borough Library's policy, another nearby university library (Rasmuson, University of Alaska/Fairbanks) and the interdependence they have on each other is mentioned. Members of this consortium have been using the WLN Conspectus for many years and are leaders in cooperative collection development in the United States.

Canterbury (New Zealand) Public Library: Collection Development Policy

Conspectus is an internationally recognized aid to collection management which is used by New Zealand libraries to measure and evaluate the quality and effectiveness of libraries' collections. This process pulls together data that quantifies stock numbers. It takes a snapshot of the collection at a particular time, measuring its age and quality. This provides a collection level to be measured against a collection goal. Conspectus measures are:

- collection level—what the collection is like now
- acquisitions commitment—at what level we are currently buying
- collection goal—what level we want the collection to be
- preservation commitment
- median age of the collection
- size of the collection
- quality of collection (number of standard titles held)

Fairbanks (Alaska) North Star Borough Public Library

The Fairbanks Public Library employs the Conspectus methodology of evaluating and assigning support levels to subject areas of the collection. This method employs established criteria for assessing subject areas within the collections. The Collection Level Indicators (Appendix H) assigned for the categories in the 24 WLN Conspectus Database divisions (Appendix I) describe the quality and depth of the collection that is available.

The Fairbanks Public Library supports cooperative collection development between libraries and has established agreements with other libraries in the state and locally. In recognition of these agreements, the library has identified and prioritized subject areas for which it will attempt to provide in-depth collections and has likewise identified subject areas for which it will rely on other cooperating libraries to provide in-depth collections. Also, in view of the resources available at the Rasmuson Library, no subject areas will be developed beyond an advanced study level (Appendix H). The library considers such factors as user surveys, community demographic studies, staff consensus, and the collection assessment, as well as the designated mission and roles, when determining these priority subject areas.

SUMMARY OF THE CONSPECTUS

The Conspectus, as a snapshot of each library's collection, summarizes the strengths of the collection and the acquisitions commitment of the library against its desired collecting intensity or goal. Whether or not it is used by an individual library or a group of libraries, each library's collection development policy should summarize the Conspectus methodologies, definitions, and terms it follows, or which are agreed to by participating institutions. Whether or not it is used for cooperative collection development, however, the assessment methodologies prescribed by the Conspectus are the same and may include any of the following:

- "Shelflist counts" or online system reports of the number of materials in the collection pertaining to the subject or topic being assessed to determine "existing collection strength." In many libraries, this analysis should include government documents, audiovisual materials, and special collections, including rare books, archives, and micromedia.
- Examination of materials on the shelves for condition, use, etc.
- Checking bibliographies, publisher catalogs, subject lists, etc., for titles held by LC or Dewey classification
- Comparing holdings and size of the local library against WorldCat, peer institutions, or collections recognized for the subject strength being assessed
- Comparing local acquisitions in the subject classification against publishers' output
- Assessing acquisition, circulation, and interlibrary loan records in the subject classification being assessed
- Age of the collection in the classification assessed
- The number of classics, notable authors, series in the subject collection being assessed
- Proceedings, foreign language materials, federal or state documents, or specialized materials held that indicate strength in the subject classification being assessed
- Preservation efforts and commitment in the subject classification being assessed

The WLN Conspectus uses the following collection codes:

- CL Current Collection (the existing collection strength)
- AC Acquisition Commitment (the amount of expenditures for material on the subject or topic
- GL Collection Goal (relative to the curriculum, user community needs, demand)
- PC Preservation Commitment

Each Collection Code employs the following indicators to describe the level at which the library attempts to build the particular subject collection:

- 0—Out of Scope
- 1—<u>Minimal Information Level</u>
- 1a—Minimal Information Level, uneven coverage (optional)
- 1b—Minimal Information Level, focused coverage (optional)
- 2—<u>Basic Information Level</u>
- 2a—Basic Information Level – Introductory (optional)
- 2b—Basic Information Level – Advanced (Optional)
- 3—<u>Study or Instructional Support Level</u>
- 3a—Basic Study
- 3b—Intermediate Study
- 3c—Advanced Study
- 4—<u>Research Level</u>
- 5—<u>Comprehensive Level</u>

The definitions of these levels are quite lengthy and can be located in the WLN Conspectus manual which can be purchased through its website. Most small to medium-sized public and academic libraries will not collect at the 4 and 5 levels because they do not seek to acquire all major published source materials, including the most specialized materials in all formats and foreign languages, required for a doctoral program. Libraries that desire resources adequate for graduate level work, but not a doctorate, or to support a specialized need in the community might acquire at 3c level if the goal is to build an extensive collection of general and specialized monographs, reference works, electronic resources, and journals, including both well-known and lesser-known authors, but not excluding selective foreign language materials. As the collection level goes up, so would the dollar expenditures for acquisitions. That is, a library at the 5 level might buy over 90% of the titles published, regardless of language, and attempt to preserve them permanently. The percentage of acquisitions would be far less at the 3c level because foreign language materials, manuscripts, and the like would be purchased selectively based on the curriculum, user needs, etc. User needs would not be relevant for a 5 level collection because the goal is to be exhaustive.

   The vast majority of academic and public libraries will build their subject collections at the 1, 1a, 1b, 2, 2a, 2b, 3, 3a, and 3b levels. The fact is that most libraries' budgets, due to inflation of serial prices, make fewer dollars available per subject and are far more selective. The percentage of publishers' output acquired would be very low for the 1 a-b level collectors (perhaps in the 10–15% range of English language materials) to as much as 60% in the 3b range, excluding foreign language publications. Libraries collecting at the 3b level, for instance, would attempt to acquire all general reference, all general periodicals, many specialized periodicals and journal indexes, all well-known authors, and all core works in English, plus a representative collection of specialized materials in all formats, to meet the needs of an upper division undergraduate student. This distinguishes a library collecting at the 3b level from the 3c level, which is intended to meet students' needs for research in master's degree programs. Thus, a university library that is expected to support a particular graduate (Master's) program, but has been very selectively acquiring only a small percentage of the English language reference and general books, journal titles, etc., would most likely report a Current Collection and Acquisition Commitment at the 3b or lower level and, therefore, say that it is not meeting its Collection Goal.

Thus, the Conspectus is not a single tool, but consists of an array of tools and is, in itself, just one aspect of a library's collection management program. Whether they do so individually or collectively, bibliographers should decide which of these methodologies to use based on the subject or topic, their experience and familiarity with the collection, and the library's collection management goals.

WLN Conspectus software allows these measures to be recorded and collection use data to be measured against the Conspectus data. Libraries may develop their own online database for recording Conspectus data. Bibliographers should make a folder for each subject or topic being assessed and place notes in it of the methodologies used for each subject or topic. This record will expedite the process when reassessing the collection. In academic libraries, the record should include notes about the curriculum, perhaps course syllabi, and college catalog course descriptions. Then, when new course or program proposals are being discussed, the folder is a convenient place to keep such information. The library's policy statement should address such record keeping as well.

In a consortium, it is a good idea for the collection assessors to examine each others' collections at least once before finalizing and publishing the results. This makes the Conspectus an effective tool for cooperating libraries to know the subject strengths and weaknesses of each library collection, library collection goals, and library acquisition commitments before assigning each library its primary collecting responsibility. Formal agreements can then prescribe duties or expectations of members relative to collection development policy. Such a process itself is of value because the cooperating librarians more fully analyze the collections, come to a consensus quicker, and do not jump to conclusions as readily. Policy statements should recap the advantages or value of collective assessments; however, the authors were not able to locate any policy statements that did so.

What many critics of the Conspectus might not understand is that libraries may select which of these methodologies will be used. Also, there are short-cuts such as random sampling that may be used to make methodologies such as bibliography checking and peer library comparisons less labor intensive. When a library adopts the Conspectus for collection development and assess-ment, its collection development policy should state that such flexibility is encouraged.

Finally, the importance of the Conspectus for the deselection and preser-vation of materials should not be ignored. The library's collection develop-ment policy should always address deselection or weeding procedures and policies that are expected to be followed. How the Conspectus is used when weeding should also be included in the same section. When a library has been assigned a primary collector status as part of a consortial agreement, the pol-icy should state how this affects deselection. Normally, primary collectors do not deselect unique copies unless there is no compelling reason to build a his-torical collection. Similarly, primary collector status should affect preserva-tion, particularly because most libraries allocate very limited budgets for the repair, binding, and other preservation techniques.

COOPERATIVE STORAGE

Another follow-on topic to cooperative collection development is cooperative storage. Successful cooperative collection development among a wide num-ber of libraries should make it easier to justify the fees that must be assessed and often spells the difference between success and failure when the libraries want to fund and staff a storage area where certain books, journals, and doc-uments can be stored for the benefit of all member libraries. In fact, all con-sortium members should benefit equally to the amount they might be assessed for the maintenance of such facilities.

Designated primary collectors in a consortium who feel compelled to re-tain unique but infrequently used copies of books and bound journals, for in-stance, will benefit from storing those items in a cooperative storage site. In academic institutions, whole programs are sometimes eliminated just as the Library Science program at Columbia was some years ago. If the library at this institution is the primary collector, but no longer has an interest in col-lecting the subject, a cooperative storage facility might be the ideal solution if no other member library wants the collections or to assume primary col-lecting responsibility.

While the authors could not locate a collection development policy that ad-dressed cooperative storage, we would suggest that statements do address the subject when members do have a cooperative storage program because it should be an important aspect of the library's collection management program. The statement should address why the library participates in the storage program (benefits), the criteria for the selection of materials that go to a storage facility, and relevant procedures and policies.

PUBLISHER OR OTHER PARTNERSHIPS

Faced with ever increasing journal subscription costs and the proliferation of new scholarly titles, members of the Association of Research Libraries in the 1990s initiated a proactive cooperative publishing agreement called the Scholarly Publishing and Academic Resources Coalition (SPARC) to encourage a less expensive alternative competition with commercial journal publishers. Over two hundred libraries across the world have joined since then and have been successful in causing some journal publishers to restrain their annual price increases, that is, to end double digit price increases. A SPARC program for print and electronic journals establishes alternative publishers for scientists and others to send their articles to for publication. High priced medical and science journal publishers have taken notice by reducing some subscriptions and keeping price increases under 10%. One SPARC electronic journal (*New Journal of Physics*) is supported by author fees, another (*Documenta Mathematica*) by the faculty in an academic department of a university member which makes it available free though the Internet. Other SPARC incubator programs aim to aggregate titles (BioOne, Columbia Earthscape, MIT CogNet). These and other SPARC programs are outlined on SPARC's web page: www.arl.org/sparc. Institutions that support SPARC programs such as these should address this matter in their collection development policies.

Cooperation among members of the Center for Research Libraries have for decades benefited many libraries, particularly the largest research level universities. One member can propose or agree to purchase and share esoteric and usually expensive research materials so that no other members need to consider acquiring the same material. Presumably, the other members will use the "savings" to acquire additional esoteric or expensive research materials for the benefit of all members.

THE "BIG DEAL" ISSUE

The "big deal" issue, as it has come to be called by many librarians, refers to the full-text article database licenses offered by such publishers as Elsevier,

Wiley InterScience, and Springer-Verlag to library consortia and university systems, or other groups of libraries. While these publishers might offer an individual library access to their print subscriptions for a premium, they will offer members of a system or consortia Internet (web) access to all of the print subscriptions held by the members, also for an additional premium. These "bundled" deals, as they are also called, have been attracting a number of libraries and consortia to participate, particularly those who may have cancelled these publishers' titles for financial reasons, or were not able to afford print subscriptions to begin with. These publishers, that is, offer library consortia and systems web access at the article level to the publishers' journal titles held collectively by the consortia or system members. For yet a higher premium, the publishers will offer access to all of the articles in all of the titles published, regardless of whether consortia members subscribe to the print titles—hence, the "big deal."

The controversial aspect of this issue has to deal with the value of the articles in the titles not held by the individual library or by the members of the consortia. Many librarians in well-funded institutions, for instance, might contend that their library already subscribes to the print titles that are valued by its community of users. Librarians in institutions where many Elsevier, Wiley, or Springer titles have been cancelled through the years might counterargue that the "big deal" affords them web access to the titles they had cancelled, as well as the titles they would like to have subscribed to had their budget been sufficient. For these institutions, the real advantage and value is represented by the cost of the non-subscribed electronic subscriptions, minus the premium paid to the publisher for their web access. Examples are as follows:

An ARL library belonging to the consortium might subscribe to 90% of the titles in Elsevier's Science Direct product and have little or no use for the few unique, unsubscribed titles held by other members that its users could access electronically by paying the publisher a premium. That library would see little value in the group deal.

A smaller university library member of the same consortium might find great value in the publisher's offer because it would gain or regain web access not only to previously dropped titles, but also to the additional titles held by other members of the consortium (or all Elsevier Science Direct titles). Many academic libraries have been forced to cancel many expensive Elsevier titles over the past two or more decades due to the huge increases in this publisher's subscriptions. If the premium paid by this smaller consortium member represents a small percentage of the library's current print subscriptions and the cost of the unsubscribed titles, the value of the Science Direct deal is likely to be many hundreds of thousands of dollars. If that library had cancelled Elsevier print subscriptions due to low use, however, others would argue that there is little value in the deal and that the library should instead use interlibrary loan to satisfy their users' needs.

Wiley and other publishers have begun to offer similar products to groups of libraries. Individual libraries belonging to such cooperative groups or consortia may wish, therefore, to address this issue in their virtual collection development policies.

ADDITIONAL REFERENCES

Bushing, M., B. Davis, and N. Powell. *Using the Conspectus Method: A Collection Assessment Handbook*. Lacey, WA: WLN, 1997.

Ferguson, A., J. Grant, and J. S. Rutstein. "The RLG Conspectus: Its Uses and Benefits." *College and Research Libraries* 49, no. 3 (1988): 197–206.

Forcier, P. C. and N. Powell. "Collection Assessment in the Pacific Northwest: Building a Foundation for Cooperation Based on the RLG Conspectus." in *Advances in Library Automation and Networking* 3 (1989): 87–121.

Gorman, G. E., and R. H. Miller, eds. *Collection Management for the 21st Century: A Handbook for Librarians*. Westport, Conn.: Greenwood Press, 1997.

Stephens, D. "The Conspectus in Alaska and How We're Using It." *PNLA Quarterly* 53 (Spring 1989): 15–16.

Wood, R. J. "The Axioms, Barriers, and Components for Cooperative Collection Development," in *Collection Management for the 21st Century: A Handbook for Librarians*, edited by Gary Gorman and R. H. Miller. Chicago: Greenwood Press, 1997): 221–248.

Wood, R. J., and K. Strauch, eds. *Collection Assessment: A Look at the RLG Conspectus*. New York: Haworth, 1992.

Appendix A

Inventory of Excerpted Library Policies

Albion College, Stockwell-Mudd Libraries: 602 E. Cass Street, Albion, Michigan 49224-1879; 517-629-0285

Albuquerque Technical Vocational Institute Libraries, Main Library: 2000 Coal SE, Albuquerque, New Mexico 87106; 505-224-3285 (reference)

Berkshore Athenaeum, Pittsfield Public Library: One Wendell Avenue, Pittsfield, Massachusetts 01201-6385; 413-499-9480

Bettendorf Public Library Information Center: 2950 Learning Campus Drive, P.O. Box 1330, Bettendorf, Iowa 52722-1330; 319-344-4175

Canterbury City Libraries: P.O. Box 1466, Gloucester Street & Oxford Terrace, Christchurch, New Zealand; (3)79-6914

Canterbury Public Library: 8 Library Road, Canterbury, Connecticut 06331-1512; 860-546-9022

Central Piedmont Community College Library: 1201 Elizabeth Avenue, P.O. Box 35009, Charlotte, North Carolina 28235; 704-330-6041

Charlotte and Mecklenburg County: *See* Public Library of Charlotte and Mecklenburg County

Clatsop Community College Library: 1680 Lexington, Astoria, Oregon 97103; 503-338-2462

College of St. Benedict: *See* St. John's University Library

College of St. Catherine, Minneapolis Campus Library & AV Services: 601 25th Avenue S., Minneapolis, Minnesota 55454; 651-690-7784

Colorado Department of Education, Colorado State Library: 201 E. Colfax Avenue, No. 309, Denver, Colorado 80203-1799; 303-866-6900

Columbia University, University Libraries: Butler Library Room 518, 535 W. 114th Street, New York, New York 10027; 212-854-2247

Cook Memorial Public Library District: 413 N. Milwaukee Avenue, Libertyville, Illinois 60048; 847-362-2900

County of Henrico Public Library: 1001 N. Laburnum Ave., Richmond, Virginia 23223; 804-22-1643

County of Los Angeles Public Library: Executive Office, 7400 E. Imperial Hwy., Downey, California 90242-3375; 562-940-8462

Cumberland County Public Library & Information Center: 300 Maiden Lane, Fayetteville, North Carolina 28301-5000; 910-483-1580

Dalhousie University, Killam Library: 6225 University Avenue, Halifax, Nova Scotia B3H 4H8; 902-494-2384

Dane County Library Service: 201 W. Mifflin Street, Madison, Wisconsin 53703-2597; 608-266-6388

Dartmouth College Library: 6025 Baker Library, Room 115, Hanover, New Hampshire 03755-3525; 603-646-2236

Duke University, William R. Perkins Library: Durham, North Carolina 27708-0190; 919-660-5800

Eugene Public Library: 100 W. 13th Avenue, Eugene, Oregon 97401; 541-682-5450

Fairbanks North Star Borough Public Library & Regional Center, Noel Wien Library: 1215 Cowles Street, Fairbanks, Alaska 99701-4313; 907-459-1020

Fermilab National Accelerator Laboratory: P.O. Box 500, MS 109, Batavia, Illinois 60510; 630-840-3401; http://fnalpubs.fnal.gov/library/cdpolicy.html

Finger Lakes Community College, Charles J. Meder Library: 4355 Lakeshore Drive, Canandaigua, New York 14424-8395; 716-394-3500, extension 371

Fitchburg State College Library: 160 Pearl Street, Fitchburg, Massachusetts 01420; 978-345-9635

Fort Vancouver Regional Library District: 1007 E. Mill Plain Boulevard, Vancouver, Washington 98663; 360-695-1561

Fresno County Public Library: 2420 Mariposa Street, Fresno, California 93721-2285; 559-488-3185

Glenview Public Library: 1930 Glenview Road, Glenview, Illinois 60025-2899; 847-729-7500

Granby Public Library: 15 N. Granby Road, Granby, Connecticut 06035; 860-653-8955

Henrico Public Library: *See* County of Henrico Public Library

Howell Carnegie District Library: 314 W. Grand River Avenue, Howell, Michigan 48843-2146; 517-546-0720

Hurt/Battelle Memorial Library of West Jefferson: 270 Lily Chapel Road, West Jefferson, Ohio 43162-1202; 614-879-8448

Indiana University–Purdue University, Fort Wayne, Walter E. Helmke Library: 2101 E. Coliseum Boulevard, Fort Wayne, Indiana 46805-1499; 219-481-6512

Jackson County Public Library: 303 W. 2nd Street, Seymour, Indiana 47274-2147; 812-522-3412

James Madison University, Carrier Library: Harrisonburg, Virginia 22807; 540-568-6691

Kenyon College, Olin-Chalmers Memorial Library: Gambier, Ohio 43022-9623; 740-427-5186

King County Library System: 300 Eighth Avenue North, Seattle, Washington 98109-5191; 206-684-6604

Kitsap Regional Library: 1301 Sylvan Way, Bremerton, Washington 98310-3498; 360-405-9100

Lakeland Community College Library: 9267 Chillicothe Road, Kirtland, Ohio 44094; 440-256-7323

Lake-Sumter Community College Library: 9501 U.S. Highway 441, Leesburg, Florida 34788-8751; 352-365-3541

Library of Michigan: 717 W. Allegan, Lansing, Michigan 48915; 517-373-1580

Library of Virginia: 800 E. Broad Street, Richmond, Virginia 23219-8000; 804-692-3592

Los Angeles Public Library: *See* County of Los Angeles Public Library

Louisville Free Public Library: 301 York Street, Louisville, Kentucky 40203-2257; 502-574-1600

Manitowoc Public Library: 707 Quay, Manitowoc, Wisconsin 54220; 920-683-4872

Marshall Public Library: 113 S. Garfield, Pocatello, Idaho 83204-5722; 208-232-1263

Medical College of Georgia, Robert B. Greenblatt Library: Medical College of Georgia Building AB, Augusta, Georgia 30912-4400; 706-721-3441

Michigan State University Library: 100 Library, East Lansing, Michigan 48824-1048; 517-353-8700

Middleton Public Library: 7425 Hubbard Avenue, Middleton, Wisconsin 53562-3117; 608-821-3440

Morton Grove Public Library: 6140 Lincoln Avenue, Morton Grove, Illinois 60053-2989; 847-965-4220

Mount Holyoke College Library, Information & Technology Services: 50 College Street, South Hadley, Massachusetts 01075-6404; 413-538-2225

National Library of Canada: 395 Wellington Street, Ottawa, Canada KIA 0N4; 613-995-9481

National Library of Wales: Aberystwyth, Ceredigion, Wales SY23 3BU

Neill Public Library: 210 N. Grand Avenue, Pullman, Washington 99163-2693; 509-334-3595

Newark Museum: 49 Washington Street, P.O. Box 540, Newark, New Jersey 07101-0540; 973-596-6550

Newark Public Library: 5 Washington Street, P.O. Box 630, Newark, New Jersey 07101-0630; 973-733-7784

North Harris Montgomery Community College District, Montgomery College Library: 3200 College Park Drive, Conroe, Texas 77384; 936-273-7392

North Vancouver District Public Library: 1280 E. 27th Street, North Vancouver, British Columbia V7J 1S1; 604-984-0286

Oakton Community College Library: 1600 E. Golf Road, Des Plaines, Illinois 60016; 847-635-1642

Oneida (TN) Public Library: 290 South Main Street, Oneida, Tennesse 37841; 423-569-8634

Pasadena Public Library: 285 East Walnut Street, Pasadena, California 91101; 626-744-4052

Pioneer Library System: 4595 Route 21 North, Canandaigua, New York 14424; 716-394-8260

Public Library of Charlotte and Mecklenburg County: 310 N. Tryon Street, Charlotte, North Carolina 28202-2176; 704-336-2002

Queens Borough Public Library, Central Library: 89-11 Merrick Boulevard, Jamaica, New York 11432; 718-990-0700

Richland Public Library: 955 Northgate Drive, Richland, Washington 99352-3539; 509-942-7450

St. John's University Libraries: 8000 Utopia Parkway, Jamaica, New York 11439; 718-990-6735

Santa Fe Community College Library: 3000 NW 83 Street, Gainesville, Florida 32606-6200; 352-395-5406

Sheridan College, Instructional Resource Center: Sheridan, Wyoming 82801; 307-674-6446

Smithsonian Institution Libraries: Constitution Avenue at 10th Street NW, NHB22 MRC154, Washington, District of Columbia 20560; 202-357-2240

Springfield College, Babson Library: 263 Alden Street, Springfield, Massachusetts 01109-3797; 413-748-3502

State Library of Victoria: 328 Swanston, Melbourne, Victoria 3000, Australia; (3)9669-9888

State University of New York at Buffalo, University Libraries: 433 Capen Hall, Buffalo, New York 14260-1625; 716-645-2967

Tufts University, Tisch Library: Professors Row, Medford, Massachusetts 02155-5816; 617-627-3345

University of Evansville, University Libraries: 1800 Lincoln Avenue, Evansville, Indiana 47722; 812-479-2482

University of Iowa Libraries: 100 Main Library, Iowa City, Iowa 52242-1420; 319-335-5867

University of Miami Libraries, Otto G. Richter Library: 1300 Memorial Drive, Coral Gables, Florida 33124-0320; 305-284-3551

University of North Texas Libraries: P.O. Box 305190, Denton, Texas 76203-5190; 940-565-3025

University of Oregon Library System: 1299 University of Oregon, Eugene, Oregon 97403-1299; 541-346-3056

University of Southern Mississippi Library: Box 5053, Hattiesburg, Mississippi 39406-5053; 601-266-4241

University of Wyoming Libraries: 13th and Ivinson, P.O. Box 3334, Laramie, Wyoming 82071-3334; 307-766-3279

Victoria and Albert Museum, National Art Library: London, England SW7 2RL

Washoe County Library: 301 S. Center Street, P.O. Box 2131, Reno, Nevada 89505; 773-785-4190

West Chester University, Francis Harvey Green Library: High Street & Rosedale Avenue, West Chester, Pennsylvania 19383; 610-436-2747

West Virginia University Libraries, Wise Library: P.O. Box 6069, Morgantown, West Virginia 26506-6069; 304-293-4040

Western Carolina University, Hunter Library: Cullowhee, North Carolina 28723-4012; 828-227-7307

Westerville Public Library: 126 South State Street, Westerville, Ohio 43081-2095; 614-882-7277

Appendix B

Intellectual Freedom Statements and Forms

The majority of these documents are available on the American Library Association's website (www.ala.org) as are the other publications cited within the text. Their inclusion here is dictated by the fact that they are widely used—with ALA's blessing—in library collection development policies.

CHECKLIST OF INTELLECTUAL FREEDOM DOCUMENTS

- Access for Children and Young Adults to Nonprint Materials
- Access to Electronic Information, Services, and Networks
- Access to Library Resources and Services Regardless of Sex, Gender Identity, or Sexual Orientation
- Challenged Materials
- Dealing with Concerns about Library Resources
- Diversity in Collection Development
- Economic Barriers to Information Access
- Evaluating Library Collections
- Exhibit Spaces and Bulletin Boards
- Expurgation of Library Materials
- Free Access to Libraries for Minors
- Freedom to Read Statement
- Freedom to View Statement
- Guidelines for the Development and Implementation of Policies, Regulations, and Procedures Affecting Access to Library Materials, Services, and Facilities
- Guidelines for the Development of Policies and Procedures regarding User Behavior and Library Usage

- Intellectual Freedom Principles for Academic Libraries
- Library Bill of Rights
- Library-Initiated Programs as a Resource
- Policy concerning Confidentiality of Personally Identifiable Information about Library Users
- Policy on Governmental Intimidation
- Request for Reconsideration of Library Resources Form
- Resolution on Access to the Use of Libraries and Information by Individuals with Physical or Mental Impairment
- Resolution on the Use of Filtering Software in Libraries
- Restricted Access to Library Materials
- Statement on Labeling
- Universal Right to Free Expression

ACCESS TO ELECTRONIC INFORMATION, SERVICES, AND NETWORKS: AN INTERPRETATION OF THE LIBRARY BILL OF RIGHTS

Introduction

The world is in the midst of an electronic communications revolution. Based on its constitutional, ethical, and historical heritage, American librarianship is uniquely positioned to address the broad range of information issues being raised in this revolution. In particular, librarians address intellectual freedom from a strong ethical base and an abiding commitment to the preservation of the individual's rights.

Freedom of expression is an inalienable human right and the foundation for self-government. Freedom of expression encompasses the freedom of speech and the corollary right to receive information. These rights extend to minors as well as adults. Libraries and librarians exist to facilitate the exercise of these rights by selecting, producing, providing access to, identifying, retrieving, organizing, providing instruction in the use of, and preserving recorded expression regardless of the format or technology.

The American Library Association expresses these basic principles of librarianship in its *Code of Ethics* and in the *Library Bill of Rights* and its Interpretations. These serve to guide librarians and library governing bodies in addressing issues of intellectual freedom that arise when the library provides access to electronic information, services, and networks.

Issues arising from the still-developing technology of computer-mediated information generation, distribution, and retrieval need to be approached and regularly reviewed from a context of constitutional principles and ALA policies so that fundamental and traditional tenets of librarianship are not swept away.

Electronic information flows across boundaries and barriers despite attempts by individuals, governments, and private entities to channel or control it. Even so, many people, for reasons of technology, infrastructure, or socioeconomic status do not have access to electronic information.

In making decisions about how to offer access to electronic information, each library should consider its mission, goals, objectives, cooperative agreements, and the needs of the entire community it serves.

The Rights of Users

All library system and network policies, procedures, or regulations relating to electronic resources and services should be scrutinized for potential violation of user rights.

User policies should be developed according to the policies and guidelines established by the American Library Association, including *Guidelines for the Development and Implementation of Policies, Regulations, and Procedures Affecting Access to Library Materials, Services, and Facilities.*

Users should not be restricted or denied access for expressing or receiving constitutionally protected speech. Users' access should not be changed without due process, including, but not limited to, formal notice and a means of appeal.

Although electronic systems may include distinct property rights and security concerns, such elements may not be employed as a subterfuge to deny users' access to information. Users have the right to be free of unreasonable limitations or conditions set by libraries, librarians, system administrators, vendors, network service providers, or others. Contracts, agreements, and licenses entered into by libraries on behalf of their users should not violate this right. Users also have a right to information, training, and assistance necessary to operate the hardware and software provided by the library.

Users have both the right of confidentiality and the right of privacy. The library should uphold these rights by policy, procedure, and practice. Users should be advised, however, that because security is technically difficult to achieve, electronic transactions and files could become public.

The rights of users who are minors shall in no way be abridged.[1]

Equity of Access

Electronic information, services, and networks provided directly or indirectly by the library should be equally, readily, and equitably accessible to all library users. American Library Association policies oppose the charging of user fees for the provision of information services by all libraries and information services that receive their major support from public funds (50.3; 53.1.14; 60.1; 61.1). It should be the goal of all libraries to develop policies concerning access to electronic resources in light of *Economic Barriers to Information Access: An Interpretation of the Library Bill of Rights* and *Guidelines for the Development and Implementation of Policies, Regulations, and Procedures Affecting Access to Library Materials, Services, and Facilities.*

Information Resources and Access

Providing connections to global information, services, and networks is not the same as selecting and purchasing material for a library collection. Determining the accuracy or authenticity of electronic information may present special problems. Some information accessed electronically may not meet a library's selection or collection development policy. It is, therefore, left to each user to determine what is appropriate. Parents and legal guardians who are concerned about their children's use of electronic resources should provide guidance to their own children.

Libraries and librarians should not deny or limit access to information available via electronic resources because of its allegedly controversial content or because of the librarian's personal beliefs or fear of confrontation. Information retrieved or utilized electronically should be considered constitutionally protected unless determined otherwise by a court with appropriate jurisdiction.

Libraries, acting within their mission and objectives, must support access to information on all subjects that serve the needs or interests of each user, regardless of the user's age or the content of the material. Libraries have an obligation to provide access to government information available in electronic format. Libraries and librarians should not deny access to information solely on the grounds that it is perceived to lack value.

In order to prevent the loss of information, and to preserve the cultural record, libraries may need to expand their selection or collection development policies to ensure preservation, in appropriate formats, of information obtained electronically.

Electronic resources provide unprecedented opportunities to expand the scope of information available to users. Libraries and librarians should provide access to information presenting all points of view. The provision of access does not imply sponsorship or endorsement. These principles pertain to electronic resources no less than they do to the more traditional sources of information in libraries.[2]

Notes

1. See *Free Access to Libraries for Minors: An Interpretation of the Library Bill of Rights*; *Access to Resources and Services in the School Library Media Program: An Interpretation of the Library Bill of Rights*; and *Access for Children and Young People to Videotapes and Other Nonprint Formats: An Interpretation of the Library Bill of Rights*.

2. See *Diversity in Collection Development: An Interpretation of the Library Bill of Rights*.

[Adopted by the ALA Council, January 24, 1996]

ACCESS TO LIBRARY RESOURCES AND SERVICES REGARDLESS OF SEX, GENDER IDENTITY, OR SEXUAL ORIENTATION: AN INTERPRETATION OF THE LIBRARY BILL OF RIGHTS

American libraries exist and function within the context of a body of laws derived from the United States Constitution and the First Amendment. The *Library Bill of Rights* embodies the basic policies which guide libraries in the provision of services, materials, and programs.

In the preamble to its Library Bill of Rights, the American Library Association affirms that *all* [emphasis added] libraries are forums for information and ideas. This concept of *forum* and its accompanying principle of *inclusiveness* pervade all six Articles of the *Library Bill of Rights* .

The American Library Association stringently and unequivocally maintains that libraries and librarians have an obligation to resist efforts that systematically exclude materials dealing with any subject matter, including sex, gender identity, or sexual orientation:

• Article I of the *Library Bill of Rights* states that "Materials should not be excluded because of the origin, background, or views of those contributing to their creation." The Association affirms that books and other materials coming from gay, lesbian, bisexual, and/or transgendered presses, gay, lesbian, bisexual and/or transgendered authors or other creators, and materials regardless of format or services dealing with gay, lesbian, bisexual and/or transgendered life are protected by the *Library Bill of Rights*. Librarians are obligated by the *Library Bill of Rights* to endeavor to select materials without regard to the sex, gender identity, or sexual orientation of their creators by using the criteria identified in their written, approved selection policies (ALA policy 53.1.5).

- Article II maintains that "Libraries should provide materials and information presenting all points of view on current and historical issues. Materials should not be proscribed or removed because of partisan or doctrinal disapproval." Library services, materials, and programs representing diverse points of view on sex, gender identity, or sexual orientation should be considered for purchase and inclusion in library collections and programs. (ALA policies 53.1.1, 53.1.9, and 53.1.11). The Association affirms that attempts to proscribe or remove materials dealing with gay, lesbian, bisexual, and/or transgendered life without regard to the written, approved selection policy violate this tenet and constitute censorship.
- Articles III and IV mandate that libraries "challenge censorship" and cooperate with those "resisting abridgement of free expression and free access to ideas."
- Article V holds that "A person's right to use a library should not be denied or abridged because of origin, age, background, or views." In the *Library Bill of Rights* and all its Interpretations, it is intended that: "origin" encompasses all the characteristics of individuals that are inherent in the circumstances of their birth; "age" encompasses all the characteristics of individuals that are inherent in their levels of development and maturity; "background" encompasses all the characteristics of individuals that are a result of their life experiences; and "views" encompasses all the opinions and beliefs held and expressed by individuals. Therefore, Article V of the *Library Bill of Rights* mandates that library services, materials, and programs be available to all members of the community the library serves, without regard to sex, gender identity, or sexual orientation. This includes providing youth with comprehensive sex education literature (ALA Policy 52.5.2).
- Article VI maintains that "Libraries which make exhibit spaces and meeting rooms available to the public they serve should make such facilities available on an equitable basis, regardless of the beliefs or affiliations of individuals or groups requesting their use." This protection extends to all groups and members of the community the library serves, without regard to sex, gender identity, or sexual orientation.

The American Library Association holds that any attempt, be it legal or extralegal, to regulate or suppress library services, materials, or programs must be resisted in order that protected expression is not abridged. Librarians have a professional obligation to ensure that all library users have free and equal access to the entire range of library services, materials, and programs. Therefore, the Association strongly opposes any effort to limit access to information and ideas. The Association also encourages librarians to proactively support the First Amendment rights of all library users, regardless of sex, gender identity, or sexual orientation.

[Adopted June 30, 1993; amended July 12, 2000, by the ALA Council; amended June 30, 2004, by the ALA Council.]

CHALLENGED MATERIALS: AN INTERPRETATION OF THE LIBRARY BILL OF RIGHTS

The American Library Association declares as a matter of firm principle that it is the responsibility of every library to have a clearly defined materials selection policy in written form that reflects the *Library Bill of Rights*, and that is approved by the appropriate governing authority.

Challenged materials that meet the criteria for selection in the materials selection policy of the library should not be removed under any legal or extra-legal pressure. The *Library Bill of Rights* states in Article I that "Materials should not be excluded because of the origin, background, or views of those contributing to their creation," and in Article II, that "Materials should not be proscribed or removed because of partisan or doctrinal disapproval." Freedom of expression is protected by the Constitution of the United States, but constitutionally protected expression is often separated from unprotected expression only by a dim and uncertain line. The Constitution requires a procedure designed to focus searchingly on challenged expression before it can be suppressed. An adversary hearing is a part of this procedure.

Therefore, any attempt, be it legal or extra-legal, to regulate or suppress materials in libraries must be closely scrutinized to the end that protected expression is not abridged.

[Adopted June 25, 1971; amended July 1, 1981; amended January 10, 1990, by the ALA Council.]

DEALING WITH CONCERNS ABOUT LIBRARY RESOURCES

As with any public service, libraries receive complaints and expressions of concern. One of the librarian's responsibilities is to handle these complaints in a respectful and fair manner. The complaints that librarians often worry about most are those dealing with library resources or free access policies. The key to successfully handling these complaints is to be sure the library staff and the governing authorities are all knowledgeable about the complaint procedures and their implementation. As normal operating procedure each library should:

Maintain a materials selection policy. It should be in written form and approved by the appropriate governing authority. It should apply to all library materials equally.

Maintain a library service policy. This should cover registration policies, programming and services in the library that involve access issues.

Maintain a clearly defined method for handling complaints. The complaint must be filed in writing and the complainant must be properly identified before action is taken. A decision should be deferred until fully considered by appropriate administrative authority. (A sample form is attached.) The process should be followed, whether the complaint originates internally or externally.

Maintain in-service training. Conduct periodic in-service training to acquaint staff, administration, and the governing authority with the materials selection policy and library service policy and procedures for handling complaints.

Maintain lines of communication with civic, religious, educational, and political bodies of the community. Library board and staff participation in local civic organizations and presentations to these organizations should emphasize the library's selection process and intellectual freedom principles.

Maintain a vigorous public information program on behalf of intellectual freedom. Newspapers, radio, and television should be informed of policies governing resource selection and use, and of any special activities pertaining to intellectual freedom.

Maintain familiarity with any local municipal and state legislation pertaining to intellectual freedom and First Amendment rights. Following these practices will not preclude receiving complaints from pressure groups or individuals but should provide a base from which to operate when these concerns are expressed. When a complaint is made, follow one or more of the steps listed below:

1. Listen calmly and courteously to the complaint. Remember the person has a right to express a concern. Use of good communication skills helps many people understand the need for diversity in library collections and the use of library resources. In the event the person is not satisfied, advise the complainant of the library policy and procedures for handling library resource statements of concern. If a person does fill out a form about their concern, make sure a prompt written reply related to the concern is sent.
2. It is essential to notify the administration and/or the governing authority (library board, etc.) of the complaint and assure them that the library's procedures are being followed. Present full, written information giving the nature of the complaint and identifying the source.
3. When appropriate, seek the support of the local media. Freedom to read and freedom of the press go hand in hand.
4. When appropriate, inform local civic organizations of the facts and enlist their support. Meet negative pressure with positive pressure.

5. Assert the principles of the *Library Bill of Rights* as a professional responsibility. Laws governing obscenity, subversive material, and other questionable matter are subject to interpretation by courts. Library resources found to meet the standards set in the materials selection or collection development policy should not be removed or restricted from public access until after an adversary hearing resulting in a final judicial determination.

6. Contact the ALA Office for Intellectual Freedom and your state intellectual freedom committee to inform them of the complaint and to enlist their support and the assistance of other agencies.

The principles and procedures discussed above apply to all kinds of resource related complaints or attempts to censor and are supported by groups such as the National Education Association, the American Civil Liberties Union and the National Council of Teachers of English, as well as the American Library Association. While the practices provide positive means for preparing for and meeting pressure group complaints, they serve the more general purpose of supporting the *Library Bill of Rights*, particularly Article III, which states that "Libraries should challenge censorship in the fulfillment of the responsibility to provide information and enlightenment."

Office for Intellectual Freedom
American Library Association
50 E. Huron Street
Chicago, IL 60611
312/280-4223
oif@ala.org

[Revised by the Intellectual Freedom Committee, January 12, 1983; November 17, 2000]

DIVERSITY IN COLLECTION DEVELOPMENT:
AN INTERPRETATION OF THE LIBRARY BILL OF RIGHTS

Throughout history, the focus of censorship has fluctuated from generation to generation. Books and other materials have not been selected or have been removed from library collections for many reasons, among which are prejudicial language and ideas, political content, economic theory, social philosophies, religious beliefs, sexual forms of expression, and other potentially controversial topics.

Some examples of censorship may include removing or not selecting materials because they are considered by some as racist or sexist; not purchasing conservative religious materials; not selecting materials about or by minorities because it is thought these groups or interests are not represented in a community; or not providing information on or materials from non-mainstream political entities.

Librarians may seek to increase user awareness of materials on various social concerns by many means, including, but not limited to, issuing bibliographies and presenting exhibits and programs. Librarians have a professional responsibility to be inclusive, not exclusive, in collection development and in the provision of interlibrary loan. Access to all materials legally obtainable should be assured to the user, and policies should not unjustly exclude materials even if they are offensive to the librarian or the user. Collection development should reflect the philosophy inherent in Article II of the *Library Bill of Rights*: "Libraries should provide materials and information presenting all points of view on current and historical issues. Materials should not be proscribed or removed because of partisan or doctrinal disapproval." A balanced collection reflects a diversity of materials, not an equality of numbers. Collection development responsibilities include selecting materials in the languages in common use in the community the library serves. Collection development and the selection of materials should be done according to professional standards and established selection and review procedures.

There are many complex facets to any issue, and variations of context in which issues may be expressed, discussed, or interpreted. Librarians have a professional responsibility to be fair, just, and equitable and to give all library users equal protection in guarding against violation of the library patron's right to read, view, or listen to materials and resources protected by the First Amendment, no matter what the viewpoint of the author, creator, or selector. Librarians have an obligation to protect library collections from removal of materials based on personal bias or prejudice, and to select and support the access to materials on all subjects that meet, as closely as possible, the needs, interests, and abilities of all persons in the community the library serves. This includes materials that reflect political, economic, religious, social, minority, and sexual issues.

Intellectual freedom, the essence of equitable library services, provides for free access to all expressions of ideas through which any and all sides of a question, cause, or movement may be explored. Toleration is meaningless without tolerance for what some may consider detestable. Librarians cannot justly permit their own preferences to limit their degree of tolerance in collection development, because freedom is indivisible.

[Adopted July 14, 1982; amended January 10, 1990, by the ALA Council.]

ECONOMIC BARRIERS TO INFORMATION ACCESS: AN INTERPRETATION OF THE LIBRARY BILL OF RIGHTS

A democracy presupposes an informed citizenry. The First Amendment mandates the right of all persons to free expression, and the corollary right to receive the constitutionally protected expression of others. The publicly supported library provides free, equal, and equitable access to information for all people of the community the library serves. While the roles, goals, and objectives of publicly supported libraries may differ, they share this common mission.

The library's essential mission must remain the first consideration for librarians and governing bodies faced with economic pressures and competition for funding.

In support of this mission, the American Library Association has enumerated certain principles of library services in the *Library Bill of Rights*.

Principles Governing Fines, Fees, and User Charges

Article I of the *Library Bill of Rights* states: "Books and other library resources should be provided for the interest, information, and enlightenment of all people of the community the library serves."

Article V of the *Library Bill of Rights* states: "A person's right to use a library should not be denied or abridged because of origin, age, background, or views."

The American Library Association opposes the charging of user fees for the provision of information by all libraries and information services that receive their major support from public funds. All information resources that are provided directly or indirectly by the library, regardless of technology, format, or methods of delivery, should be readily, equally, and equitably accessible to all library users.

Libraries that adhere to these principles systematically monitor their programs of service for potential barriers to access and strive to eliminate such barriers when they occur. All library policies and procedures, particularly those involving fines, fees, or other user charges, should be scrutinized for potential barriers to access. All services should be designed and implemented with care, so as not to infringe on or interfere with the provision or delivery of information and resources for all users. Services should be reevaluated regularly to ensure that the library's basic mission remains uncompromised.

Librarians and governing bodies should look for alternative models and methods of library administration that minimize distinctions among users based on their economic status or financial condition. They should resist the temptation to impose user fees to alleviate financial pressures, at long-term cost to institutional integrity and public confidence in libraries.

Library services that involve the provision of information, regardless of format, technology, or method of delivery, should be made available to all library users on an equal and equitable basis. Charging fees for the use of library collections, services, programs, or facilities that were purchased with public funds raises barriers to access. Such fees effectively abridge or deny access for some members of the community because they reinforce distinctions among users based on their ability and willingness to pay.

Principles Governing Conditions of Funding

Article II of the *Library Bill of Rights* states: "Materials should not be proscribed or removed because of partisan or doctrinal disapproval."

Article III of the *Library Bill of Rights* states: "Libraries should challenge censorship in the fulfillment of their responsibility to provide information and enlightenment."

Article IV of the *Library Bill of Rights* states: "Libraries should cooperate with all persons and groups concerned with resisting abridgment of free expression and free access to ideas."

The American Library Association opposes any legislative or regulatory attempt to impose content restrictions on library resources, or to limit user access to information, as a condition of funding for publicly supported libraries and information services.

The First Amendment guarantee of freedom of expression is violated when the right to receive that expression is subject to arbitrary restrictions based on content.

Librarians and governing bodies should examine carefully any terms or conditions attached to library funding and should oppose attempts to limit through such conditions full and equal access to information because of content. This principle applies equally to private gifts or bequests and to public funds. In particular, librarians and governing bodies have an obligation to reject such restrictions when the effect of the restriction is to limit equal and equitable access to information.

Librarians and governing bodies should cooperate with all efforts to create a community consensus that publicly supported libraries require funding unfettered by restrictions. Such a consensus supports the library mission to provide the free and unrestricted exchange of information and ideas necessary to a functioning democracy.

The Association's historic position in this regard is stated clearly in a number of Association policies: 50.4 "Free Access to Information," 50.8 "Financing of Libraries," 51.2 "Equal Access to Library Service," 51.3 "Intellectual Freedom," 53 "Intellectual Freedom Policies," 59.1 "Policy Objectives," and 60 "Library Services for the Poor."

[Adopted by the ALA Council, June 30, 1993.]

EVALUATING LIBRARY COLLECTIONS:
AN INTERPRETATION OF THE LIBRARY BILL OF RIGHTS

The continuous review of library materials is necessary as a means of maintaining an active library collection of current interest to users. In the process, materials may be added, and physically deteriorated or obsolete materials may be replaced or removed in accordance with the collection maintenance policy of a given library and the needs of the community it serves. Continued evaluation is closely related to the goals and responsibilities of all libraries and is a valuable tool of collection development. This procedure is not to be used as a convenient means to remove materials presumed to be controversial or disapproved of by segments of the community. Such abuse of the evaluation function violates the principles of intellectual freedom and is in opposition to the Preamble and Articles I and II of the *Library Bill of Rights*, which state: "The American Library Association affirms that all libraries are forums for information and ideas, and that the following basic policies should guide their services."

1. Books and other library resources should be provided for the interest, information, and enlightenment of all people of the community the library serves. Materials should not be excluded because of the origin, background, or views of those contributing to their creation.
2. Libraries should provide materials and information presenting all points of view on current and historical issues. Materials should not be proscribed or removed because of partisan or doctrinal disapproval.

The American Library Association opposes such "silent censorship" and strongly urges that libraries adopt guidelines setting forth the positive purposes and principles of evaluation of materials in library collections.
[Adopted February 2, 1973; amended July 1, 1981, by the ALA Council.]

EXHIBIT SPACES AND BULLETIN BOARDS:
AN INTERPRETATION OF THE LIBRARY BILL OF RIGHTS

Libraries often provide exhibit spaces and bulletin boards. The uses made of these spaces should conform to the *Library Bill of Rights*: Article I states, "Materials should not be excluded because of the origin, background, or views of those contributing to their creation." Article II states, "Materials should not be proscribed or removed because of partisan or doctrinal disapproval." Article VI maintains that exhibit space should be made available "on an equitable basis, regardless of the beliefs or affiliations of individuals or groups requesting their use."

In developing library exhibits, staff members should endeavor to present a broad spectrum of opinion and a variety of viewpoints. Libraries should not shrink from developing exhibits because of controversial content or because of the beliefs or affiliations of those whose work is represented. Just as libraries do not endorse the viewpoints of those whose work is represented in their collections, libraries also do not endorse the beliefs or viewpoints of topics that may be the subject of library exhibits.

Exhibit areas often are made available for use by community groups. Libraries should formulate a written policy for the use of these exhibit areas to assure that space is provided on an equitable basis to all groups that request it.

Written policies for exhibit space use should be stated in inclusive rather than exclusive terms. For example, a policy that the library's exhibit space is open "to organizations engaged in educational, cultural, intellectual, or charitable activities" is an inclusive statement of the limited uses of the exhibit space. This defined limitation would permit religious groups to use the exhibit space because they engage in intellectual activities, but would exclude most commercial uses of the exhibit space.

A publicly supported library may designate use of exhibit space for strictly library-related activities, provided that this limitation is viewpoint neutral and clearly defined.

Libraries may include in this policy rules regarding the time, place, and manner of use of the exhibit space, so long as the rules are content neutral and are applied in the same manner to all groups wishing to use the space. A library may wish to limit access to exhibit space to groups within the community served by the library. This practice is acceptable provided that the same rules and regulations apply to everyone, and that exclusion is not made on the basis of the doctrinal, religious, or political beliefs of the potential users.

The library should not censor or remove an exhibit because some members of the community may disagree with its content. Those who object to the content of any exhibit held at the library should be able to submit their complaint and/or their own exhibit proposal to be judged according to the policies established by the library.

Libraries may wish to post a permanent notice near the exhibit area stating that the library does not advocate or endorse the viewpoints of exhibits or exhibitors.

Libraries that make bulletin boards available to public groups for posting notices of public interest should develop criteria for the use of these spaces based on the same considerations as those outlined above. Libraries may wish to develop criteria regarding the size of material to be displayed, the length of time materials may remain on the bulletin board, the frequency with which material may be posted for the same group, and the geographic area from which notices will be accepted.

[Adopted July 2, 1991, by the ALA Council; amended June 30, 2004, by the ALA Council.]

EXPURGATION OF LIBRARY MATERIALS:
AN INTERPRETATION OF THE LIBRARY BILL OF RIGHTS

Expurgating library materials is a violation of the *Library Bill of Rights*. Expurgation as defined by this interpretation includes any deletion, excision, alteration, editing, or obliteration of any part(s) of books or other library resources by the library, its agent, or its parent institution (if any). By such expurgation, the library is in effect denying access to the complete work and the entire spectrum of ideas that the work intended to express. Such action stands in violation of Articles I, II, and III of the *Library Bill of Rights*, which state that "Materials should not be excluded because of the origin, background, or views of those contributing to their creation," that "Materials should not be proscribed or removed because of partisan or doctrinal disapproval," and that "Libraries should challenge censorship in the fulfillment of their responsibility to provide information and enlightenment."

The act of expurgation has serious implications. It involves a determination that it is necessary to restrict access to the complete work. This is censorship. When a work is expurgated, under the assumption that certain portions of that work would be harmful to minors, the situation is no less serious.

Expurgation of any books or other library resources imposes a restriction, without regard to the rights and desires of all library users, by limiting access to ideas and information.

Further, expurgation without written permission from the holder of the copyright on the material may violate the copyright provisions of the United States Code.

[Adopted February 2, 1973; amended July 1, 1981; amended January 10, 1990, by the ALA Council.]

FREE ACCESS TO LIBRARIES FOR MINORS:
AN INTERPRETATION OF THE LIBRARY BILL OF RIGHTS

Library policies and procedures that effectively deny minors equal and equitable access to all library resources available to other users violate the *Library Bill of Rights*. The American Library Association opposes all attempts to restrict access to library services, materials, and facilities based on the age of library users.

Article V of the *Library Bill of Rights* states, "A person's right to use a library should not be denied or abridged because of origin, age, background, or views." The "right to use a library" includes free access to, and unrestricted use of, all the services, materials, and facilities the library has to offer. Every restriction on access to, and use of, library resources, based solely on the chronological age, educational level, literacy skills, or legal emancipation of users violates Article V.

Libraries are charged with the mission of developing resources to meet the diverse information needs and interests of the communities they serve. Services, materials, and facilities that fulfill the needs and interests of library users at different stages in their personal development are a necessary part of library resources. The needs and interests of each library user, and resources appropriate to meet those needs and interests, must be determined on an individual basis. Librarians cannot predict what resources will best fulfill the needs and interests of any individual user based on a single criterion such as chronological age, educational level, literacy skills, or legal emancipation.

Libraries should not limit the selection and development of library resources simply because minors will have access to them. Institutional self-censorship diminishes the credibility of the library in the community, and restricts access for all library users.

Children and young adults unquestionably possess First Amendment rights, including the right to receive information in the library. Constitutionally protected speech cannot be suppressed solely to protect children or young adults from ideas or images a legislative body believes to be unsuitable for them.[1] Librarians and library governing bodies should not resort to age restrictions in an effort to avoid actual or anticipated objections, because only a court of law can determine whether material is not constitutionally protected.

The mission, goals, and objectives of libraries cannot authorize librarians or library governing bodies to assume, abrogate, or overrule the rights and responsibilities of parents. As "Libraries: An American Value" states, "We affirm the responsibility and the right of all parents and guardians to guide their own children's use of the library and its resources and services." Librarians and governing bodies should maintain that parents—and only parents—have the right and the responsibility to restrict the access of their children—and only their children—to library resources. Parents who do not want their children to have access to certain library services, materials, or facilities should so advise their children. Librarians and library governing bodies cannot assume the role of parents or the functions of parental authority in the private relationship between parent and child.

Lack of access to information can be harmful to minors. Librarians and library governing bodies have a public and professional obligation to ensure that all members of the community they serve have free, equal, and equitable access to the entire range of library resources regardless of content, approach, format, or amount of detail. This principle of library service applies equally to all users, minors as well as adults. Librarians and library governing bodies must uphold this principle in order to provide adequate and effective service to minors.

Note

1. See Erznoznik v. City of Jacksonville, 422 U.S. 205 (1975) "Speech that is neither obscene as to youths nor subject to some other legitimate proscription cannot be suppressed solely to protect the young from ideas or images that a legislative body thinks unsuitable [422 U.S. 205, 214] for them. In most circumstances, the values protected by the First Amendment are no less applicable when government seeks to control the flow of information to minors. See also Tinker v. Des Moines School Dist., *supra. Cf.* West Virginia Bd. of Ed. v. Barnette, 319 U.S. 624 (1943)."

[Adopted June 30, 1972; amended July 1, 1981; July 3, 1991, June 30, 2004, by the ALA Council.]

THE FREEDOM TO READ STATEMENT

The freedom to read is essential to our democracy. It is continuously under attack. Private groups and public authorities in various parts of the country are working to remove or limit access to reading materials, to censor content in schools, to label "controversial" views, to distribute lists of "objectionable" books or authors, and to purge libraries. These actions apparently rise from a view that our national tradition of free expression is no longer valid; that censorship and suppression are needed to counter threats to safety or national security, as well as to avoid the subversion of politics and the corruption of morals. We, as individuals devoted to reading and as librarians and publishers responsible for disseminating ideas, wish to assert the public interest in the preservation of the freedom to read.

Most attempts at suppression rest on a denial of the fundamental premise of democracy: that the ordinary individual, by exercising critical judgment, will select the good and reject the bad. We trust Americans to recognize propaganda and misinformation, and to make their own decisions about what they read and believe. We do not believe they are prepared to sacrifice their heritage of a free press in order to be "protected" against what others think may be bad for them. We believe they still favor free enterprise in ideas and expression.

These efforts at suppression are related to a larger pattern of pressures being brought against education, the press, art and images, films, broadcast media, and the Internet. The problem is not only one of actual censorship. The shadow of fear cast by these pressures leads, we suspect, to an even larger voluntary curtailment of expression by those who seek to avoid controversy or unwelcome scrutiny by government officials.

Such pressure toward conformity is perhaps natural to a time of accelerated change. And yet suppression is never more dangerous than in such a time of social tension. Freedom has given the United States the elasticity to endure strain. Freedom keeps open the path of novel and creative solutions, and enables change to come by choice. Every silencing of a heresy, every enforcement of an orthodoxy, diminishes the toughness and resilience of our society and leaves it the less able to deal with controversy and difference.

Now as always in our history, reading is among our greatest freedoms. The freedom to read and write is almost the only means for making generally available ideas or manners of expression that can initially command only a small audience. The written word is the natural medium for the new idea and the untried voice from which come the original contributions to social growth. It is essential to the extended discussion that serious thought requires, and to the accumulation of knowledge and ideas into organized collections.

We believe that free communication is essential to the preservation of a free society and a creative culture. We believe that these pressures toward conformity present the danger of limiting the range and variety of inquiry and expression on which our democracy and our culture depend. We believe that every American community must jealously guard the freedom to publish and to circulate, in order to preserve its own freedom to read. We believe that publishers and librarians have a profound responsibility to give validity to that freedom to read by making it possible for the readers to choose freely from a variety of offerings.

The freedom to read is guaranteed by the Constitution. Those with faith in free people will stand firm on these constitutional guarantees of essential rights and will exercise the responsibilities that accompany these rights.

We therefore affirm these propositions:

It is in the public interest for publishers and librarians to make available the widest diversity of views and expressions, including those that are unorthodox, unpopular, or considered dangerous by the majority. Creative thought is by definition new, and what is new is different. The bearer of every new thought is a rebel until that idea is refined and tested. Totalitarian systems attempt to maintain themselves in power by the ruthless suppression of any concept that challenges the established orthodoxy. The power of a democratic system to adapt to change is vastly strengthened by the freedom of its citizens to choose widely from among conflicting opinions offered freely to them. To stifle every nonconformist idea at birth would mark the end of the democratic process. Furthermore, only through the constant activity of weighing and selecting can the democratic mind attain the strength demanded by times like these. We need to know not only what we believe but why we believe it.

Publishers, librarians, and booksellers do not need to endorse every idea or presentation they make available. It would conflict with the public interest for them to establish their own political, moral, or aesthetic views as a standard for determining what should be published or circulated. Publishers and librarians serve the educational process by helping to make available knowledge and ideas required for the growth of the mind and the increase of learning. They do not foster education by imposing as mentors the patterns of their own thought. The people should have the freedom to read and consider a broader range of ideas than those that may be held by any single librarian or publisher or government or church. It is wrong that what one can read should be confined to what another thinks proper.

It is contrary to the public interest for publishers or librarians to bar access to writings on the basis of the personal history or political affiliations of the author. No art or literature can flourish if it is to be measured by the political views or private lives of its creators. No society of free people can flourish that draws up lists of writers to whom it will not listen, whatever they may have to say.

There is no place in our society for efforts to coerce the taste of others, to confine adults to the reading matter deemed suitable for adolescents, or to inhibit the efforts of writers to achieve artistic expression. To some, much of modern expression is shocking. But is not much of life itself shocking? We cut off literature at the source if we prevent writers from dealing with the stuff of life. Parents and teachers have a responsibility to prepare the young to meet the diversity of experiences in life to which they will be exposed, as they have a responsibility to help them learn to think critically for themselves. These are affirmative responsibilities, not to be discharged simply by preventing them from reading works for which they are not yet prepared. In these matters values differ, and values cannot be legislated; nor can machinery be devised that will suit the demands of one group without limiting the freedom of others.

It is not in the public interest to force a reader to accept the prejudgment of a label characterizing any expression or its author as subversive or dangerous. The ideal of labeling presupposes the existence of individuals or groups with wisdom to determine by authority what is good or bad for others. It presupposes that individuals must be directed in making up their minds about the ideas they examine. But Americans do not need others to do their thinking for them.

It is the responsibility of publishers and librarians, as guardians of the people's freedom to read, to contest encroachments upon that freedom by individuals or groups seeking to impose their own standards or tastes upon the community at large; and by the government whenever it seeks to reduce or deny public access to public information. It is inevitable in the give and take of the democratic process that the political, the moral, or the aesthetic concepts of an individual or group will occasionally collide with those of another individual or group. In a free society individuals are free to determine for themselves what they wish to read, and each group is free to determine what it will recommend to its freely associated members. But no group has the right to take the law into its own hands, and to impose its own concept of politics or morality upon other members of a democratic society. Freedom is no freedom if it is accorded only to the accepted and the inoffensive. Further, democratic societies are more safe, free, and creative when the free flow of public information is not restricted by governmental prerogative or self-censorship.

It is the responsibility of publishers and librarians to give full meaning to the freedom to read by providing books that enrich the quality and diversity of thought and expression. By the exercise of this affirmative responsibility, they can demonstrate that the answer to a "bad" book is a good one, the answer to a "bad" idea is a good one. The freedom to read is of little consequence when the reader cannot obtain matter fit for that reader's purpose. What is needed is not only the absence of restraint, but the positive provision of opportunity for the people to read the best that has been thought and said. Books are the major channel by which the intellectual inheritance is handed down, and the principal means of its testing and growth. The defense of the freedom to read requires of all publishers and librarians the utmost of their faculties, and deserves of all Americans the fullest of their support.

We state these propositions neither lightly nor as easy generalizations. We here stake out a lofty claim for the value of the written word. We do so because we believe that it is possessed of enormous variety and usefulness, worthy of cherishing and keeping free. We realize that the application of these propositions may mean the dissemination of ideas and manners of expression that are repugnant to many persons. We do not state these propositions in the comfortable belief that what people read is unimportant. We believe rather that what people read is deeply important; that ideas can be dangerous; but that the suppression of ideas is fatal to a democratic society. Freedom itself is a dangerous way of life, but it is ours.

This statement was originally issued in May of 1953 by the Westchester Conference of the American Library Association and the American Book

Publishers Council, which in 1970 consolidated with the American Educational Publishers Institute to become the Association of American Publishers.

[Adopted June 25, 1953; revised January 28, 1972, January 16, 1991, July 12, 2000, June 30, 2004, by the ALA Council and the AAP Freedom to Read Committee.]

GUIDELINES FOR THE DEVELOPMENT AND IMPLEMENTATION OF POLICIES, REGULATIONS, AND PROCEDURES AFFECTING ACCESS TO LIBRARY MATERIALS, SERVICES, AND FACILITIES

Publicly supported libraries exist within the context of a body of law derived from the United States Constitution and appropriate state constitutions, defined by statute, and implemented by regulations, policies, and procedures established by their governing bodies and administrations. These regulations, policies, and procedures establish the mission of the library, define its functions, services, and operations and ascertain the rights and responsibilities of the clientele served by the library.

Publicly supported library service is based upon the First Amendment right of free expression. The publicly supported library provides free and equal access to information for all people of the community it serves. Thus, publicly supported libraries are governmental agencies designated as limited public forums for access to information. Libraries that make meeting rooms, exhibit spaces, and/or bulletin boards available for public use are also designated as limited public forums for the exchange of information.

Many libraries adopt administrative policies and procedures regulating the organization and use of library materials, services, and facilities. These policies and procedures affect access and may have the effect of restricting, denying, or creating barriers to access to the library as a public forum, including the library's resources, facilities, and services. Library policies and procedures that impinge upon First Amendment rights are subject to a higher standard of review than may be required in the policies of other public services and facilities.

Policies, procedures, or regulations that may result in denying, restricting, or creating physical or economic barriers to access to the library's public forum must be based on a compelling government interest. However, library governing authorities may place reasonable and narrowly drawn restrictions on the time, place, or manner of access to library resources, services, or facilities, provided that such restrictions are not based upon arbitrary distinctions between individuals or classes of individuals.

The American Library Association has adopted the *Library Bill of Rights* and Interpretations of the *Library Bill of Rights* to provide library governing authorities, librarians and other library staff, and library users with guidelines on how constitutional principles apply to libraries in the United States of America.

The American Library Association's Intellectual Freedom Committee recommends that publicly supported libraries use the following guidelines, based on constitutional principles, to develop policies, regulations, and procedures.

All library policies, regulations, and procedures should be carefully examined to determine if they may result in denying, restricting, or creating barriers to access. If they may result in such restrictions, they:

1. should be developed and implemented within the legal framework that applies to the library. This includes: the United States Constitution, including the First and Fourteenth Amendments, due process and equal treatment under the law; the applicable state constitution; federal and state civil rights legislation; all other applicable federal, state and local legislation; and applicable case law;
2. should cite statutes or ordinances upon which the authority to make that policy is based, when appropriate;
3. should be developed and implemented within the framework of the *Library Bill of Rights* and its Interpretations;
4. should be based upon the library's mission and objectives;
5. should only impose restrictions on the access to, or use of library resources, services, or facilities when those restrictions are necessary to achieve the library's mission and objectives;
6. should narrowly tailor prohibitions or restrictions, in the rare instances when they are required, so they are not more restrictive than needed to serve their objectives;
7. should attempt to balance competing interests and avoid favoring the majority at the expense of individual rights, or allowing individual users' rights to interfere materially with the majority's rights to free and equal access to library resources, services, and facilities;
8. should avoid arbitrary distinctions between individuals or classes of users, and should not have the effect of denying or abridging a person's right to use library resources, services, or facilities based upon arbitrary distinctions such as origin, age, background, or views;
9. In the *Library Bill of Rights* and all of its Interpretations, it is intended that: "origin" encompasses all the characteristics of individuals that are inherent in the circumstances of their birth; "age" encompasses all the characteristics of individuals that are inherent in their levels of development and

maturity; "background" encompasses all the characteristics of individuals that are a result of their life experiences; and "views" encompasses all the opinions and beliefs held and expressed by individuals;

10. should not target specific users or groups of users based upon an assumption or expectation that such users might engage in behavior that will materially interfere with the achievement of substantial library objectives;

11. must be clearly stated so that a reasonably intelligent person will have fair warning of what is expected;

12. must provide a means of appeal;

13. must be reviewed regularly by the library's governing authority and by its legal counsel.

14. must be communicated clearly and made available in an effective manner to all library users;

15. must be enforced evenhandedly, and not in a manner intended to benefit or disfavor any person or group in an arbitrary or capricious manner;

16. Libraries should develop an ongoing staff training program designed to foster the understanding of the legal framework and principles underlying library policies and to assist staff in gaining the skill and ability to respond to potentially difficult circumstances in a timely, direct, and open manner. This program should include training to develop empathy and understanding of the social and economic problems of some library users;

17. should, if reasonably possible, provide adequate alternative means of access to information for those whose behavior results in the denial or restriction of access to any library resource, service, or facility.

[Adopted by the ALA Intellectual Freedom Committee, June 28, 1994]

GUIDELINES FOR THE DEVELOPMENT OF POLICIES AND PROCEDURES REGARDING USER BEHAVIOR AND LIBRARY USAGE

Libraries are faced with problems of user behavior that must be addressed to ensure the effective delivery of service and full access to facilities. Library governing bodies must approach the regulation of user behavior within the framework of the ALA Code of Ethics, the *Library Bill of Rights*, and the law, including local and state statutes, constitutional standards under the First and Fourteenth Amendments, due process, and equal treatment under the law.

Publicly supported library service is based upon the First Amendment right of free expression. Publicly supported libraries are recognized as limited public forums for access to information. At least one federal court of appeals has recognized a First Amendment right to receive information in a public library. Library policies and procedures that could impinge upon such rights are subject to a higher standard of review than may be required in the policies of other public services and facilities.

There is a significant government interest in maintaining a library environment that is conducive to all users' exercise of their constitutionally protected right to receive information. This significant interest authorizes publicly supported libraries to maintain a safe and healthy environment in which library users and staff can be free from harassment, intimidation, and threats to their safety and well-being. Libraries should provide appropriate safeguards against such behavior and enforce policies and procedures addressing that behavior when it occurs.

In order to protect all library users' right of access to library facilities, to ensure the safety of users and staff, and to protect library resources and facilities from damage, the library's governing authority may impose reasonable restrictions on the time, place, or manner of library access.

The American Library Association's Intellectual Freedom Committee recommends that publicly supported libraries use the following guidelines, based upon constitutional principles, to develop policies and procedures governing the use of library facilities:

1. Libraries are advised to rely upon existing legislation and law enforcement mechanisms as the primary means of controlling behavior that involves public safety, criminal behavior, or other issues covered by existing local, state, or federal statutes. In many instances, this legal framework may be sufficient to provide the library with the necessary tools to maintain order.
2. If the library's governing body chooses to write its own policies and procedures regarding user behavior or access to library facilities, services, and resources, the policies should cite statutes or ordinances upon which the authority to make those policies is based.
3. Library policies and procedures governing the use of library facilities should be carefully examined to ensure that they are not in violation of the *Library Bill of Rights*.
4. Reasonable and narrowly drawn policies and procedures designed to prohibit interference with use of the facilities and services by others, or to prohibit activities inconsistent with achievement of the library's mission statement and objectives, are acceptable.
5. Such policies and the attendant implementing procedures should be reviewed frequently and updated as needed by the library's legal counsel for compliance with federal and state constitutional requirements, federal and

state civil rights legislation, all other applicable federal and state legislation, and applicable case law.

6. Every effort should be made to respond to potentially difficult circumstances of user behavior in a timely, direct, and open manner. Common sense, reason, and sensitivity should be used to resolve issues in a constructive and positive manner without escalation.

7. Libraries should develop an ongoing staff training program based upon their user behavior policy. This program should include training to develop empathy and understanding of the social and economic problems of some library users.

8. Policies and regulations that impose restrictions on library access:

   a. should apply only to those activities that materially interfere with the public's right of access to library facilities, the safety of users and staff, and the protection of library resources and facilities;

   b. should narrowly tailor prohibitions or restrictions so that they are not more restrictive than needed to serve their objectives;

   c. should attempt to balance competing interests and avoid favoring the majority at the expense of individual rights, or allowing individual users' rights to supersede those of the majority of library users;

   d. should be based solely upon actual behavior and not upon arbitrary distinctions between individuals or classes of individuals. Policies should not target specific users or groups of users based upon an assumption or expectation that such users might engage in behaviors that could disrupt library service;

   e. should not restrict access to the library by persons who merely inspire the anger or annoyance of others. Policies based upon appearance or behavior that is merely annoying or which merely generates negative subjective reactions from others, do not meet the necessary standard. Such policies should employ a reasonable, objective standard based on the behavior itself;

   f. must provide a clear description of the behavior that is prohibited and the various enforcement measures in place so that a reasonably intelligent person will have both due process and fair warning; this description must be continuously and clearly communicated in an effective manner to all library users;

   g. to the extent possible, should not leave those affected without adequate alternative means of access to information in the library;

   h. must be enforced evenhandedly, and not in a manner intended to benefit or disfavor any person or group in an arbitrary or capricious manner.

The user behaviors addressed in these Guidelines are the result of a wide variety of individual and societal conditions. Libraries should take advantage of the expertise of local social service agencies, advocacy groups, mental health professionals, law enforcement officials, and other community resources to develop community strategies for addressing the needs of a diverse population.

[Adopted by the Intellectual Freedom Committee, January 24, 1993; rev. November 17, 2000.]

INTELLECTUAL FREEDOM PRINCIPLES FOR ACADEMIC LIBRARIES: AN INTERPRETATION OF THE LIBRARY BILL OF RIGHTS

A strong intellectual freedom perspective is critical to the development of academic library collections and services that dispassionately meet the education and research needs of a college or university community. The purpose of this statement is to outline how and where intellectual freedom principles fit into an academic library setting, thereby raising consciousness of the intellectual freedom context within which academic librarians work. The following principles should be reflected in all relevant library policy documents.

1. The general principles set forth in the *Library Bill of Rights* form an indispensable framework for building collections, services, and policies that serve the entire academic community.
2. The privacy of library users is and must be inviolable. Policies should be in place that maintain confidentiality of library borrowing records and of other information relating to personal use of library information and services.
3. The development of library collections in support of an institution's instruction and research programs should transcend the personal values of the selector. In the interests of research and learning, it is essential that collections contain materials representing a variety of perspectives on subjects that may be considered controversial.
4. Preservation and replacement efforts should ensure that balance in library materials is maintained and that controversial materials are not removed from the collections through theft, loss, mutilation, or normal wear and tear. There should be alertness to efforts by special interest groups to bias a collection though systematic theft or mutilation.
5. Licensing agreements should be consistent with the *Library Bill of Rights*, and should maximize access.
6. Open and unfiltered access to the Internet should be conveniently available to the academic community in a college or university library. Content filtering devices and content-based restrictions are a contradiction of the academic

library mission to further research and learning through exposure to the broadest possible range of ideas and information. Such restrictions are a fundamental violation of intellectual freedom in academic libraries.

7. Freedom of information and of creative expression should be reflected in library exhibits and in all relevant library policy documents.

8. Library meeting rooms, research carrels, exhibit spaces, and other facilities should be available to the academic community regardless of research being pursued or subject being discussed. Any restrictions made necessary because of limited availability of space should be based on need, as reflected in library policy, rather than on content of research or discussion.

9. Whenever possible, library services should be available without charge in order to encourage inquiry. Where charges are necessary, a free or low-cost alternative (e.g., downloading to disc rather than printing) should be available when possible.

10. A service philosophy should be promoted that affords equal access to information for all in the academic community with no discrimination on the basis of race, values, gender, sexual orientation, cultural or ethnic background, physical or learning disability, economic status, religious beliefs, or views.

11. A procedure ensuring due process should be in place to deal with requests by those within and outside the academic community for removal or addition of library resources, exhibits, or services.

12. It is recommended that this statement of principle be endorsed by appropriate institutional governing bodies, including the faculty senate or similar instrument of faculty governance.

[Approved by ACRL Board of Directors: June 29, 1999; Adopted July 12, 2000, by the ALA Council.]

LIBRARY BILL OF RIGHTS

The American Library Association affirms that all libraries are forums for information and ideas, and that the following basic policies should guide their services.

1. Books and other library resources should be provided for the interest, information, and enlightenment of all people of the community the library serves. Materials should not be excluded because of the origin, background, or views of those contributing to their creation.

2. Libraries should provide materials and information presenting all points of view on current and historical issues. Materials should not be proscribed or removed because of partisan or doctrinal disapproval.
3. Libraries should challenge censorship in the fulfillment of their responsibility to provide information and enlightenment.
4. Libraries should cooperate with all persons and groups concerned with resisting abridgment of free expression and free access to ideas.
5. A person's right to use a library should not be denied or abridged because of origin, age, background, or views.
6. Libraries which make exhibit spaces and meeting rooms available to the public they serve should make such facilities available on an equitable basis, regardless of the beliefs or affiliations of individuals or groups requesting their use.

[Adopted June 18, 1948. Amended February 2, 1961, and January 23, 1980, inclusion of "age" reaffirmed January 23, 1996, by the ALA Council.]

LIBRARY-INITIATED PROGRAMS AS A RESOURCE: AN INTERPRETATION OF THE LIBRARY BILL OF RIGHTS

Library-initiated programs support the mission of the library by providing users with additional opportunities for information, education, and recreation. Article I of the *Library Bill of Rights* states: "Books and other library resources should be provided for the interest, information, and enlightenment of all people of the community the library serves."

Library-initiated programs take advantage of library staff expertise, collections, services, and facilities to increase access to information and information resources. Library-initiated programs introduce users and potential users to the resources of the library and to the library's primary function as a facilitator of information access. The library may participate in cooperative or joint programs with other agencies, organizations, institutions, or individuals as part of its own effort to address information needs and to facilitate information access in the community the library serves.

Library-initiated programs on site and in other locations include, but are not limited to, speeches, community forums, discussion groups, demonstrations, displays, and live or media presentations.

Libraries serving multilingual or multicultural communities should make efforts to accommodate the information needs of those for whom English is a second language. Library-initiated programs that cross language and cultural barriers introduce otherwise underserved populations to the resources of the library and provide access to information.

Library-initiated programs "should not be proscribed or removed [or canceled] because of partisan or doctrinal disapproval" of the contents of the program or the views expressed by the participants, as stated in Article II of the *Library Bill of Rights*. Library sponsorship of a program does not constitute an endorsement of the content of the program or the views expressed by the participants, any more than the purchase of material for the library collection constitutes an endorsement of the contents of the material or the views of its creator.

Library-initiated programs are a library resource, and, as such, are developed in accordance with written guidelines, as approved and adopted by the library's policy-making body. These guidelines should include an endorsement of the *Library Bill of Rights* and set forth the library's commitment to free and open access to information and ideas for all users.

Library staff select topics, speakers, and resource materials for library-initiated programs based on the interests and information needs of the community. Topics, speakers, and resource materials are not excluded from library-initiated programs because of possible controversy. Concerns, questions, or complaints about library-initiated programs are handled according to the same written policy and procedures that govern reconsiderations of other library resources.

Library-initiated programs are offered free of charge and are open to all. Article V of the *Library Bill of Rights* states: "A person's right to use a library should not be denied or abridged because of origin, age, background, or views."

The "right to use a library" encompasses all the resources the library offers, including the right to attend library-initiated programs. Libraries do not deny or abridge access to library resources, including library-initiated programs, based on an individual's economic background or ability to pay.

[Adopted January 27, 1982; amended June 26, 1990; July 12, 2000, by the ALA Council.]

POLICY CONCERNING CONFIDENTIALITY OF PERSONALLY IDENTIFIABLE INFORMATION ABOUT LIBRARY USERS

"In a library (physical or virtual), the right to privacy is the right to open inquiry without having the subject of one's interest examined or scrutinized by others. Confidentiality exists when a library is in possession of personally identifiable information about users and keeps that information private on their behalf" (*Privacy: An Interpretation of the Library Bill of Rights*).

The ethical responsibilities of librarians, as well as statutes in most states and the District of Columbia, protect the privacy of library users. Confidentiality extends to "information sought or received and resources consulted, borrowed, acquired, or transmitted" (*ALA Code of Ethics*), and includes, but is not limited to, database search records, reference interviews, circulation records, interlibrary loan records and other personally identifiable uses of library materials, facilities, or services.

The First Amendment's guarantee of freedom of speech and of the press requires that the corresponding rights to hear what is spoken and read what is written be preserved, free from fear of government intrusion, intimidation, or reprisal. The American Library Association reaffirms its opposition to "any use of governmental prerogatives that lead to the intimidation of individuals or groups and discourages them from exercising the right of free expression as guaranteed by the First Amendment to the U.S. Constitution" and "encourages resistance to such abuse of governmental power . . ." (ALA Policy 53.4). In seeking access or in the pursuit of information, confidentiality is the primary means of providing the privacy that will free the individual from fear of intimidation or retaliation.

The American Library Association regularly receives reports of visits by agents of federal, state, and local law enforcement agencies to libraries, asking for personally identifiable information about library users. These visits, whether under the rubric of simply informing libraries of agency concerns or for some other reason, reflect an insensitivity to the legal and ethical bases for confidentiality, and the role it plays in the preservation of First Amendment rights, rights also extended to foreign nationals while in the United States. The government's interest in library use reflects a dangerous and fallacious equation of what a person reads with what that person believes or how that person is likely to behave. Such a presumption can and does threaten the freedom of access to information. It also is a threat to a crucial aspect of First Amendment rights: that freedom of speech and of the press include the freedom to hold, disseminate, and receive unpopular, minority, extreme, or even dangerous ideas.

The American Library Association recognizes that law enforcement agencies and officers may occasionally believe that library records contain information that would be helpful to the investigation of criminal activity. The American judicial system provides the mechanism for seeking release of such confidential records: a court order, following a showing of *good cause* based on *specific facts*, by a court of competent jurisdiction.[1]

The American Library Association also recognizes that, under limited circumstances, access to certain information might be restricted due to a legitimate national security concern. However, there has been no showing of a plausible probability that national security will be compromised by any use made of unclassified information available in libraries. Access to this unclassified information should be handled no differently than access to any other information. Therefore, libraries and librarians have a legal and ethical responsibility to protect the confidentiality of all library users, including foreign nationals.

Libraries are one of the great bulwarks of democracy. They are living embodiments of the First Amendment because their collections include voices of dissent as well as assent. Libraries are impartial resources providing information on all points of view, available to all persons regardless of origin, age, background, or views. The role of libraries as such a resource must not be compromised by an erosion of the privacy rights of library users.

Note

1. See *Confidentiality and Coping With Law Enforcement Inquiries: Guidelines for the Library and its Staff*, ALA Office for Intellectual Freedom, available on the Web at http://www.ala.org/oif/ifissues.

[Adopted July 2, 1991; amended June 30, 2004, by the ALA Council]

POLICY ON GOVERNMENTAL INTIMIDATION

The American Library Association opposes any use of governmental prerogatives that lead to the intimidation of individuals or groups and discourages them from exercising the right of free expression as guaranteed by the First Amendment to the U.S. Constitution. ALA encourages resistance to such abuse of governmental power and supports those against whom such governmental power has been employed. See figure B.1.

[Adopted February 2, 1973; amended July 1, 1981; June 30, 2004, by the ALA Council.]

RESOLUTION ON ACCESS TO THE USE OF LIBRARIES AND INFORMATION BY INDIVIDUALS WITH PHYSICAL OR MENTAL IMPAIRMENT

Whereas, The Intellectual Freedom Committee is concerned with freedom of access; and

Whereas, The *Library Bill of Rights* states that "books and other library resources should be provided for the interests, information, and enlightenment of all people of the community the library serves" and "a person's right to use a library should not be denied or abridged . . ."; and

Request for Reconsideration of Library Resources

IMPORTANT: The entire form must be completed in order for an item to be reconsidered. PLEASE PRINT.

Date: _____

Request initiated by: _____

Address: _____

Telephone: _____

Complainant represents:
___ him/herself
___ organization

FORMAT: ___Book ___Video ___Audio cassette ___CD
___Book on tape ___other (specify) _____

Author/artist/director: _____

Title:_____

Publisher/producer: _____

1. Did you read/view/listen to the entire item?

_____

_____

2. To what do you object? (Cite pages, scenes, etc.)

_____

_____

Figure B.1   Library resource form.

3. To what do you approve? (Cite pages, scenes, etc.)

_____

_____

4. What do you believe is the theme of this book/video/audio recording?

_____

_____

5. What do you feel might be the result of reading/viewing/hearing this material?

_____

_____

6. Are you aware of the judgment of this material by critics?

_____

_____

7. What would you like the library to do about this item?

_____

_____

8. What alternative book/video/audio recording of equal quality do you recommend that will convey a similar perspective?

_____

_____

Signature _____

Whereas, Federal and state constitutional and statutory laws forbid public institutions from discriminating against handicapped individuals, i.e., persons who have a physical or mental impairment; and

Whereas, Court opinions have clearly interpreted said laws as proscribing discrimination against persons who have acquired immune deficiency syndrome ("AIDS"), AIDS-related complex ("ARC"), or who test positive for the human immunodeficiency virus ("HIV"); and

Whereas, The American Medical Association and the United States Department of Health and Human Services have opined that while the human immunodeficiency virus that causes AIDS is a contagious disease, it cannot be transmitted by casual contact; now, therefore be it

Resolved, That the *Library Bill of Rights* of the American Library Association which ensures access to library facilities, materials, and services by all people of the community includes individuals with physical or mental impairments; and be it further

Resolved, That the American Library Association deplores discrimination against and denial or abridgment of library and information access to persons of all ages who have acquired immune deficiency syndrome ("AIDS"), AIDS-related complex ("ARC"), or who test positive for the human immunodeficiency virus ("HIV").

[Adopted January 13, 1988, by the ALA Council.]

RESTRICTED ACCESS TO LIBRARY MATERIALS:
AN INTERPRETATION OF THE LIBRARY BILL OF RIGHTS

Libraries are a traditional forum for the open exchange of information. Attempts to restrict access to library materials violate the basic tenets of the Library Bill of Rights.

Some libraries place materials in a "closed shelf," "locked case," "adults only," "restricted shelf," or "high-demand" collection. Some libraries have applied filtering software to their Internet stations to prevent users from finding targeted categories of information, much of which is constitutionally protected. Some libraries block access to certain materials by placing other barriers between the user and those materials.

Because restricted materials often deal with controversial, unusual, or sensitive subjects, having to ask a librarian or circulation clerk for access to them may be embarrassing or inhibiting for patrons desiring the materials. Requiring a user to ask for materials may create a service barrier or pose a language-skills barrier. Even when a title is listed in the catalog with a reference to its restricted status, a barrier is placed between the patron and the publication. (See also "Statement on Labeling.") Because restricted materials often feature information that some people consider objectionable, potential library users may be predisposed to think of the materials as objectionable and, therefore, be reluctant to ask for access to them.

Limiting access by relegating materials into physically or virtually restricted or segregated collections or restricting materials by creating age-related, linguistic, economic, psychological, or other barriers violates the Library Bill of Rights. However, some libraries have established restrictive policies to protect their materials from theft or mutilation, or because of statutory authority or institutional mandate. Such policies must be carefully formulated and administered to ensure they do not violate established principles of intellectual freedom. This caution is reflected in ALA policies, such as "Evaluating Library Collections," "Free Access to Libraries for Minors," "Preservation Policy," and the ACRL "Code of Ethics for Special Collections Librarians."

In keeping with the "Joint Statement on Access" of the American Library Association and Society of American Archivists, libraries should avoid accepting donor agreements or entering into contracts that impose permanent restrictions on special collections. As stated in the "Joint Statement," it is the responsibility of libraries with such collections "to make available original research materials in its possession on equal terms of access."

All proposals for restricted access collections should be carefully scrutinized to ensure that the purpose is not to suppress a viewpoint or to place a barrier between certain patrons and particular content. A primary goal of the library profession is to facilitate access to all points of view on current and historical issues.

[Adopted February 2, 1973; amended July 1, 1981; July 3, 1991; July 12, 2000; June 30, 2004, by the ALA Council.]

STATEMENT ON LABELING: AN INTERPRETATION OF THE LIBRARY BILL OF RIGHTS

Labeling is the practice of describing or designating materials by affixing a prejudicial label and/or segregating them by a prejudicial system. The American Library Association opposes these means of predisposing people's attitudes toward library materials for the following reasons:

1. Labeling is an attempt to prejudice attitudes and as such, it is a censor's tool.
2. Some find it easy and even proper, according to their ethics, to establish criteria for judging publications as objectionable. However, injustice and

ignorance rather than justice and enlightenment result from such practices, and the American Library Association opposes the establishment of such criteria.

3. Libraries do not advocate the ideas found in their collections. The presence of books and other resources in a library does not indicate endorsement of their contents by the library.

A variety of private organizations promulgate rating systems and/or review materials as a means of advising either their members or the general public concerning their opinions of the contents and suitability or appropriate age for use of certain books, films, recordings, or other materials. For the library to adopt or enforce any of these private systems, to attach such ratings to library materials, to include them in bibliographic records, library catalogs, or other finding aids, or otherwise to endorse them would violate the *Library Bill of Rights*.

While some attempts have been made to adopt these systems into law, the constitutionality of such measures is extremely questionable. If such legislation is passed which applies within a library's jurisdiction, the library should seek competent legal advice concerning its applicability to library operations.

Publishers, industry groups, and distributors sometimes add ratings to material or include them as part of their packaging. Librarians should not endorse such practices. However, removing or obliterating such ratings—if placed there by or with permission of the copyright holder—could constitute expurgation, which is also unacceptable.

The American Library Association opposes efforts which aim at closing any path to knowledge. This statement, however, does not exclude the adoption of organizational schemes designed as directional aids or to facilitate access to materials.

[Adopted July 13, 1951. Amended June 25, 1971; July 1, 1981; June 26, 1990, by the ALA Council.]

THE UNIVERSAL RIGHT TO FREE EXPRESSION:
AN INTERPRETATION OF THE LIBRARY BILL OF RIGHTS

Freedom of expression is an inalienable human right and the foundation for self-government. Freedom of expression encompasses the freedoms of speech, press, religion, assembly, and association, and the corollary right to receive information.

The American Library Association endorses this principle, which is also set forth in the Universal Declaration of Human Rights, adopted by the United Nations General Assembly. The Preamble of this document states that ". . .

recognition of the inherent dignity and of the equal and inalienable rights of all members of the human family is the foundation of freedom, justice, and peace in the world. . ." and ". . . the advent of a world in which human beings shall enjoy freedom of speech and belief and freedom from fear and want has been proclaimed as the highest aspiration of the common people. . . ."

Article 18 of this document states: "Everyone has the right to freedom of thought, conscience, and religion; this right includes freedom to change his religion or belief, and freedom, either alone or in community with others and in public or private, to manifest his religion or belief in teaching, practice, worship, and observance."

Article 19 states: "Everyone has the right to freedom of opinion and expression; this right includes freedom to hold opinions without interference and to seek, receive, and impart information and ideas through any media regardless of frontiers."

Article 20 states: "(1) Everyone has the right to freedom of peaceful assembly and association. (2) No one may be compelled to belong to an association."

We affirm our belief that these are inalienable rights of every person, regardless of origin, age, background, or views. We embody our professional commitment to these principles in the *Library Bill of Rights* and *Code of Ethics*, as adopted by the American Library Association.

We maintain that these are universal principles and should be applied by libraries and librarians throughout the world. The American Library Association's policy on International Relations reflects these objectives:

". . . to encourage the exchange, dissemination, and access to information and the unrestricted flow of library materials in all formats throughout the world."

We know that censorship, ignorance, and limitations on the free flow of information are the tools of tyranny and oppression. We believe that ideas and information topple the walls of hate and fear and build bridges of cooperation and understanding far more effectively than weapons and armies.

The American Library Association is unswerving in its commitment to human rights and intellectual freedom; the two are inseparably linked and inextricably entwined. Freedom of opinion and expression is not derived from or dependent on any form of government or political power. This right is inherent in every individual. It cannot be surrendered, nor can it be denied. True justice comes from the exercise of this right.

We recognize the power of information and ideas to inspire justice, to restore freedom and dignity to the oppressed, and to change the hearts and minds of the oppressors.

Courageous men and women, in difficult and dangerous circumstances throughout human history, have demonstrated that freedom lives in the human heart and cries out for justice even in the face of threats, enslavement, imprisonment, torture, exile, and death. We draw inspiration from their example. They challenge us to remain steadfast in our most basic professional responsibility to promote and defend the right of free expression.

There is no good censorship. Any effort to restrict free expression and the free flow of information aids the oppressor. Fighting oppression with censorship is self-defeating.

Threats to the freedom of expression of any person anywhere are threats to the freedom of all people everywhere. Violations of human rights and the right of free expression have been recorded in virtually every country and society across the globe.

In response to these violations, we affirm these principles:

- The American Library Association opposes any use of governmental prerogative that leads to the intimidation of individuals that prevents them from exercising their rights to hold opinions without interference, and to seek, receive, and impart information and ideas. We urge libraries and librarians everywhere to resist such abuse of governmental power, and to support those against whom such governmental power has been employed.
- The American Library Association condemns any governmental effort to involve libraries and librarians in restrictions on the right of any individual to hold opinions without interference, and to seek, receive, and impart information and ideas. Such restrictions pervert the function of the library and violate the professional responsibilities of librarians.
- The American Library Association rejects censorship in any form. Any action that denies the inalienable human rights of individuals only damages the will to resist oppression, strengthens the hand of the oppressor, and undermines the cause of justice.
- The American Library Association will not abrogate these principles. We believe that censorship corrupts the cause of justice, and contributes to the demise of freedom.

[Adopted by the ALA Council, January 16, 1991]

Bibliography

American Library Association, Reference and Adult Services Division, Collection Development and Evaluation Section. "The Relevance of Collection Development Policies: Definition, Necessity, and Applications," *RQ.* 33 (Fall 1993) 65–74.

Boon, George. "Evaluation of the Collection," *Library Trends.* 22 (January 1974) 265–304.

Bushing, M., B. Davis, and N. Powell. *Using the Conspectus Method: A Collection Assessment Handbook.* Lacey, WA: WLN, 1997.

Cargill, J. S. "Collection Development Policies: An Alternative Viewpoint," *Library Acquisition, Practice and Theory.* 1 (1984) 47–49.

Clark, L., ed. *Guide to Review of Library Collections: Preservation, Storage, and Withdrawal.* Chicago: American Library Association, 1991.

Columbia University. "Collection Development Policies: Digital Libraries": http://www.columbia.edu/cu/libraries/about/colldev/digital-library.htm

Evans, G. Edward. *Developing Library and Information Center Collections.* 4th ed. Englewood, CO: Libraries Unlimited, 2000. Includes Chapter 3: "Collection Development Policies."

Evans, G. Edward, and Sandra M. Heft. *Introduction to Technical Services.* 6th ed. Englewood, Colo.: Libraries Unlimited, 1994.

Fedunok, Suzanne. "Hammurabi and the Electronic Age: Documenting Electronic Collecting Decisions," *RQ.* 36:1 (Fall 1996) 86–90. Covers commonly used elements found in electronic information collection development policy statements acquired by an ALA committee.

Ferguson, Anthony W., Joan Grant, and Joel S. Rutstein. "The RLG Conspectus: Its Uses and Benefits," *College and Research Libraries.* 49:3 (May 1988) 197–206.

Forcier, Peggy, and N. Powell. "Collection Assessment in the Pacific Northwest: Building a Foundation for Cooperation Based on the RLG Conspectus" in *Advances in Library Automation and Networking.* 3 (1989) 87–121.

Futas, Elizabeth, ed. *Collection Development Policies and Procedures.* 3rd ed. Phoenix, AZ: Oryx, 1995.

Gabriel, Michael R. *Collection Development and Collection Evaluation: A Sourcebook.* Metuchen, NJ: Scarecrow, 1995.

Gardner, Richard K. *Library Collections: Their Origin, Selection, and Development.* New York: McGraw-Hill, 1981.

Gessesse, Kebede. "Collection Development and Management in the Twenty-First Century with Special Reference to Academic Libraries: An Overview," *Library Management.* 21:6/7 (2000) 365–72. Argues that the new electronic media must be addressed by library collection development policies.

Gorman, G. E., and B. R. Howes. *Collection Development for Libraries.* London: Bowker-Saur, 1989.

Gorman, G. E., and R. H. Miller, eds. *Collection Management for the 21st Century: A Handbook for Librarians.* Westport, Conn.: Greenwood, 1997.

Hall, Blaine. *Collection Assessment Manual for College and University Libraries.* Phoenix, AZ: Oryx, 1985.

Hall, Blaine. "Writing the Collection Assessment Manual," *Collection Management.* (Fall–Winter 1984) 49–61.

Harloe, Bart, ed. *Guide to Cooperative Collection Development.* Chicago: American Library Association, 1994.

Hazen, Dan C. "Collection Development Policies in the Information Age," *College & Research Libraries.* 56 (January 1995) 29–31.

Intner, Sheila S. "The Ostrich Syndrome: Why Written Collection Development Policies Are Important," *Technicalities.* 16 (July/August 1996) 1ff.

Johnson, Margaret Ann. *Collection Management for the 21st Century.* Westport, Conn.: Greenwood, 1997. Includes chapter "Collection Development Policies and Electronic Information Resources."

Johnson, P. "Collection Policies for Electronic Resources," *Technicalities.* 18:6 (June 1998) 10–12.

Kertesz, C. "The Unwanted Gift: When Saying 'No Thanks' Isn't Enough," *American Libraries.* 32:3 (March 2001) 34–36. Recommends that collection development policies specify those gifts considered to be acceptable, list relevant evaluative criteria, incorporate an appeals process, and allow for flexibility.

Lane, M. T. *Selecting and Organizing State Government Publications.* Chicago: American Library Association, 1987.

Liestman, Daniel. "Reference Collection Management Policies: Lessons from Kansas; review of reference collection development policies from academic libraries in Kansas," *College & Undergraduate Libraries.* 8:1 (2001) 79–112.

Lowe, J. L., and S. Henson. "Government Publications for School and Small Public Libraries," *Collection Management.* 11, no. 3/4 (1989): 141–50.

Magrill, Rose Mary, and John Corbin. *Acquisitions Management and Collection Development in Libraries.* 2nd ed. Chicago: American Library Association, 1989.

Mandal, B. R., S. Datta, and S. K. Dey. "Collection Development in Biomedical Science: New Media," *IASLIC Bulletin.* 44:3 (September 1999) 117–23. Analyzes role of a collection development policy in helping libraries deal with the information explosion, budget cuts, rising material costs, and storage shortages.

McClure, Charles, and Peter Hernon. *Users of Academic and Public GPO Depository Libraries.* Washington, D.C.: Government Printing Office, 1989.

Monk, John S. *Collection Development Policy.* Columbus, OH: Eisenhower National Clearinghouse, The Ohio State University, September 1996. p. 31 Report Number ENC-97-017.

Morehead, Joseph. "Govzines on the Web: A Preachment," *Serials Librarian.* 23, no. 3/4 (1997) 17–30.

Morehead, Joseph, and M. Fetzer. *Introduction to United States Government Information Sources.* 6th ed. Englewood, Colo.: Libraries Unlimited, 1999.

Ogburn, Joyce L. "T2: Theory in Acquisition Revisited," *Library Acquisitions Practice and Theory.* 21 (Summer 1997) 168ff.

Ostendorf, J. E. "Internet Policies for Public Libraries," *Georgia Librarian.* 34:4 (Winter 1997) 4–7.

Pastine, M., ed. *Collection Development: Past and Future.* New York: Haworth, 1996.

Pearlmutter, Jane. "Which Online Resources Are Right for Your Collection?" *School Library Journal.* 45:6 (June 1999) 27–29. Discusses virtual collection development policies.

Phillips, Faye. "Congressional Papers: Collection Development Policies," *The American Archivist.* 58 (Summer 1995) 258–69.

Pierce, S. J., ed. *Weeding and Maintenance of Reference Collections.* New York: Haworth, 1990.

Sauer, Cynthia K. "Doing the Best We Can? The Use of Collection Development Policies and Cooperative Collecting Activities at Manuscript Repositories: survey of U.S. repositories," *The American Archivist.* 64:2 (Fall/Winter 2001) 308–49.

Scholtz, James C. *Video Collection Development in Multi-Type Libraries.* 2nd ed. Westport, Conn.: Greenwood, 2002. Includes chapter "Developing Video Collection Development Policies to Accommodate Existing and New Technologies."

Sears, J. L., and M. K. Moody. *Using Government Information Sources.* Phoenix, Ariz.: Oryx, 1994.

Smith, D. H., ed. *Management of Government Document Collections.* Englewood, Colo.: Libraries Unlimited, 1993.

Snow, Richard. "Collection Development Policies, Collection Manuals, and Louisiana's Academic Libraries," *LLA Bulletin.* 56 (Summer 1993) 21–27.

Snow, Richard. "Wasted Words: The Written Collection Development Policy and the Academic Library," *Journal of Academic Librarianship.* 22:3 (May 1996) 191–94.

Spencer, M. D. *Free Publications from U.S. Government Agencies.* Englewood, Colo.: Libraries Unlimited, 1989.

Stephens, Annabel K. *Public Library Collection Development in the Information Age.* Binghamton, NY: Haworth, 1998. Includes chapter "The Public Library Planning Process: Its Impact on Collection Development Policies and Practices."

Stephens, D. "The Conspectus in Alaska and How We're Using It." *PNLA Quarterly* 53 (Spring 1989): 15–16.

Stierholtz, K. "U.S. Government Documents in the Electronic Era: Problems and Promise," *Collection Management.* 21, no. 1 (1996) 41–56.

Strong, R. "A Collection Development Policy Incorporating Electronic Formats," *Journal of Interlibrary Loan, Document Delivery and Information Supply.* 9:4 (1999) 53–64.

Stueart, Robert D., and Barbara B. Moran. *Library and Information Center Management.* Englewood, Colo.: Libraries Unlimited, 1998.

University of Oregon Libraries. "Collection Development Policy for Internet Resources": http://libweb.uoregon.edu/colldev/intres.html. First published September 14, 2000; last updated September 14, 2000.

University of Tennessee, Knoxville, Libraries. "Electronic Resources Collection Development Policy": http://toltec.lib.utk.edu/%7Ecolldev/elrescd.html. First published May 1998.

University of Texas at Austin. General Libraries. "Digital Library Collection Development Framework": http://www.lib.utexas.edu/cird/Policies/Subjects/framework.html. Last updated March 29, 1999.

Van Zijl, Carol. "The Why, What, and How of Collection Development Policies," *South African Journal of Library and Information Science.* 66:3 (September 1998) 99–106.

Vogel, Kristin D. "Integrating Electronic Resources Into Collection Development Policies," *Collection Management.* 21:2 (1996) 65–76.

White, Howard D. *Brief Tests of Collection Strength: A Methodology for All Types of Libraries.* Westport, CT: Greenwood, 1995.

Whiteside, Ann Baird, Pamela Born, and Adeane Alpert Bregman. *Collection Development Policies for Libraries and Visual Collections in the Arts.* Laguna, CA: Art Libraries Society of North America, 2000.

Wiemers, Eugene, et al. "Collection Evaluation: A Practical Guide to the Literature," *Library Acquisitions Practice and Theory.* 8:1 (1984) 65–78.

Wilkinson, Patrick. "Beyond the Federal Depository Library Program," *Journal of Government Information.* 23, no. 3 (1996): 411–17.

Wood, Richard J. "The Axioms, Barriers, and Components for Cooperative Collection Development," in *Collection Management for the 21st Century: A Handbook for Librarians*, edited by Gary Gorman and R. H. Miller. Chicago: Greenwood, 1997. pp. 221–48.

Wood, Richard J., and Katina Strauch, eds. *Collection Assessment: A Look at the RLG Conspectus.* New York: Haworth, 1992.

Yale University Library. "Licensing Digital Information: A Resource for Librarians": http://www.library.yale.edu/~llicense/index.shtml. Last updated January 14, 2001.

Index

academic libraries, 9, 32, 38, 72, 93; acquisition methods, 159–72; appendixes, 212; audio-visual materials, 89; background statements, 10–11; bibliographies, 208; "big deal" issue, 232–33, 271–73; book vs. electronic access, 231–32; budget allocation and funding statements, 38–39; collection development objectives, 42–43; collection evaluation, 196–98; collection maintenance, 181–82; comic art, 113–18; definition of terms or glossary, 204; document delivery, 134; format statements, 55–57; gift and exchange statements, 173–76; government publication section, 72–82; intellectual freedom statements, 143, 148–53; local history and genealogy, 105–6; mission, goal, and objective statements, 21; oral history, 111–13; purpose statements, 6; rare books, 108–11; reserve, materials on, 134–35; resource sharing statements, 126–28; resources identified in policies, treatment of specific, 84–85, 89; responsibility statements, 16–17; selection aid checklist, 137–38; serials, 84–85, 115; special collection statements, 95–100, 105–6, 108–11; specific evaluative criteria, 44–47; subject archives, 111–18; target audience statements, 33; weeding statements, 187–88. *See also* community colleges; Conspectus

acceptable use policies, 242

Access to Electronic Information, Services, and Networks [ALA document], 280–283

access to electronic resources. *See* policy components for online electronic resources

Access to Library Resources and Services Regardless of Sex, Gender Identity, or Sexual Orientation [ALA document], 283–85

acquisition methods identified in policies, 158–70

Albion College, Stockwell-Mudd Libraries, 44–46, 89, 126–27

Albuquerque Technical Vocational Institute Libraries, 11, 55, 57–58

allocation of electronic resources, 234–35

American Civil Liberties Union, 147

About the Authors

Frank W. Hoffmann (PhD, University of Pittsburgh; MLS, Indiana University) is professor of library science at Sam Houston State University. His teaching responsibilities include library collection development, reference/information services, organization of collections, and research methods. He has worked in libraries in Indiana, Tennessee, and Pennsylvania and has written over thirty books relating to librarianship and popular music, including more than a dozen titles for Scarecrow Press.

Richard J. Wood (PhD and MLS, University of Pittsburgh) is director of university libraries at the University of South Alabama and was formerly the director of university libraries at the Citadel and Sam Houston State University. He has published monographs and scholarly articles on a wide range of subjects, most notably the Conspectus, electronic information collections and services in academic institutions, and copyright.